Behind the Cameras:

Minnesotans in the Movies, volume II

Behind the Cameras:

Minnesotans in the Movies, volume II

Rolf Canton

NODIN PRESS

Acknowledgments

I would like to thank the Moving Images Section of the Library of Congress; David Ouse, researcher from the Duluth Public Library; Tamim Haron, computer assistant; and Ben Nelson, formerly of the Minnesota Film Board.

Also, the Hastings Public Library; the Stillwater Public Library; the family of John Goodell; The Stearns County History Center; the Hinckley Fire Museum; Crow Wing County History Center; The University of Minnesota's Eric Sevareid Library at the School of Journalism and Mass Communication; the Minneapolis Public Main Library's Special Collections' vertical files; the St. Paul Public Library's Special Collections; *Current Biographies* and the *New York Times Obits* of the Hennepin County Southdale Library; Cretin School in St. Paul; and the IMDb.

ISBN 13: 978-1-932472-53-5
ISBN 10: 1-932472-53-0
Library of Congress Control Number: 2007938608
Editing, design, and layout: John Toren

Nodin Press is a division of Micawber's, Inc.
530 North Third Street, Suite 120,
Minneapolis, MN 55401

This Book Is Dedicated to:

Barbara Flanagan, longtime columnist for
the *Star-Tribune* newspaper. Her columns were the
inspiration for this book and for the companion volume
Minnesotans in the Movies (2006).

Al Milgrom, founder and artistic director of the
U Film Society at the University of Minnesota. He has
served the Twin Cities with devotion in offering excellent
films from all over the world in their original languages.

Bill Irvine, former owner-manager of the Parkway Movie
Theater. He has been dedicated to serving excellent movies at
inexpensive prices with the best popcorn in town.

Tom Letness and associates who refurbished
the Heights Movie Theater in Columbia Heights, which
offers classic movies from Hollywood's golden years.

Foreword

It has arrived at last—*Behind the Cameras: Minnesotans in the Movies, Volume 2*. It's a book for the casual moviegoer as well as the hard-core film buff. Following up on his best-selling book about movie stars and character actors with Minnesota connections, here Rolf Canton explores the careers of Minnesotans who worked *behind* the scenes in the movie industry. Some of them are familiar to all of us. Others deserve to be better known.

A few of the many entries included are producers Ted Mann, Mike Todd, Sarah Pillsbury, and Bill Pohlad; directors the Coen Brothers, Ali Selim, and Jack Smight; screenwriters F. Scott Fitzgerald, Judith Guest, and Pat Proft; Composers Bob Dylan, Jimmy Jam Harris and Terry Lewis; and editors John Stag Hanson and Stephen Rivkin.

Minnesotan Leroy Shield has a huge following in Europe on the strength of the incidental music he composed for the Laurel & Hardy, Our Gang, and Charlie Chase comedies. And it was enlightening for me to discover that my favorite animator, Ward Kimball, is from Minnesota. He worked on many of Disney's classic cartoons including *Snow White*, and was responsible for creating the screen persona of Jiminy Cricket.

Rolf Canton has researched many sources, including old newspaper clippings and county historical society records, to give the reader the most comprehensive information possible on the Minnesotans who have enriched our lives by bringing the craft of making films to the level of high art. It's a fascinating read and an essential sourcebook for anyone interested in film history.

– Bob DeFlores
Film historian and archivist

Contents

Producers

W. R. Frank	**1**
Ted Mann	**5**
Byron McKinney	**9**
Sarah Pillsbury	**10**
Bill Pohlad	**14**
Mike Todd	**16**
Pat Wells	**21**

Directors

Hy Averback	**24**
Earl Bellamy	**26**
Jack Conway	**29**
Terry Gilliam	**31**
John Goodell	**35**
John Hanson	**37**
George Roy Hill	**41**
Jerome Hill	**46**
Peter Markle	**48**
David Burton Morris	**50**
Gordon Parks	**54**
Charles Reisner	**56**
Ali Selim	**59**
Jack Smight	**62**
Stephen Sommers	**65**
John Griffith Wray	**68**

Screenwriters

Houston Branch	**70**
Sidney Buchman	**72**
Vincent Bugliosi	**76**
Joel & Ethan Coen	**78**
F. Scott Fitzgerald	**83**
Al Franken	**86**
Eleanore Griffin	**88**
Frank Gruber	**91**
Judith Guest	**94**
Mark Steven Johnson	**95**
Jerome Odlum	**98**
Pat Proft	**100**
Allen Rivkin	**102**
John Monk Saunders	**104**
Jack Sher	**107**
Max Shulman	**109**
C. Gardner Sullivan	**112**

Editors

John Stag Hanson	**115**
Stephen E. Rivkin	**118**

Composers

Bob Dylan	**120**
"Jimmy Jam" Harris & Terry Lewis	**123**
S.L. Rothafel	**126**
Roy Shield	**129**

Animator

Ward Kimball   **131**

Art Director

Harry Oliver   **134**

Technical Director/ Special Effects

Peter Stolz   **137**

Minnesota Authors whose Works have been Made into Films

Charles Baxter   **140**

Jon Hassler   **142**

Thomas Heggen   **144**

Sinclair Lewis   **147**

Tim O'Brien   **151**

Martha Ostenso   **153**

Anne Tyler   **155**

Will Weaver   **157**

Laura Ingalls Wilder   **159**

Kathleen Winsor   **166**

Movies Made in Minnesota   **168**

About the Author   **196**

MINNESOTANS WHO HAVE WON OSCARS
FOR WORK DONE BEHIND THE CAMERA

Bob Dylan (2000)
Best Song "Things Have Changed" from *Wonder Boys*

Joel & Ethan Coen (1996)
Best Screenplay for *Fargo*

Cray Research Supercomputer (1985)
Technical Oscar (shared)

Prince (1984)
Best Musical Composition & Song: "When Doves
        Cry" from *Purple Rain*

Donald Anderson and Diana Reiners of 3M (1984)
Technical Oscar for a new magnetic film that
        improved sound recording

Sarah Pillsbury (1979)
Best Short Film, *Board & Care*

Dr. Mohammed S. Nozari of 3M (1982)
Technical Oscar for a protective coating to make film
        prints last longer

George Roy Hill (1973)
Oscar for Best Director, *The Sting*

Dr. Philip V. Palmquist of 3M (1968)
Technical Oscar for development of a successful
        embodiment of the reflex background
        projection system for composite
        cinematography. First used in
        2001: A Space Odyssey

Todd AO Sound Department (1961)
Best Sound, *West Side Story* (shared with
      the Goldwyn Studio Sound Dept.)

Todd AO Sound Department (1960)
Best Sound, *The Alamo* (shared with
      the Goldwyn Studio Sound Dept.)

Todd AO Sound Department (1958)
Best Sound, *South Pacific*

The Todd AO Corp. and Westrex Corp. (1957)
Technical Oscar for a method of producing
      and exhibiting wide-film motion pictures.

Mike Todd (as Producer, 1956))
Best Picture, *Around the World in 80 Days*

Jerome Hill (as director, 1957)
Best Documentary, *Albert Schweitzer*

Todd AO Sound Department (1955)
Best Sound recording, *Oklahoma*

Sidney Buchman (1941)
Best Screenplay, *Here Comes Mr. Jordan*

Eleanore Griffin (1938)
Best Original Story, *Boys Town*
      (shared with Dore Schary)

John Monk Saunders (1930)
Best Original Story, *Dawn Patrol*

Producers

W. R. Frank

Wilfred Robert Frank
Born 16 April 1892, Mpls, MN
Died 25 May 1960, Mpls, MN

W. R. "Bill" Frank had an elegant lion-like head of wavy gray hair, with black bushy eyebrows, dark eyes, and a genial smile. The roly-poly, good natured Mrs. Frank (Lucille née Buffenmeyer), a former teacher, ran the family's bakery and gift shop by day and their restaurant by night. The highlight dishes at the Boulevard Twins Restaurant at 5315 Lyndale Avenue South were the fried chicken (or hamburger) in a basket followed by a banana split, and then a movie. Bill Frank was the first to offer dinner and a movie on one $2.50 ticket.

Bill was born in Northwestern Hospital on Chicago Avenue and 28th Street to John Robert Frank and Mary J. Yost, who lived across the street from the Minneapolis Courthouse and City Hall. The couple also produced a daughter, Corrine.

By the age of eight Bill Frank was burning to get into business. He loved having a product or service and selling it. His first plan was to open a restaurant with his mother serving as cook. He planned to pay her $100 a week. Some of the food would come from his father's garden, which always provided more than the family could eat themselves. No doubt the restaurant that his Grandma Turner ran across from City Hall provided the impetus for this precocious vision, but Bill's attraction to restaurants remained strong 'til he died.

At Minneapolis Central High School Bill played football (he was an All-City end), hockey and baseball, yet he had time for after-school and weekend jobs like working at the old Nicollet Hotel on Washington Avenue at Hennepin, janitor work at a church, delivering news-

1

papers, peddling garden equipment, and selling ice cream at the Lake Harriet Pavilion. By 1910, his senior year, Bill had $400 saved up and was ready to invest in a business.

After seeing just three movies, Bill knew that he had found his future business. Yes, Bill would be a movie man.

Frank's first movie house was the Excelsior, created by renovating a vacant store for an estimated $200. A friend from Excelsior, Ray Steadman, recommended the site. A classmate, Howard Hall, who also had $400, was ready for the business world, too. However, the estimate was short by $600 so the final bill took all their capital investment. With benches and an Edison projector bought from the recently defunct Wonderland Amusement Park at 36th Street and 42nd Avenue, the theater opened on a Sunday in the spring of 1910, and brought in $17.70 that first day. The film was *Babes in the Bullrushes* preceded by Steadman himself singing "I Am the Guy Who Put Salt in the Ocean," giving the public, in all, a half hour show.

Business was good all summer even with temperatures at 100 degrees. During the July 4th showing Frank sat on a 200-lb cake of ice and fanned himself while he collected admissions. He even chopped a hole in the roof to let the hot air escape. Unfortunately it rained the next day and many people got wet. So, necessity, being the mother of invention, he made a tin lid over the hole, which he could open or close as needed. He acted as his own thermostat.

While accumulating five more theaters, Bill found time to attend the University of Minnesota. When the U.S. entered World War I, he enlisted. Bill's mother ran his theaters for him during the War, but upon his return he found he had only two theater properties left because of economic stresses. He tried tent shows briefly and also became associated with the original Orpheum Theatre at 7th off Hennepin, until vaudeville died and the theater was left empty. This theater was renamed the Seventh Street Theatre while a new Orpheum was built in 1921 at 910 Hennepin Avenue South. The Radisson Parking Ramp replaced the old Orpheum.

In 1920 Bill jumped on the radio bandwagon. He was a partner in manufacturing Northland Radios for a while, and in 1925 he started broadcasts of the Minneapolis Symphony Orchestra in open air settings in small towns where he had already shown movies to outdoor crowds. This was aired through WCCO Radio, which was originally at 8 on the dial. He also produced a magazine with summer schedules of shows.

By 1944 W. R. Frank had opened no less than twenty-one theaters in the Twin Cities metro area and beyond. Among them were the Excelsior Theatre, which became the Tonka and later the Excelsior Dock at 26 Water Street; the West Twins in West St. Paul; the Rosebud Twins at 1506 East Lake St, which later became the Avalon; the Franklin Theatre at 1307 Franklin Ave. E; and the Boulevard Twins. He had four out-state theaters: a theater and a drive-in theater in Owatonna; a theater in Hutchinson; and a drive-in in Willmar.

The West Twins opened in February, 1939, at 924 Robert Street in West St. Paul, and the city's mayor led 350 guests to the adjoining West Inn for a formal dinner before the film. The art deco theater had 1,200 seats, glass bricks, neon lights, curving steel handrails, and a circular lobby with a blue terrazzo floor. The revolving tower had neon letters four feet high and was once a prominent feature on the West St. Paul skyline. The auditorium was built in a stadium style, the screen was 16 by 23 feet. The lobby walls were adorned with seven-foot high blue mirrors and the ceiling was lit by indirect lighting. The opulence notwithstanding, the West Twins lasted only thirty years.

The Boulevard Twins in South Minneapolis was a 1,000-seat theater offering red velour seats, a large gift shop, and a broad staircase leading to the plush-red second floor dining room. The casual, family-style restaurant sat next to the lobby. The theater opened in March of 1933. It was divided in two in 1978 and closed as a movie house in 1999. Hollywood Video is there now. However, the marquee still says "Boulevard" arched over the important notice: "Park In Rear" meaning free parking. Through the 1960s dinner and a movie was still only $2.50. "Twins" meant theater and restaurant.

The Avalon, sporting a lovely tower, lasted from 1931 to 1984. The Franklin began in 1914 but has been vacant as a movie house for twenty-five years.

Because of friction with film distributors Frank eventually decided to make his own films, and in 1941 he and attorney Robert McDonald joined forces with William Dieterle, a distinguished film director with RKO Studios, to produce *All That Money Can Buy* (1941) starring Walter Huston and Edward Arnold. It was a great hit and Frank bought the full rights to it later. Its original title was *The Devil and Daniel Webster*. Bosley Crowther of the *New York Times* hailed this movie as one of the year's best.

Frank's second Dieterle-directed film was *Syncopation* (1942), an all-star music show starring Charlie Barnet, Harry James, Benny Goodman and Gene Krupa backing up stars Jackie Cooper, Adolph Menjou and teen actress Bonita Granville. Cooper's trumpet playing was dubbed by Bunny Berrigan. The film parallels the development of jazz through the life of a young trumpeter from Chicago and his New Orleans girlfriend as they read Walt Whitman to each other and follow hot jazz.

The Adventures of Martin Eden (1942) was Frank's third film as co-producer and this time Columbia was the production studio. His fourth, *Enemy of Women* (1944), followed the life of Goebbels, Adolf Hitler's propaganda minister.

Film number five was *A Boy, a Girl and a Dog* (1946) starring Sharyn Moffett, Jerry Hunter, Harry Davenport (Doctor Mead in *Gone with the Wind*) and Lionel Stander. The film was shot entirely in Minnesota.

Frank's sixth motion picture, *The Great Dan Patch*, was also filmed in Minnesota. Frank was the sole producer for this one. The film is sentimental, technically uneven, and historically inaccurate, yet it also has endearing qualities.

In 1951 he produced *Cry Danger* starring Rhonda Fleming and Dick Powell. Also in the cast are William Conrad, who played Marshal Matt Dillon on radio's *Gunsmoke*, Minneapolis-born announcer, Hy Averback and Richard Erdman.

Rhonda Fleming is at her charming best here, and the bantering dialogue is good—the kind that served Powell so well in radio's *Richard Diamond, Private Eye*. Powell came to the Twin Cities for the film's première at the West Twins and the Boulevard Twins.

Bill Frank's last production was *Sitting Bull* (1954) starring J. Carrol Naish as Sitting Bull, Iron Eyes Cody, Mary Murphy, Dale Robertson and Douglas Kennedy in the role of General George Armstrong Custer. Sidney Salkow directed again for Frank. Frank had made a deal with the Mexican government to provide citizens to portray Indians and some of the capital as well as much of the setting for location shooting. This was another United Artists production shot in cinemascope with magnificent New Eastman Color.

Bill Frank loved ice cream but he grew to hate smoking and was the first to try to ban smoking in movie theaters. This made some movie-goers angry. He had stopped smoking as a young man and rarely drank alcohol yet loved fatty foods like fried chicken and ice cream. He died at age 68 of a heart attack.

W. R. Frank, Jr, a Harvard graduate and ex-marine who served in Korea, loved ice cream, too, but he added peanut butter to his ice cream and died even earlier. Bill, Jr. co-produced only one film, *The Wrestler* (1974) starring wrestling champion, Verne Gagne, who was executive producer of the film.

Shortly after their marriage in 1927 he and Lucille were able to move into 4501 Moorland Avenue in "Old Edina," where they lived until he died. They also had a lake home on Lake Minnetonka's Carmen's Bay next to then-governor Luther Youngdahl.

Ted Mann

Born 16 April 1916,
Wishek, ND
Died 15 January 2001,
Los Angeles, CA

Twenty-one year-old Ted Mann picked a bad year to enter the movie theater business. In 1935 people were lining up for bread, not movie tickets. Yet for him it turned out to be the right time. He leased the Selby Theater in St. Paul for $100 a month. Some people may have gone without bread this or that day but the Selby stayed afloat while the nation continued to suffer from the effects of the Great Depression. In time, Mann would own some twenty-five theaters in the Twin Cities. Later he would produce a half-dozen films and TV series and own a large chain of movie houses across the nation. He would also marry one of the prettiest women in the world, actress Rhonda Fleming.

Mann's first movie-house job was as assistant manager of the Metro Theater in St. Paul. There he sold tickets, made popcorn, sold the candies and soda pop, ran the projector, and cleaned up afterward—a one-man operation. In 1936 he re-opened the Oxford Theater in St. Paul. He bought the Gem Theater three years later and in 1941 built a bowling center next to the Oxford. In 1942 he acquired the Metro and in 1943 the Royal Theater of St. Paul.

In 1944, he met Don Guttmann, who became a partner in buying the Dickerman chain of five theaters. They also built theaters in Compton, California, and Duluth, where Mann became President of Skyline Drive-in Theater Organization and Director of Minnesota Entertainment Enterprises. In 1945 Mann bought the World and Alvin Theaters in Minneapolis and the World in St. Paul, while selling off all his other theaters except the Duluth drive-in. He and Guttmann also operated an industrial banking house in Los Angeles.

Ted had been a Diamond Belt finalist in the light-heavyweight boxing division but had put on weight since, and was now a two-hundred pound man, though he remained active playing handball at the YMCA and walking every morning around Lake of the Isles, which was near his home at 2731 Dean Boulevard. Good-looking, robust, and barrel-chested, Mann prided himself on youthful vigor, and often engaged in fencing matches with one of his ushers, Roger James Dunn, while the features were playing. Ted also golfed on occasion.

Through the 1940s, 50s and 60s Mann was buying up movie houses and eventually owned twenty-five of them in Minnesota. His Minneapolis theaters were the Academy, Downtown Mann (formerly the RKO Pan), Downtown World, State, Orpheum, Edina, Westgate, Uptown, Campus, Park Cinerama, Mann Southtown, France Avenue Drive-in, Suburban World and Varsity. In St. Paul he had the Grand-view, Highland, Strand, St. Paul World, and Orpheum. He sold most of them to General Cinema in 1970. Mann's office was in the Academy so he kept that one until the new Mann theatre was completed at 708 S. Hennepin Avenue.

Mann bought up movie houses like a kid collecting baseball cards, but in time that was no longer enough. He wanted to produce movies. He had run T*he Sound of Music* (1965) at his Academy Theatre for ninety-five weeks, seven weeks short of two full years, selling more than 700,000 tickets for a gross income of $1.4 million. Mann was convinced, in light of these impressive figures, that a well-made movie that really clicked with the public, especially the youth of America, would make a bundle. He pondered several such projects and talked actively with Robert Evans, President of Paramount Pictures, who agreed to pay all the costs—if they liked the project. He also entered into discussions with Robert Wise, who had produced of *The Sound of Music* about film producing prospects.

Mann told the *Minneapolis Tribune* in 1966, "Most of the best films being shown today are being made by the independents, because too many of the big people in the big film companies have simply lost touch with what people want to see. I don't claim to be a director, but I do think I know what kind of a film people are going to see… I know from experience."

Finally, Ted decided to produce *The Illustrated Man* (1969) based on three short stories by science fiction writer Ray Brad-bury, who was widely read by college-aged kids at that time. He hired Minneapolis-born director Jack Smight to make the film and Oscar-winner Rod Steiger, also very hot in the 60s, to star in it, along with Claire Bloom. Warner Bros, with partners, distributed it. Howard Kreitsek, the screenplay writer, was also a producing partner. Though the film was somewhat confused and wandering, it also contained intriguing elements and may be considered a moderate success.

Ted's second venture into film production was *Buster and Billie* (1973) with Jan-Michael Vincent and Pamela Sue Martin, for Columbia Studios. Paramount Studio's *Lifeguard* (1976), which starred Sam Elliott, was Ted's first experience as an executive producer, which means his main job was to raise money for the costs of production. In both this and his next film, *The Nude Bomb* (aka *Maxwell Smart and the Nude Bomb*) for Universal Studios, he worked with Ron Silverman. He and Silverman also co-produced *Brubaker* (1980) with Robert Redford at Twentieth Century-Fox; and *Krull* (1983, aka *Dragons of Krull*; aka *Dungeons and Dragons*) for Columbia.

One painful event in the otherwise lucky life of Ted Mann was his divorce from Ida, his wife of thirty-four years. They had married in 1934. He convinced her that he was worth only a half-million dollars. It turned out his real worth was close to $6 million. In 1978 Ida tried to get more from him.

So, what was Mann's financial worth? Because of increased flack about his owning so many theaters, there were some inquiries as to his having an illegal monopoly in movie-house ownership in Minnesota. These charges, well-founded or not, may have figured into his decision to sell twenty-one theaters to General Cinema Corporation for $6 million in 1970. Not long after the deal he moved to Los Angeles to become more deeply involved as a film producer. In 1973 he bought Sid Grauman's Chinese Theatre and renamed it Mann's Chinese Theatre.

In 1975 Mann bought the National General Theatre chain of movie houses for $67.5 million and renamed it Mann Theatres. During the next ten years he expanded the chain from 276 to 360 screens, and in 1986 he sold the company to Gulf & Western Oil, which also owned Paramount Pictures, for $220 million. However, he stayed on as chairman, retiring in 1991 at which time the company boasted about 500 screens nationwide.

Barbara Flanagan, columnist for the *Star-Tribune*, once described Ted as a "remarkable man who always seemed to be ahead of his time. When he had a hunch, he'd follow it." And Irv Letofsky recalled, "For a guy of his achievement, Ted was a very quiet, almost shy guy. I know people who worked for him, and they said Ted was tough, not unkind, but tough." Letofsky had been a columnist and entertainment writer for the *Minneapolis Tribune* but became a TV critic for the *Hollywood Reporter*. Irv also wrote some skits for Dudley Riggs' Brave New Workshop. Timothy D. Kehr, a promoter for Columbia Records, a rock music critic, advertiser, and occasional producer for band concerts, said, "Ted Mann was accessible to people. I was just a young man with some ideas I wanted to bounce off him. He saw me and gave me some pointers. He was always business-like but he could laugh easily, too."

In recognition of his outstanding contributions to the local arts scene, in 1993 the University named its new 1,250-seat auditorium on the West Bank of the Mississippi the Ted Mann Concert Hall. (Mann's two-and-a-half million gift to the University had helped bring the building's twelve-and-a-half million price tag within reach.) At the ribbon cutting ceremony Ted said, "The star is the hall. I'm just the benefactor."

During the final decade of his life Mann became more involved with TV. He was always curious about what the young people were thinking and wanting, and as a writer he contributed to *O.C. and Stiggs* (1987); *Slimer! And the Real Ghostbusters* (1988); *Millenium* (1996); *Space Truckers* (1996); *Total Security* (1997); and *Judging Amy* (1999). He produced episodes of *NYPD Blue* (1993); *Millenium* (1996); and *Space Truckers* (1996), and appeared as an actor in *NYPD Blue* and *Space: Above and Beyond* (1995).

Mann died at eighty-five from complications of a stroke, survived by actress Rhonda Fleming, whom he had married on January 15, 1977; daughters Roberta Benson and Victoria Simms; a sister, Edythe; and four grandchildren. His younger brother, Marvin, had predeceased him by seven years. Marvin, born in 1925, a forty-year resident of St. Paul's Highland Park, had two sons, Stephen and Benji, who followed their father and uncle into show business, and two daughters, Pamela Margolis and Penny Cody, both of Minneapolis. Marvin and Ted had two sisters, Belle Lerman and Edythe Mark, both of California. Ted's proper name was Abraham but he also went by Alec as a boy. His parents, Ben and Sarah Mann, lived at 805 Jewett Place in North Minneapolis.

What was Ted Mann's secret formula to a successful career in the movie theater business? He said, "Give the public a good theater with conveniences ala 1961, give them a good picture, then tell them what you're playing."

Ted was also a decent singer who loved to be the last one out of piano bars such as Richard's on 4th Street next to the Grain Exchange.

That can be tough on a guy who prides himself on being up at 6 a.m. for his morning walk, and also the first one in the office every morning. But he did it. He did it all! So, hats off to this Polar graduate of Minneapolis North High, Class of '34!!

Byron H. McKinney

Born 11 March 1918,
Scranton, AK.
Died 30 January 2007,
Mpls, MN.

Byron produced the most-watched film in the world, *To Fly* (1976), which has been running almost continuously at the Smithsonian's Air and Space Museum in Washington, D.C. for over thirty years. The film runs eight times a day, six days a week. Just think of the millions of people who have sat in the museum's audience to see the history of flight since this ground-breaking IMAX film premiered during the inauguration of the Air and Space Museum in 1976.

Though born in Scranton, New Jersey, Byron actually grew up in Conway, Arkansas, and graduated from Hendrix College there in 1939. As soon as he got his sheepskin, he lit out for the East Coast to act in the theater, his earliest dream. He worked as a radio actor/announcer, an apt medium to apply his resonant bass-baritone voice before World War II service.

Byron gained experience in flying in the U.S. Navy during World War II, serving in the Pacific Theater of Operations. Following the war he returned to the States to marry Doreen Robertson in 1946. They relocated to New York City where Byron joined the American Theatre Wing, through which he established the first TV training course. In 1948 he became one of the only two directors at the new Dumont Television Network. Later, he became a producer for the J. Walter Thompson Company, one of the nation's largest advertising agencies.

In 1969, as an executive producer, he joined Francis Thompson, Inc., an Academy Award-winning documentary film production company, and produced *City Out of Wilderness*, *The Feast of the Gods*, *Legacy...Andrew W. Mellon Remembered*, and *Col-*

lecting America, before moving on to form his own company, the Byron McKinney Associates.

By this time McKinney had well-established contacts with major corporations such as TWA, Pan Am, American Airlines, Mobil, and Exxon Oil Companies, and he put those contacts to good use drumming up the financing for *To Fly*, which several airline companies contributed to, *Energy! Energy!* (1982), and *Parade* (1987).

One project he strove hard to launch was a documentary on bandstands in America. He was fascinated by the role of the bandstand in community life during the early days of small-town America. It was the center of a town in more ways than one. Entertainment and business were conducted there and shops were built out from that center. His aim was to underscore the ways that bandstands had assisted in our growth of democracy. He had a script, loads of visuals, and the title, but the title he had selected, *And the Band Played On* (1993), was lifted, so to speak, by Pillsbury-Sanford Productions, for a documentary about AIDS. During the course of the 1990s many of Byron's cronies retired and his contacts in business circles dwindled. The bandstand film never got made.

Byron and his wife Doreen retired to Edina, Minnesota, to live near their daughter, Marcia, and her husband, John Diracles. Doreen died a few years later. They have another daughter, Kim Engelsman, of Yardley, PA.. and three grandchildren. Nowadays Byron's passions are the arts, travel, and antiques.

Sarah Pillsbury

Born 1951, New York

Though born in New York, Sarah Pillsbury spent some ten years of her early life in Orono, Minnesota, on Brackett's Point, just north of Lake Minnetonka. She didn't finish up with her original class at Northrop Collegiate School in 1969, however, leaving Northrop early to attend an East Coast prep school before entering Yale University. At Yale Sarah immersed herself in film studies, though she delayed graduation by a year to live in Africa and study its special problems. Upon graduation in 1974 she moved to Los Angeles and began her film career as associate producer for *The California Reich* (1975) which was nominated for an Academy Award for Best Documentary Feature. She also attended UCLA Film School.

In 1976 Pillsbury co-founded Liberty Hill Foundation, a progressive organization formed to alleviate inner city problems in Los Angeles. This group has given seven million dollars to worthy grassroots community groups such as the Korean Immigrant Workers Association, the Bus Riders' Union and welfare rights organizations. The following year she was a crew member of David Lynch's *Eraserhead* (1977). And these two elements—innovating film-making and a social conscience—were to define her career for decades to come.

Sarah treaded carefully in the film world, where one can easily gamble too much too soon and "take a bath," wisely focusing on small-scale, moderate-budget films. Nor were her motives for limiting film costs entirely self-interested. "People are starving in this world," she once remarked. "People are homeless. In my mind, it's literally sinful to spend an outrageous amount of money (on a film)."

Pillsbury co-produced Ron Ellis's script, *Board and Care* (1979) which won an Oscar for Best Short Film. A year later she met Midge Sanford. The two quickly recognized that their ideas about film were similar and they became business partners. By 1982 they had dug up the necessary capital to form Pillsbury-Sanford Productions.

What sorts of topics attracted Pillsbury-Sanford? Their films have explored Down Syndrome, the AIDS virus, surrogate partnering, women's self-discovery, and the complexities of group dynamics. Yet their films remain "character-driven." Another hallmark of Pillsbury-Sanford films is that women occupy the prominent jobs, all things being equal, such as director, screenwriter, cinematographer, and editor.

After careful deliberation of Leona Barisch's screenplay, the two hired Susan Seidelman to direct *Desperately Seeking Susan* (1985) and cast Madonna and Rosanna Arquette in the starring roles. This cult favorite is set in downtown New York City. Arquette is a bored suburban housewife who answers the more intriguing ads in the personals columns. By this means she makes the acquaintance of Manhattan girl Madonna, who introduces her to a very different slice of life. The film has all the best elements of the classic screwball comedies, it's funny with thrills, and it has appealed to a diverse audience.

Pillsbury followed up this success with *River's Edge* (1986), which was also widely praised, its downbeat tone and chaotic, depressing storyline notwithstanding. The film follows the lives of a teenager and his morally bankrupt friends after he casually murders his girlfriend. It stars Crispin Glover, Keanu Reeves (in a real breakthrough performance) and Dennis Hopper. David Denby of *New York* magazine said, "A brilliant, messy little picture, another triumph for the independent film movement...."

Eight Men Out (1988) once again turned challenging material into solid cinema. Written and directed by John Sayles, the film stars John Cusack, D. B. Sweeney, David Strathairn, Charlie Sheen, and Christopher Lloyd in a recount of the 1919 Chicago White Sox team who took bribes to lose the World Series. Though this absorbing drama has some great ensemble acting, distribution was a problem. Major studios were leery of the less-than-heroic subject matter and the absence of a real star. Finally, Orion Pictures said yes.

Immediate Family (1989) is about a rich but childless couple that wants to adopt the unborn child of a poor, unmarried teenager. This was the first script that Pillsbury and Sanford did not initiate themselves. Rather, director Jonathan Kaplan approached the two because he thought that they might, as women and mothers, be amenable to the adoption theme. Glenn Close and James Woods play the infertile couple and Mary Stuart Masterson does a great job as the pregnant, unmarried teen. Critics found the film warmhearted but predictable.

In 1991 Pillsbury and her production partner moved beyond commercial film channels to produce a TV docudrama, *Seeds of Tragedy* (Fox-TV). This film follows coca beans from the farm fields of South American to the street of Los Angeles and shows the many ways that the bean, and the drugs that are made from it, affect the lives of those who deal with it. The team returned to the Hollywood mainstream the next year with *Love Field* (1992), directed once again by Kaplan. It stars Michele Pfeiffer as a Dallas hairdresser who identifies so strongly with Jacqueline Kennedy that when the president is assassinated she feels compelled to attend his funeral. Her encounters along the way to the funeral provide the grist for this surprisingly subtle and satisfying little drama.

Returning to TV, Pillsbury-Sanford struck gold with *And the Band Played On* (1993, HBO Telefilm) which won an Emmy and an Independent Spirit Award. The film tracked the discovery and management of the AIDS epidemic, the history of which was generally not well-known until Randy Shilts's best-selling book told the story. The film brought the epidemic to the attention of an even wider audience.

The next film the two produced together was a chestnut, *How to Make an American Quilt* (1995), starring Minnesota-born Winona Ryder, Jean Simmons, the poet Maya Angelou, Anne Bancroft, Ellen Burstyn, Kate Capshaw, Kate Nelligan, and Rip Torn. Halliwell described it as "a formulaic film that manages to be a humane and enjoyable celebration of feminism without being merely an exercise in nostalgia, illuminating the struggles and triumphs of its participants in their unexceptional lives."

Pillsbury's perchance for exploring poorly-understood personal afflictions continued with *The Tic Code* (1999) a predictable but engaging film starring Gregory Hines as a saxophone player with Tourette's Syndrome. The same year the team also produced *The Joyriders* and *The Love Letter*.

Pillsbury is currently a lecturer at the University of California-Santa Barbara. She has received a Tercentennial Medal from Yale University; she has lectured at the American Film Institute; she is on several advisory boards including the Minnesota Film Board. She and her husband, Richard Kletter, have two grown children, Nora and Will. She lives in Venice, California. She is described as "an extremely outgoing and spontaneous woman; a non-linear thinker who produces a constant flow of creative ideas. Despite her more public successes, her private priorities still are her love and care for her family and for humanity."

When asked if she felt great power being a producer and holding the purse strings, she replied that no one holds all the power. You still have to cajole someone here or plead with someone there or negotiate about this or that. She observed that only Charlie Chaplin and Woody Allen have ever had virtual total control.

In 1999 Blake School presented her with its Outstanding Alumni Award.

Bill Pohlad

Born 1955,
Minneapolis, MN

W hen you have endless amounts of money you can afford to make movies. Bill is the third and youngest son of Carl and Eloise (O'Rourke) Pohlad. Father Carl, a self-made billionaire, recently appeared in the Fortune 500 list of America's richest men at $2.3 billion.

Carl himself didn't have it quite so easy. He was the son of a railroad brakeman. Both he and Eloise were born in Iowa, and they met on a blind date at the Iowa Hawkeye/Minnesota Gopher football game in 1946. It was love at first sight, and the two were married five months later on April 22, 1947. The marriage lasted fifty-six years, ending only with Eloise's death.

Bill began his film career making short documentaries and in-flight programming for Northwest Airlines. His first foray into feature films came with *Old Explorers* (1991). Jim Cada and Mark Keller wrote the original script as a skit for Dudley Riggs' ETC Theatre at Seven Corners in Minneapolis, with Jim Lawless and Warren Frost playing two elderly men who swap wild tales about daring adventures. The show was held over for weeks and weeks, and it occurred to Pohlad that the material might be worthy of turning into a film.

After reworking the script, Pohlad hired old pros James Whitmore and Jose Ferrer to play the leads and secured time at Paisley Park in Chanhassen to shoot the film. It did not receive serious distribution, however, and Pohlad stayed away from commercial features for quite a while, except for doing a turn as second unit director for *Little Big League* (1994), a film made partly in Minnesota.

A friend of Pohlad's, an aficionado of "A Prairie Home Companion," contacted him about video-taping the 30th Anniversary Show (2004), which he agreed to do. Then word got out that Robert Altman wanted to direct a movie of the show. Garrison Keillor, the show's creator, wrote the script and Pohlad financed it. Stars Meryl Streep, Tommy Lee Jones, Kevin Kline, Lily Tomlin, and Woody Harrelson led the usual cast for a fine cinematic romp.

In between the video-taping and the filming of *A Prairie Home Companion* (2006) Pohlad co-financed *Brokeback Mountain* (2005), a cowboy love story that made a fine showing at the Academy Awards, and *I'm Going To Tell You a Secret* (2005), a film of Madonna's 2004 national tour.

Chris Hewitt of the *St. Paul Pioneer Press* recently noted that all the films produced by Bill Pohlad, diverse as they are, have one thing in common: They're good. And Stephanie N. Mehta of *Fortune* magazine identified Pohlad as one of several new, deep-pocket, outsider-producers with loads of ready cash to invest in a film they happen to like. One investor may go into twenty movies to spread his risk and do well in the long run because there is no certain way to foresee success except that movies that cost over $100 million to make are much more certain to bring a decent profit than cheaper-to-produce films. Pohlad's perspective is totally different. If he likes it, he invests.

However, Bill Pohlad is never in a hurry to make up his mind. He takes his time to feel certain that this or that film is a good fit for him. "For me, this is about love of movies, not a business deal or because there's a big opportunity to make money," Pohlad says, in spite of the fact that **Brokeback Mountain** cost only $13 million to make and grossed $175 million in its first year. "I'm proud of the fact that our slate consists almost 100% of movies I love and have a strong creative connection to." Pohlad is said to have the "aesthetic approach." Others call him the "dream financier," who can fulfill the dreams of art-house writers/directors like Robert Altman.

This new breed of money men has taken some of the risk off the major studios and, as long as they occasionally produce hits, they will stay a factor in movie production, says Robert Evans, longtime CEO of Paramount Pictures. The ones who get skittish and want only quick profits will not last in the business once they hit a losing streak.

"Bill has a sense of nuance, a very literate manner," observed James Schamus, main producer of **Brokeback Mountain** and co-President of Focus Features. He invited Pohlad into co-financing the film. He added, "People often come to Hollywood looking to invest in films and, generally, the industry treats them the way a boy who just gets a new BB gun treats a tin can on his back fence. But Bill has been extremely smart and strategic about his entry into the business and how he goes about his business."

His temper, or lack thereof, is also something new. "Whether it has to do with my being from Minnesota or some kind of attitude, I've had a really good time with these people," Pohlad said. "I've tried to deal with them as a regular guy." He added, "I'm not a big fan of publicity—I don't like to blow my own horn. I prefer a low profile but I also don't want to be rude."

Bill has hobnobbed with Madonna, Nicole Kidman, Robert Downey, Jr., Steven Soderbergh and the list is growing. Kidman plays the title role in *Fur: An Imaginary Portrait of Diane Arbus* (2006), one of Pohlad's recent films that was neither popular or critically esteemed. "It's been intriguing to connect with these talented people on a one-to-one basis," Pohlad said. "Madonna was a joy to work with. She expects a lot from herself." He noted that Kidman and Downey were polar opposites, "Nicole is very studied and super-prepared. Downey is like a loose cannon, totally spontaneous."

Staying at the rate of two films a year, *The Chicago 10* (2007) and *Into the Wild* (2007) are Pohlad's newest films to date. Pohlad's most ambitious upcoming project, *Che* with Steven Soderbergh directing, will star Benicio Del Toro as the Cuban revolutionary who fought alongside of Fidel Castro and later became a cult hero.

Early in his career Pohlad made documentaries on Prince and Joe Dowling, the Artistic Director of the Guthrie Theater. He founded River Road Entertainment in 1987 and keeps his office on the fortieth floor of a downtown Minneapolis office building while also maintaining a presence in Hollywood. He and wife, Michelle, and their son, Oliver, still live in Minneapolis. Why? "I don't like Los Angeles. My family had a fair amount of contact with the entertainment business while I was growing up, and even though I like the business, there was something about the Los Angeles scene that I didn't want to get caught up in... I have a better perspective from here."

Mike Todd

Avrom "Abe" Goldbogen
Born 22 June 1907, Mpls, MN
Died 23 March 1958, NM

Mike Todd was always running out of his father's house to embark on some scheme and he was always hollering to one of his older brothers, "Gimme my toat." His brothers called him toaty or toady for several years because of this. Only when he entered show business did he realize that Abe Goldbogen didn't have a theatrical ring, so he became Mike Toad, which was further modified to Mike Todd. Mike was the English equivalent of Moishe, his grandfather's name.

Todd's father, Chaim, and his grandfather were Orthodox rabbis in Poland but pogroms in the early 1900s forced them to emigrate to America. When Chaim arrived in Minneapolis, he found that the Jewish community already had a rabbi and couldn't support a second one so he did a variety of jobs to make ends meet for his family. Mike was seventh of eight children. His mother was Sophia Hellerman Goldbogen. His older brothers were Joe, Frank and Carl; one older sister was Sarah; a younger brother was David. They lived in Minneapolis for ten years and in the Oxboro Heath part of Bloomington for a year and a half before moving to the near northwest side of Chicago in 1918, where Chaim finally found a congregation that needed a rabbi.

The family remembered that Mike liked the garbage man and he used to tag along with him on his route collecting trash. Little four-year old Mike sat on the man's lap and held the horse's reins. He occasionally spotted some unusual piece of junk that he would rescue to trade or sell later. He moved on to establish a shoe-shining business, parking himself in front of a Hennepin Avenue brothel. The business was brisk, but his presence irritated the madam, who therefore commissioned him to walk up and down Hennepin Avenue handing out advertising cards. For every card that brought a customer Mike received a quarter. Mike passed out the cards but he missed the piano music coming from inside the brothel—perhaps his first brush with show business.

Mike described his first regular job. "I worked for a pitchman in Minneapolis... and I had a knife through my neck. I was known as a shill and I had to get the tip, which means the crowd...Now this pitchman, Doc Benton, was probably the guy who started me in show business and I was about seven years old." That would 1914.

His younger brother Dave described another of Mike's ventures. "Attracted on Saturdays by such stirring serials as *Stingeree*, he began hanging around the Zone Picture Palace in our neighborhood. (The Zone was built around 1913 at 1300 Sixth Avenue South.) By helping to set up the folding chairs and cleaning up after the shows, he so ingratiated himself with the manager that he landed himself a job. Among his other duties was to station himself at the side door to make sure that no kids could sneak in. Todd drew fifteen cents a week for his work but he soon found a way to supplement this salary when, during the First World War, an amusement tax skyrocketed the admission to six cents. Todd dropped the word around the neighborhood that if you came to the side door, not only could you have the benefit of the original five cents admission, but two could come in for that price. Todd was doing great until one day a couple of kids went up to the box office and demanded the two-for-five-cents admission, whereupon the manager booted out his "side-door partner."

Early in life Mike Todd figured out how to turn adversity into opportunity. He was nine when his tonsils were removed. The day after the surgery he returned to school and charged each classmate two cents to look down his tonsil-less throat.

When the Minneapolis Working Boys Marching Band started up, Mike fell in love with the splendid uniforms and decided to join in. He saved money from his small ventures and bought a cornet from a hock shop. He learned some John Philip Sousa tunes, auditioned and joined the band. About this time he saw some live shows such as Gilbert & Sullivan's *Mikado*. (As an adult he later produced *The Hot Mikado*, which earned him some nice profits.)

Mike loved being where the action was, and it was an easy trip downtown from his family's homes at 1137 Emerson Avenue North (1910), 622 Lyndale Avenue North (1912), and 718 Girard Avenue North (1913 to 1917). When the family moved to Oxboro Heath, in the vicinity of Old Shakopee Road and Lyndale Avenue South, he was very unhappy. But his father Chaim ran a general store there, so ten-year old Mike contented himself with commuting to the city (probably taking the Dan Patch Railroad to the depot at 54th & Nicollet Avenue and taking the street car downtown from there.) He indulged himself with as much food and entertainment as he could afford. He did not believe in saving money. What he didn't give to his parents, he spent. A favorite stop was the Baltimore Dairy Lunch where a quarter could buy a Delmonico-styled feast, albeit the Minneapolis version.

Mike's formal education came to an end after sixth grade. The family moved to Chicago and Mike was enrolled in seventh grade in junior high school but was caught running a crap game during a recess on school grounds. His lookout guard for the event was Jack E. Leonard, the comedian, who became his life-long chum. Todd said he was going to pay Leonard but never did, or so Jack later claimed.

By thirteen Mike was attracted to the pharmaceutical business and he persuaded a druggist to train him. At thirteen he was the youngest person in the state of Illinois to win an assistant pharmaceutical license. At fifteen he started a bricklayers college and he was, of course, president of the college. That folded when graduates of the program found they couldn't get the jobs he had promised them.

A little before his sixteenth birthday Todd married Bertha Freshman. They eloped on Valentine's Day, 1923, to be married by a justice of the peace in Crown Point, Indiana. Bertha was the eldest of seven children. She was poised, attractive and an honors student AND she thought she could handle Mike Todd. They had one child, Mike Todd, Jr. The marriage to Bertha lasted twenty-three years, but Bertha never really adjusted to Mike's unstable, roller-coaster life. He was a big spender, big gambler, big risk-taker, and there was just too much insecurity. Often he didn't come home at night preferring to stay out with gambling buddies like Damon Runyon. By the age of twenty-three Mike Todd had made and lost two fortunes.

Todd's life as a theater producer began at the Chicago World's Fair in 1933-34. In the French section he created a ballet/striptease show in which a beautiful girl with moth-like wings dances around a large burning candle. Her gauze wings catch fire, her costume burns up and suddenly she's naked. It was called "The Flame Dance." Mike toured the country with this show and with another naughty show called "At Home A Broad." Both did well for him.

His first grand success in the "legitimate theater" was buying the play *Harvey*. He first saw it in Boston. That production included a six-foot rabbit on stage with star Frank Fey. Todd told the director that the rabbit had to go but the rest of the show was great! The rabbit went and *Harvey* became a smash hit, closing after 1,175 performances—the fifth longest running show in Broadway history—at the Forthy-eighth Street Theatre, which had previously been considered a jinxed venue.

Mike came to know several Broadway persons quite well over the years. He and Damon Runyon often went to the race tracks together in the afternoons and played gin rummy at night. Playwright George S. Kaufman was another boon companion. Strip-dancer Gypsy Rose Lee became a "special" friend while Mike was working to produce a play about her life. In order to establish himself on Broadway quickly Mike allowed a phony feud to hit the press about how he and Billy Rose were fighting about something. Rose married Fanny Brice after she left Nick Arnstein, a wild gambler, and their story is told in the movie *Funny Lady* (1975) starring Barbra Streisand. During those days Mike was known as "The Boy Genius."

Bertha Todd died in 1946, and a year later Todd married Joan Blondell, who had recently divorced Dick Powell. Todd brought his new bride to Minnesota where he picked up a copy of his birth certificate, which now boasted a doctored-up birthdate, thanks to the cooperation of Senator Hubert Humphrey. With the flick of a pen and the slipping of cash into Humphrey's pocket, Mike was suddenly two years younger. Or so the story goes.

The marriage to Blondell didn't last, and in 1957 Todd married Elizabeth Taylor. That very happy union lasted just over a year, ending with Todd's untimely death in a plane crash in the mountains of New Mexico during a storm. He and Liz had one child, Liza Todd, who was Elizabeth's last child.

Liz was his girlfriend when he was organizing the casting of his one hands-on film marvel, *Around the World in 80 Days* (1956). Mike wanted his cast to be star-studded and it was. David Niven headed the cast in the role of the gambler-traveler, Phineas Fogg, the epitome of an English gentleman who is ever punctual and proper. For Fogg's valet, Passepartou, Todd chose Cantinflas, who was very popular in Mexico and Latin America. Not only was he a fine selection for the part but Todd was aware of the gross receipts that the Latin countries could contribute to his block-buster if it boasted an international cast. To bolster this image he persuaded dancer, Jose Greco, and his dance company to provide the entertainment to Fogg in Spain before his Mediterranean Sea crossing. The horse-faced comic, Fernadel, led them in a buggy ride to the Eifel Tower in Paris just prior to the balloon crossing of the Alps.

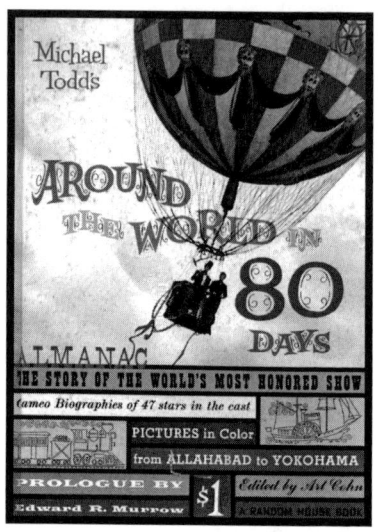

Some of the stars Todd rounded up were still in their heyday, such as Frank Sinatra, but the film also boasted a long list of aging or retired stars including Marlene Dietrich, Ronald Colman (who was begged back to be a railway inspector in India) and Colonel Tim McCoy who led the cavalry for one final time against the marauding Indians. Joe E. Brown still had one great movie ahead of him, *Some Like It Hot* (1958), but Buster Keaton, Jack Oakie, Edmund Lowe, and Victor McLaughlin were at the end of their careers. The one new face was Shirley MacLaine who was starring as the female lead for the first time ever. She played an Indian princess who is rescued by Fogg and Passepartou and marries Fogg in London at the conclusion of his madcap journey around the world.

Mike Todd was only the producer for the film but following in the David Selznick mold, he virtually directed it as well. When the Academy Award announced that *Around the World in 80 Days* (1956) had won the Oscar for Best Picture, Mike marched up to the microphone and thanked the Academy for their wise and judicious selection of his film as being the best that year. He said he felt like a winner of the triple-double as he announced his forthcoming marriage to Elizabeth Taylor and also the recent racetrack successes of a horse he owned.

Simultaneously with producing this giant film, Mike had scientists and engineers studying different ways to enhance the audio elements of film. This became Todd AO Corporation, which had a wonderful run of its own by garnering technical Academy Awards in Sound for *Oklahoma* (1955), *South Pacific* (1958), *The Alamo* (1960) and *West Side Story* (1961). The Todd AO Corp. and Westrex Corp shared the 1957 Technical Oscar for the Todd AO System, for its method of producing and exhibiting wide-film motion pictures. Six Oscars in seven years is phenomenal to say the least!

Two years later Todd was traveling in a small plane, "The Lucky Liz," when, flying grossly overweight and at the limit of its altitude capacity, its engine failed and it crashed into the mountains of New Mexico killing everyone on board.

Patrick Wells

Born 1943, Wayzata, MN

Pat Wells is a super-clean-living guy, but he has one vice. He is addicted to movies, particularly the making of movies. His formed the habit in 1981 during his involvement with the Minnesota-made film, The Personals, written and directed by Peter Markle. Pat did the fund-raising, the executive producer's primary job. No funds, no film. He had previously been a Board Member and fund-raiser for the Cricket Theatre in Northeast Minneapolis. His motto in school: "No sweat!"

How did Markle find his angel (finance man)? They both used the same insurance agent, who thought the two might benefit from getting better acquainted. They had played on the same high school hockey at Blake School in Hopkins, though Wells was a senior on the team and Markle was only a freshman. Both had a passion for hockey. Wells later played on the 1965 Middlebury College (VT) championship team that won the NCAA, East Coast, Division II Title; and Markle played for Yale and for the U.S. Hockey Team, the best of the best of American hockey players.

Pat raised all the $425,000 total budget for *The Personals* and $100,000 of that went just to pay for the rights to certain pop songs used for background music. Markle wrote, directed, co-produced, and did the camerawork. Stephen E. Rivkin, an acquaintance from making industrial films, edited. Rivkin, lead actor Bill Shoppert, and others became associate producers.

The film tells a touching yet humorous tale of a divorced man (Shoppert) looking for new love in the Personals column of newspapers. He finds love with Karen Landry and learns a bit about life in the process. This film was made entirely in the Twin Cities and features roller-skating around Lake Calhoun and other urban sites. The whole community seemed to support the film. The Cooper-Park Cinerama ran the film for twelve weeks straight. Wells and Markle persuaded New World Pictures to distribute it nationally. It received good reviews in the *Los Angeles Times*, the *New York Times*, the *Washington Post*, the *Village Voice* and *Variety*. In time it turned a profit.

On the strength of the film's success, both Wells and Markle moved to Hollywood. Their next venture together was *Hot Dog...The Movie* (1983), an action-comedy hit, followed by *Youngblood* (1986). Patrick invested in *Hot Dog*, which had a $2.5 million budget and earned gross receipts of over $20 million. It was distributed by M-G-M/United Artists. He co-produced and co-wrote *Youngblood* with Markle. This film cost $5 million to make and brought in a gross of $15 million domestically and $25 million gross worldwide. It was distributed by United Artists. It starred Rob Lowe and Patrick Swayze. A year earlier Pat had been associate producer for *Space Rage*, and he had developed a $3.2 million budget for a science fiction thriller called *Vestron* starring Richard Farnsworth in 1985.

The budgets grew with each film, and in 1988 Pat optioned the book and developed a $12 million spy-thriller called *Honor Bound* starring Tom Skerritt. Next came *The Cellar* (1990), a $1.8 million fantasy/horror film shot on location in Tucson, Arizona, for Indian Neck Entertainment.

By far the biggest film challenge to date was his co-producing with Lawrence Kasdan the film *I Love You to Death* (1990) with Kevin Kline, Tracy Ullmann, William Hurt, Joan Plowright, River Phoenix, and Keanu Reeves. This Tri-Star film, which Kasdan also directed, had a budget of $22 million and received excellent reviews.

For his most recent film Well's returned to his Minnesota roots to produce *Herman, USA* (2001, aka *Taking a Chance on Love*), for which he raised capital of $5 million. The film opened in fifty-six theaters in the Upper Midwest while playing in 125 screens in all nationally. Through a quirk of rotten luck the domestic release came three days after the destruction of the World Trade Center towers in New York City on September 11, 1991, and only a sprinkling of customers showed up to see this poignant romantic comedy. It was directed by Bill Seamans, founder and early director of the Cricket Theatre.

Wells, who heralds from old English stock and had relatives who came over on the Mayflower in 1620, attended Blake School throughout his school years and graduated in 1961. He graduated from Middlebury College, Vermont, in 1965, with a degree in Economics and studied industrial relations in graduate school at the University of Minnesota. He served in the U.S. Army, 1966-67, discharged as a First Lieutenant. Pat was awarded the Army Commendation Medal for training recruits with learning disabilities and behavioral problems and most of those did go to Vietnam, a tribute to his executive abilities. He was the Company Commander of this group at Fort Knox, Kentucky.

In his other business life Patrick was an owner and Executive Vice President of Lundgren Bros. Construction, Inc. 1970-80; President of Lundgren Bros. Remodeling, 1991-96. He and his co-owner sold the company to U.S. Homes in 1999. It was later bought by Lenard Homes, the biggest home builder in the U.S..

Wells has written a book: *Free Rides: How to Get High without Drugs* (1991); republished as *Stoned Free: How to Get High without Drugs* (1995). He has appeared frequently on local radio shows and the public speaker circuit, speaking on spiritual topics such as Near Death Experiences. He is President of God's Dream L.L.C. currently developing five films with themes on human spirituality. *At Jesus' Side*, an animated, romantic tragicomedy, was completed at the end of 2006. In high school Pat was well known for hosting fine parties; riding horses, and skiing, acting in the class play, *Finian's Rainbow*, and for his calm, cheerful attitude. He is still well known for working hard to finish up the jobs he starts.

Directors

Hy Averback

*Born 21 October 1920,
Minneapolis, MN
Died 14 October 1997,
Los Angeles, CA*

Hy lived briefly at 624 Sixth Avenue North, at 619 Aldrich Ave.
No. and at 909 Oliver Ave. No. but his
parents, Lewis and Rebecca, moved
away from Minneapolis in 1931, when
Hy was eleven. By that time Hy had completed the John Hay Elementary School next to Lincoln Junior High. His father was a barrel maker
and occasionally a peddler.

Though Hy eventually distinguished himself as an actor, film
and TV director, and producer, it is as a radio announcer that he first
became known to the American public. His first important radio
job was on *The Sealtest Village Store* (1943-1948), a musical variety
show and spin-off from *The Rudy Vallee Show*. St. Paul's Joan Davis
began the run as proprietress of the mythical store. Jack Haley from
The Wizard of Oz was her helper. Hy came on board for announcing
duties in 1945, at the age of twenty-five, just as Davis and Haley were
leaving. Hy jumped over to CBS for his next gig, announcing for the
comedy *Sweeney and March* (1946), in which Bob Sweeney and Hal
March offered a series of unrelated comic skits. (March would later
become the famous TV quiz master of *The $64,000 Question*.)

Back with NBC, Hy announced for *The Jack Paar Show*, a situation comedy series that ran as the 1947 summer replacement for *The
Jack Benny Show*. Jack Benny, incidentally, discovered Jack Paar during World War II on Guadalcanal when Paar was entertaining troops.
One of the show's writers at the time was Larry Gelbart, who went on
to write for Broadway shows and for TV's *M*A*S*H**, where he met
Averback again, who was then directing shows.

Hy announced for *The Bob Hope Show* from 1948 to 1950. The
show had begun in 1935, and guests such as Judy Garland, Frances

Langford, and Jerry Colonna appeared often. Announcing duties had been handled by Bill Goodwin, Art Baker, Larry Keating from Saint Paul, and Wendell Niles, born in Twin Valley, Minnesota. Doris Day was a regular guest while Hy was with the show.

He returned to CBS as an actor in the crime drama, *Broadway Is My Beat*, joining the cast when the show moved from New York to Hollywood in 1949. Hy's final major radio job came in 1950 when he joined the cast of *Presenting Charles Boyer*, a romantic drama in which Boyer played a stereotypical French lover-cad-adventurer.

Averback's real directing began in 1957 with the TV series *The Real McCoys*. He graduated to *The Rogues* in 1964, a very sophisticated and wry-humored, though ultimately short-lived mystery series with a great cast that included David Niven, Charles Boyer, Robert Coote, Gladys Cooper, and Gig Young. Averback also directed episodes of *The Rockford Files, Columbo, The Love Boat II, The Dukes of Hazard,* and *Murder, She Wrote.*

Hy was executive producer to the 1965 TV series *F Troop*. He produced *The Don Rickles Show* in 1972 and the *Big Eddie* series (1975).

In 1975 Hy won an Emmy for Outstanding Direction in a Comedy Series with the *M*A*S*H** episode "Alcoholic Unanimous," which also won him a Director's Guild Award. In 1976 he won the Director's Guild Award for the *M*A*S*H** episode "Bombed" and he again won the Emmy for the Outstanding Direction in a Comedy Series with "Sons & Bowlers" of the 1981-82 season of *M*A*S*H**. Hy ended up directing nineteen episodes.

Averback-directed movies made for TV include *A Guide for the Married Woman* (1978), *The New Maverick* (1978), *The Night Rider* (1979), *She's in the Army Now* (1981), *Where the Boys Are '84* (1984), *The Last Precinct* (1986), *The Rubber Gun Squad* (1977) and *The Magnificent Magical Magnet of Santa Mesa* (1977), starring Roseville actress Loni Anderson.

Hy's three principal film parts were in *The Benny Goodman Story* (1956, as William Alexander), *Four Girls in Town* (1956, as Bob Trapp), and *How to Succeed in Business without Really Trying* (1967, as the second executive). In those day he was also a regular cast member on *Our Miss Brooks Show* (as Mr. Romero), *The NBC Comedy Hour, The Saturday Night Revue,* and NBC's *Tonight*. He was also a regular narrator for the *Meet Corliss Archer show* in 1954.

Hy's film debut was significant. He played Harry the Bookie in *Cry Danger* (1951), a film starring Rhonda Fleming and Dick Powell and produced by W. R. Frank, the first film producer from Minnesota.

Hy produced one commercial feature film, *Chamber of Horrors* (1966). He was also a production manager for the TV series *Meet Corliss Archer* (1954). He appeared on the *I Love Lucy* show in 1953 and 1955. Eventually Hy touched all the bases in Hollywood, hitting homers in radio and TV and directing some of the best episodes of *M*A*S*H*.

Earl F. Bellamy

Born 11 March 1917,
Minneapolis, MN
Died 30 November 2003,
Albuquerque, NM

Earl broke into directing as a "second unit" man or assistant director in movies, and later moved into television where he directed more than 1,600 episodes.

The Bellamy family moved from Minneapolis to Los Angeles, California, in 1920, when Earl was three. Papa's experience as a railroad engineer qualified him to run the steam engine powering the Gaylord Hotel in Hollywood. Young Earl went on to Hollywood High and graduated in 1935, after which he picked up a job as a messenger at Columbia Studios. "I was there a week and I knew what I wanted to do," Earl later told the *Albuquerque Journal*.

He worked his way up to production clerk and, finally, in 1939, he made his debut as assistant director in *Blondie Takes a Vacation* (1939). He took some night courses in drama, largely in order to better understand actors. He said later, "I have always respected the actors I've worked with and, as a director, I wanted to keep them relaxed." His on-set motto as a director was "no strain." "If someone flubbed their lines, no strain. Everyone I've worked with has appreciated it."

Earl worked as an assistant with some top-flight directors including Fred Zinnemann, George Cukor, and George Stevens. While working on Shirley Temple's *Kiss and Tell* (1945), Earl got his draft notice. He was assigned to a Navy film training unit, "I really enjoyed it," Bellamy told the *Times* in 2002. "I had a lieutenant who was a great officer but knew absolutely nothing about making movies, so I had quite a bit of creative control."

By the late 1940s Earl was assistant-directing higher class, B-budget pictures like *The Fuller Brush Girl* (1949) starring Lucille Ball and Minneapolis-raised Eddie Albert. An exciting change of pace presented itself when he was hired to help introduce *The Lone Ranger* to TV audiences, directing twenty-seven episodes (six months' worth) for the show's debut season. Strangely, Bellamy was attracted to the hectic pace of early TV filming.

When he returned to assisting on feature films, they were more often A-budget, quality films such as *Born Yesterday* (1950) with Judy Holliday and Broderick Crawford, directed by George Cukor; *Sirocco* (1951) with Humphrey Bogart; *Ten Tall Men* (1951) with Burt Lancaster; *The Marrying Kind* (1952) with Judy Holliday; *Salome* (1953) with Rita Hayworth, Stewart Granger, Charles Laughton; *Let's Do It Again* (1953) with Jane Wyman and Ray Milland; *From Here to Eternity* (1953) with Burt Lancaster and Deborah Kerr, directed by Fred Zinnemann; *It Should Happen to You* (1954) with Judy Holliday and Jack Lemmon; and *A Star Is Born* (1954) starring Judy Garland and James Mason.

Turning to TV nearly full-time, in 1953 Bellamy directed *General Electric Theater* and four other series in quick succession. He directed the film *Seminole Uprising* (1955) starring George Montgomery and William Fawcett; then returned to TV with *Sergeant Preston of the Yukon* (1955).

Some of the scads of TV series he directed were *Lassie*; *The Adventures of Rin Tin Tin*; *M Squad*; *Perry Mason*; *Leave It to Beaver*; *Wagon Train*; *The Donna Reed Show*; *I Spy*; *Get Smart*; *Starsky and Hutch*; *The Love Boat*; *Fantasy Island*; *Rawhide*; *McHale's Navy*; *Hart to Hart*; and *M*A*S*H*.

Some of his twenty features were *Blackjack Ketchum, Desperado* (1956); *Toughest Gun in Tombstone* (1958); *Stagecoach to Dancer's Rock* (1962); *Fluffy* (1965); *Munster, Go Home* (1966, he had already directed several episodes in the 1964 season of *The Munsters*); *Three Guns for Texas* (1968); *Sidecar Racers* (1975); *Sidewinder* (1977); and *Magnum Thrust* (1981).

After a very satisfying 1984-85 season directing seventeen episodes of *Trapper John, M.D.*, Earl retired. He had been working in the movie and TV biz for fifty years. Bellamy died at the age of eighty-six. He was survived by Gail, his wife of twenty-six years; three children: Earl J., Michael and Karen; five grandchildren; and eleven great grandchildren. They had lived in Rio Rancho since 1991.

He was in TV in its embryo stages where they did fast set ups and fast "takes;" there was little time to rehearse and do several takes as you can in the movies. Most certainly there is no other Minnesota director with so many TV directing credits and possibly none others in the United States. Earl could and did deliver fast, quality products within any schedule. And he loved the stress of it!

"The interesting thing about television was that, in those days, you had six days to put together an hour-long show and three days for a half-hour show. It was possible to do two shows a week," he told the *Albuquerque Journal*. "That was the fun of it, because you'd get a new script and a new cast. If you were doing features, which were a lot of fun, it was a long and drawn-out process. With TV, you're through with one show in six days, and now you've got another one to do with a new script, and off you go again." He once said, "I got hooked on television." He was TV's most sought-after director.

Ernest Borgnine, who worked with Bellamy on the 1960s hit comedy series, *McHale's Navy*, remembered the "no strain" approach. "It was wonderful working with him because he made everything so enjoyable. When you worked with him, there was plenty of time for laughter all the time," Borgnine told the *Times*. Robert Wagner, the star of *Hart to Hart*, said, "He used to have a wonderful saying, and that was when you finished a shot. He'd say, 'First rate' and that's what he was."

Boyd Magers, who publishes *Western Clippings*, said of Bellamy, "... to me, the important thing about Earl was his irrepressible spirit. It rubbed off on everybody he knew and came into contact with." In 2002, a year before he died, Bellamy won the Golden Boot Award from the Motion Picture and Television Fund for his contributions to the Western film genre. He also won a Director's Guild Award for his work on assistant directing *From Here to Eternity*.

Earl learned something important from George Cukor, that everybody has something to contribute—even the guy who sweeps the stage. "I remember Cukor one time used a suggestion that turned into a very funny moment. In *It Should Happen to You* there's a scene where Peter Lawford was about to kiss Judy Holliday. 'Just a minute' she said as she removed her earrings. 'Now.' It was the prop man's idea to take off the jewelry."

Jack Conway

Born 17 July 1886,
Graceville, MN
Died 11 October 1952,
Pacific Palisades, CA

Jean Harlow's favorite director was Jack Conway. M-G-M also loved him as he was "Mr. Dependable" who delivered a steady flow of solidly-directed films for twenty-five years. Yet he had acted and directed in oodles of movies in the silent days before the formation of Metro-Goldwyn-Mayer in 1924.

Jack was born in Graceville, which lies in Big Stone County on the western edge of Minnesota as it borders South Dakota. It's a small prairie town, pheasant and goose country, surrounded by wheat and potato farmers who also give some acreage to sugar beets, soy beans, and corn. It also borders on Indian Country as the Lakota Sioux were neighbors in Sisseton across the Sioux River in South Dakota. And there were lots of Indians in the Dakotas in those days, only ten years after the Little Big Horn slaughter of Custer's Seventh Cavalry in Southeastern Montana.

Jack Conway was born among pioneers, settlers, sod-busters, and Indians in an age preceding the airplane by seventeen years, the automobile by ten, radio by thirty-plus and movies by fifteen years. Instead of airplanes there were kites to fly in the summer skies; instead of autos there were buckboards, Conestoga wagons, and prairie schooners and sleighs in winter. Life was a lot quieter and there was more time to dream.

Jack's parents, James and Hanna, were born in Ireland. Hugh was the third of four surviving children from nine pregnancies. They were farmers. Jack had a much older sister, Mary, a much older brother, Stephen, and a slightly younger brother, Frank. He attended a one-room school house through his mid-teens. He had become a "legit actor" in Santa Barbara by 1907. By 1909 he had drifted into the moving picture business and joined the D. W. Griffith Stock Company. He was the male lead in *Her Indian Hero* (1912), which was also his debut as a director. This is reputedly the first feature film shot in Hollywood, produced by the old Nestor Motion Picture Company. His stature as an actor grew rapidly as he both starred in (with Gladys Brockwell) and directed *An Old Armchair* (1913) and he achieved true star status in *Valley of the Moon* (1914, as Billy Roberts), taken from a Jack London story. D. W. Griffith, Hollywood's first master director, was Jack's mentor in directing. After 1914 he began phasing out of acting to devote himself to directing.

Jack directed his (and M-G-M's) first sound film, *Alias Jimmy Valentine* (1928), a comedy-drama about crooks, with Lionel Barrymore. He went on to direct *Our Modern Maidens* (1929) with Joan Crawford; and Lon Chaney in his last film and only sound film, *The Unholy Three* (1930). Lon Chaney, Sr. was known as the Man of a Thousand Faces and he created a couple of new ones for this film.

After this picture he directed all the major stars at M-G-M Studios. including Robert Montgomery, Grace Moore, and Walter Huston until bad health brought on his early retirement in 1948.

Conway directed John Barrymore in *Arsène Lupin* (1932) in a story about a French jewel thief; Wallace Beery in *Viva Villa* (1934), the life of Mexican revolutionist, Pancho Villa; and Ronald Colman in *A Tale of Two Cities* (1935), the classic film of Charles Dickens' novel.

The first of his four films directing Jean Harlow was *Red-Headed Woman* (1932) followed by *The Girl from Missouri* (1934) and two of their finest films ever, *Libeled Lady* (1936) also starring Spencer Tracy, Myrna Loy, and William Powell; and *Saratoga* (1937), Harlow's last film before dying of kidney failure. *Libeled Lady* was nominated for an Oscar for Best Picture. *Saratoga* also stars Clark Gable, who also co-starred with Harlow in the classic *Red Dust* (1932). Anita Loos wrote this as well as the first two of the Harlow-Conway films.

Conway and Gable were good friends both on and off the set, and sometimes fished and hunted together. In fact, Conway's tales of the Western Minnesota–Dakota prairie brought Gable on hunting missions there with Jimmy Robinson, former Sports Editor of the *Minneapolis Star*, as his host.

Jack's other great films include *A Star Is Born* (1937) starring Janet Gaynor; *A Yank at Oxford* (1938) starring Robert Taylor and Vivien Leigh; *Boom Town* (1940); *The Hucksters* (1947) with Gable, Deborah Kerr, Ava Gardner and Sydney Greenstreet; and *Julia Misbehaves* (1948) starring Greer Garson.

Jack suffered a minor heart attack from a pulmonary disorder in 1948. He hung on for four years but was never able to work again. He was survived by his wife, Virginia, the daughter of silent film star Francis X. Bushman. They had two sons, Patrick and Michael, and a daughter, Mrs. Rosemary Foster. Pat became an actor on contract to M-G-M. Jack died in his showplace home on Sunset Boulevard.

Terry Gilliam

*Terence Vance Gilliam
Born 22 November 1940,
Minneapolis, MN*

Now 3M has two meanings. Terry Gilliam connects Monty Python to Minnesota to movies. (The other 3M is Minnesota Mining & Manufacture or something like that.) Terry was raised on the western shore of Medicine Lake at 2539 Lakeview Blvd, Elmhurst District, Plymouth, and went through Beacon Heights Elementary School. His third grade teacher was Josephine Buckley, a longtime resident of the City of Medicine Lake. He played in the nearby swamps and wooded areas and even built a three-story treehouse.

At age ten Terry got a paper route, though his parents supported the enterprise only reluctantly, as Minnesota's dark, cold, winter mornings can be tough on little kids. All his customers knew when Terry was coming because they could hear him whistling. At eleven Terry, his younger siblings Sherry Lee and Scott, his mother, Beatrice, (who shared these tidbits of his childhood with the author), and James Hall Gilliam moved to Los Angeles. There he matriculated at Occidental College and founded a campus humor magazine, *Fang*, in the early 1960s.

Gilliam graduated with a degree in political science and sped off to New York hoping to meet and work for Harvey Kurtzman, a founder-creator of *Mad Magazine*. Kurtzman now published *Help* and as luck would have it, he needed some. His associate editor had just resigned, and Terry got the job. One of his memorable works was a fumetti strip which showed John Cleese as a man falling in love with his daughter's Barbie doll. *Help* folded in 1965 and Terry wandered around Europe for a while, but ended up back in L. A. illustrating children's books. He moved on to being an art director for an advertising agency.

He met John Cleese when Cleese was on a comedy tour through California. In 1967 Terry moved to London to further develop his zany artistic taste in animation and he did freelance illustration work for the *Sunday Times Magazine*. He also worked for "Car-toons and

Surf-toons" and the *Londoner* magazine. Then he re-connected with Cleese who invited him to join a group of five British-born comedy writers for a TV series. He soon became good friends with his new colleagues Terry Jones and Michael Palin. Their first effort together was *Do Not Adjust Your Set* (1967) followed by *Broaden Your Mind* (1968), starring Michael Palin, though Terry Jones and Gilliam also appear briefly.

They now dubbed themselves Monty Python's Flying Circus, which was also the name of their popular TV comedy show. Initially, Terry provided a collage of photographs and cut-out illustrations. Full animation arrived with the film compilation of sketches from the TV show, *And Now for Something Completely Different* (1971), and it gave The Monty Python Show a look and identity that was quite different from any other show then or now.

Terry appeared only incidentally in these "Python" movies. His primary contributions were as an animator and writer, though he also became a fine director and, of necessity, a producer. Actually, none of these TV writers sought to be actors but they felt that no actors would be very eager to perform their material so they all volunteered themselves. By the way, Graham Chapman, John Cleese, and Eric Idle (also a cartoonist) wrote for David Frost whom they later parodied in their sketches.

Terry kept freelancing on the side, creating the title shots for the movie, *Cry of the Banshee* (1970) for example. The next year he provided twenty-five minutes of animation for ABC's *The Marty Feldman Comedy Machine*. In 1972 he shot his first commercial for the British Gas Board and created the title sequence for a CBS special on William Shakespeare.

The team's next film, *Monty Python and the Holy Grail* (1975) finally won over American audiences, who had been only mildly impressed with *And Now for Something Completely Different*. Gilliam co-directed with Terry Jones. He both wrote and directed his next film, *Jabberwocky* (1975). This starred Michael Palin though Terry Jones and Gilliam appear briefly. The Pythons followed separate ventures after *Holy Grail* but reunited for *Monty Python's Life of Brian* (1979) and *Monty Python's Meaning of Life* (1983) both directed by Terry Jones with Gilliam acting in both and directing the Crimson Permanent Assurance sequence of the second film. The public loved *Life of Brian*, a "what if..." spoof in which a would-be messiah named Brian is mistaken for Jesus and later crucified. In *Meaning of Life* we see gruesome sketches on organ transplants, sex, death and a restaurant scene in which an obese man explodes from overeating.

Mr. Gilliam's first book came out in 1978, *Animations of Mortality*. A few years later he appeared with Dan Ackroyd and Chevy Chase in *Spies Like Us*.

After the success of *The Life of Brian*, which Terry had designed, Handmade Films wanted to work with him. However, they rejected his idea for *Brazil* and agreed to *Time Bandits*. That film really made a name for Gilliam in the film industry.

For *Time Bandits* (1981) most of the Pythons worked but not all. Though it took Gilliam one weekend to come up with the story, it became the biggest money-maker among the Python films. Palin co-wrote this film with Gilliam though Terry directed it. It is about a boy who meets six dwarves who have stolen a map of the Holes in Time and Space from the Supreme Being. The boy goes with them as they meet King Agamemnon (Sean Connery), Robin Hood (John Cleese) and Napoleon (Ian Holm). Shelly Duvall plays a dual role as star-crossed lovers with Palin both on the Titanic and in Sherwood Forest. On the strength of the film offers came to Terry to direct several others including *The Princess Bride* (1987). He rejected them all for his pet project, *Brazil*.

Brazil (1985) led Terry deep into film noir, satire, and tasteless chaos, for which he is proud. Tom Stoppard and Charles McKeown joined him in writing the script about a lowly clerk, Sam Lowry (Jonathan Pryce), in the Ministry of Information Retrieval. The film has some parallels to *1984* in that there is the ever-present repressive bureaucracy watching everyone and tripping them up. Sam falls in love with a beautiful revolutionary (Kim Griest) and his best friend (Michael Palin) becomes his torturer. Robert De Niro and Bob Hoskins make cameo appearances as air conditioner repairmen who are beseeched to lead our heroes to freedom. Ian Richardson also appears.

Universal Studios was unhappy with *Brazil* and refused to run the uncut version anywhere, even though it won the L. A. Film Critics Best Picture Award. It didn't do well at the box office either, perhaps because Universal refused to promote and distribute it as a normal film. They hated the dark view of life it presented and wanted a happy ending, which they added against Terry's wishes. Meanwhile, Gilliam himself was nominated for a Best Original Screenplay Oscar.

The Adventures of Baron Munchausen (1988) was an expensive film with lavish sets, perhaps to its detriment. It was a joint Great Britain-German production. John Neville plays the Baron, famous in literature for his outlandish lies and wild tales. Eric Idle plays his squire. Uma Thurman and Oliver Reed also appear. The Munchhausen tales are a rich blend of reality and fantasy that are designed to cast a spell on the viewer. And yet, although the film was nominated for several technical Oscars, Gilliam's writing and directing did not connect much with audiences, and the film was a box-office flop.

Gilliam returned to a more conventional film style, and greater audience appeal, with *The Fisher King* (1991) which starred Robin Williams and Mercedes Ruehl, who received an Oscar for her performance. An ex-disc jockey (Jeff Bridges) wants salvation and thinks he can find it through a tramp (Robin Williams) who was once a medieval historian. Ruehl plays the long-suffering yet understanding girlfriend. Though the film is ostensibly derived from Chrétien de Troyes's epic *Perceval*, the connections are tenuous, and flights of imagination by both Gilliam and Williams seal the film's success.

Twelve Monkeys (1995) was a critical success. Set in 2035, it tells the story of a convict who is sent back to 1996 to learn more about a virus that has killed off much of the population. Brad Pitt won an Oscar nomination and Bruce Willis was also effective, though many critics felt too much was going on in the film (or in Gilliam's mind), that was bleak and pointless—a psychotic's bad dream.

Fear and Loathing in Las Vegas (1998) written and directed by Gilliam, is based on a book by the gonzo journalist and drug guru Hunter S. Thompson. A journalist and his lawyer get into drugs in a big way in Vegas and embark on a surreal trip. The film sports a fine cast including Johnny Depp, Benicio Del Toro, Ellen Barkin, Gary Busey, Cameron Diaz, Christina Ricci, Lyle Lovett, and Harry Dean Stanton, but viewers reactions varied from "bizarre masterpiece" to "Ten Worst of All Time" lists.

Gilliam has long been interested in making a film about the Spanish knight, Don Quixote. The film has never been completed, but in 2003 a funny and heart-breaking documentary *Lost in La Mancha*, was made about the difficulties the project presents, starring Gilliam and Johnny Depp. Terry's last completed film to date is *Tideland* (2005) which was widely considered to be a misguided mess.

Some have speculated that Gilliam's desire to draw and do animations derives from the fact that his father was a painter. But his father was a *car* painter. Maybe it was the fumes?

John D. Goodell

*Born 30 September 1909,
Omaha, NE
Died 4 April 2004,
St. Paul, MN*

John Goodell was a Renaissance Man who taught ballroom dancing and played the organ as a youth, later designed floating pen holders, floating ashtrays, and other corporate gifts, and went on to invent transfer robots and teaching machines. His natural curiosity led him eventually into the field of industrial motion pictures, and several of his productions won Industrial Oscars. Those Oscars encouraged him to make commercial films, one of which, *It's Always a New Beginning* (1974), earned John a Hollywood nomination for the Oscar for Best Documentary. He and his film crew traveled over five continents and twenty-six countries for four years following in the footsteps of several doctors from the Institute for Achievement of Human Potential, recording how children in various parts of the world learn. (The film lost out to a documentary about rodeos.)

Listening to Goodell discuss the macro-concept of a highly technical procedure or the micro-detail of how the system really worked and where it could be modified or improved, you would never know that he had been a high school drop-out. When John was ten, he tested as equivalent to a thirteen year-old, and that summer the *Pioneer Press* ran a story on the prodigy. He had been collecting butterflies in glass jars, and when asked if a butterfly has intelligence, he replied that "it hasn't any ability to smell or see but has a sense that directs it to a food patch." When asked why he had taken up this hobby, he replied, "It was the mostest fun for the leastest money."

John was the son of Edwin and Vera Goodell of 2315 Harney Street (St. Claire Apartments), in Omaha, Nebraska. His dad was a traveling salesman and his mother an organist. His uncle, H. B. Watts, was a manager of the Strand Theater in St. Paul.

In the 1930s and 40s John worked as a consulting engineer for several companies, though he also worked as a ballroom dance teacher at the Arthur Murray Dance Studios. It was there that he met Bernadette Michel, whom he married in 1943. They had five children: Mary, John Gregory, Thomas, Caroline and Daniel. The first two were born when the family lived on Marshall Avenue and the last three at

1420 Sumner Avenue in Highland Park.

Goodell became the president of Minnesota Electronics Corp in 1946, and later moved on to several other engineering firms. He was Manager of the New Products Department of Brown & Bigelow, St. Paul, 1955-57, where he designed the floating penholders and ashtrays, based on the principle of opposing magnets.

John edited the *Journal of Computing Systems*, 1955-56, writing articles on magnetic structures; electronic circuitry; and special sensing systems—biological, electrical and mechanical. And during the 1950s he was also introduced to the Japanese game of Go (which means "surround"). John, Bernadette and all five children became active Go players. John studied with Takao Matsuda, the Western World Champion for many years, and he even became President of the American Go Association. To excel in Go one needs to know oodles of Japanese proverbs such as "A Go player never quite makes it to his parents' funerals." In 1957, John wrote and published *The World of Ki*, (1957) a book about board games that focused on Go.

In 1958 the family moved to Greenwich, Connecticut, where Goodell became manager of New Product Development for CBS Laboratories (Columbia Broadcasting System). During his stay there Goodell invented the cassette tape recorder for 3M. The family moved to Silver Spring, Maryland, in 1960, where John became President of Robodyne Division of U.S. Industries. Two years later he took a position as Corporate Technical Director of the firm.

In 1963, while employed at Robodyne, John began to write, film, and produce his award-winning industrial motion pictures. A few years later he left Robodyne and moved back to Saint Paul, to 355 Kenneth St. in Highland Park. *Summer of Decision* and *Two Lives in Ten Minutes* were two of his early films, but *It's Always a New Beginning* brought him serious attention and an Oscar nomination.

John and son Dan later made the first-ever film of a gorilla giving birth. In other films he discusses the "double brain" (left and right brain) and the mysteries of creative thought, and we see a computer model of a right brain operating at lightning speed. We are left with a powerful impression of the body/mind as a jumble of energy centers in motion every second of our lives. As we rebuild cells, we have new beginnings. Guthrie actor James Lawless narrated the script. The Uptown Theater in South Minneapolis was one of the many sites where this 90-minute documentary was shown.

In 1982 Goodell was itchy to direct another film and he wrote the script for *Jackpot*. It had a traditional story line about a struggling grocery store owner who makes a deal with Satan, a deal that gives him the power to gamble in Las Vegas and Atlantic City without losing. However, his deal is threatened with exposure when a casino boss becomes suspicious of his unending winning streak. The cast of local actors included Paul Davies, a well known psychic in Minnesota (as the Devil); Warren Frost, Assistant Professor of Theater and Television at the University of Minnesota at the time; Peter Michael Goetz, a popular Guthrie Theatre actor; James Lawless, and Shirley Venard. Two years later Goodell seems to have remade the film with the title, *Satan's Touch*. In that version Lou Bellamy, Founder and Artistic Director of St. Paul's Penumbra Theatre, replaced Goetz, who had moved to New York.

At the age of sixty-two Goodell was involved in a motorcycle accident and spent three months in traction. Thoroughly bored at St. Joseph's Hospital in St. Paul, he gave himself a crash course in orthopedic medicine and then designed a splint-traction device to be used in bed *or* in a wheelchair, allowing a patient to return home weeks earlier than before.

Goodell died of natural causes at the age of ninety-four, survived by Bernadette, his wife of nearly sixty years, and his five children. He had explored many facets of life in his ninety-four years—philosophy, travel, electronics, physics, Go, mathematics, painting, poetry, novels, and was fascinated right up to the end with life's infinite possibilities.

John Hanson

Born 7 March 1942,
St. Paul, MN

John Hanson produces, directs and writes documentaries. He sports quite a robust, gray handlebar moustache and looks like a cross between a nineteenth-century immigrant and a hippie. He won a Camera d'Or Award at the Cannes International Film Festival for *Northern Lights* and also the Grand Prize at the Figueria Da Foz Internacionale de Cinema in Portugal, along with fourteen other awards.

Many of Hanson's earlier documentaries center on rural activities on the northern plains. For example, *Western Coal* (1974) deals with strip mining in Montana, Wyoming and the Dakotas; and *Prairie Fire*

(1977), is a history of the populist, agrarian Non-Partisan League of North Dakota, which flourished between 1915 and 1921.Fellow North Dakotan Rob Nilsson worked with him on these films.

Northern Lights (1978) an outgrowth of the thirty-minute *Prairie Fire*, was John and Rob's first feature. The 95-minute film featured Susan Lynch, Robert Behling, and Joe Spano plus a few dozen non-professional actors. It was broadcast on PBS's American Playhouse and won the Neil Simon Award for Best Screenplay in a Television Dramatic Series. The next spring it was shown at the Cannes Film Festival and won a Camera d'Or for Best First Feature.

The film deals with the Non-Partisan League's opposition to the Eastern establishment of grain merchants and railroad and banking trusts, which seemed to be dictating all aspects of the lives of North Dakota farmers during the 1910s. It focuses on a young farmer who must balance his energies between his new bride, the family farm, and the political activities of the Non-Partisan League. In one well-filmed segment we witness a day of harvesting during an early winter blizzard. Camerawoman Judy Irola deserves special notice for her masterful use of light in this feature, (and also in some of Hanson's earlier documentaries).The narrator was ninety-one-year-old Henry Martinson, a former League member. The film cost $200,000; most of the cast and crew worked on a deferred payment plan.

Following the success of *Northern Lights*, Hanson embarked on another feature film, *Wildrose* (1984). It's set on Minnesota's Iron Range, though it also has a few scenes set in Bayfield, Wisconsin, where miners sometimes found employment in the commercial fishing industry after the mines closed for the season. The story focuses on the challenges that one woman faces finding and keeping work in an industry that has traditionally been dominated by men. It features Lisa Eichhorn, Tom Bower, James Cada, James Stowell, Stephen Yoakam, and Bill Shoppert, and was selected for the respected New Films/New Directors series at the Museum of Modern Art in New York. It was also a finalist for the Critics Prize at the Venice Film Festival. Hanson lived on Ely Lake near Eveleth (1980-82) while working on the film, socializing with the miners to probe the nuances of the environment and social ethos. One mine was given over to his camera crew as a set.

Wildrose was premiered in Virginia, Minnesota, in 1984. It had theatrical distribution, was shown on HBO, and later released on home video.

The next year Hanson patched together *Troubled Waters* (1985) a documentary about Lake Superior commercial fishermen. Three years later he completed *Traveling Light*, a feature-length one-man show by James Stowell, from his play of the same name. It was filmed on the St. Paul waterfront and screened at the Sundance Festival. Stowell also performed solo in *Talking Pictures* (1990), an hour-long show co-produced with Twin Cities Public TV. It aired on KTCA-TV, and won a regional Emmy.

Shimmer (1993) set in Toledo, Iowa, was shown at the Heartland Film Festival where it won the Crystal Heart Award. It's based on a play by John J. O'Keefe, and features Tom Bower and Mary Beth Hurt. It was aired on PBS's American Playhouse and later screened at film festivals in Toronto, Chicago, and Locarno, Italy.

Hanson also produced a public television special, "A Sense of Place," written by Minnesota writers Paul Gruchow and Diane Glancy. Another co-producing project is "Rhythm Is the Soul of Life," a documentary portrait of the great Nigerian teacher and drummer Babatunde Olantunji. A dramatic feature as yet untitled is in the planning stages.

Though Hanson was born in Saint Paul, he spent his earliest years in Iowa before his family moved on to North Dakota where he grew up in a Norwegian-American community. He and his sister were sent to live with his mother's parents while his father served in the army in World War II. His mother soon joined them and when the war ended his father returned and the family eased into a conventional 1950s life.

At fifteen, because of a successful paper route, Hanson earned a scholarship from the *Minneapolis Star Tribune* to attend Phillips Exeter Academy in New Hampshire. No one in his family had ever heard of a prep school even though his parents had received higher educations. "I took the train to Bismarck," John recalled, "changed in Chicago, changed in Boston, and then arrived in New Hampshire. At the station I arrived in my Levis while the other boys were already in their coats and ties." Later that day the school's director of admissions took him to Brooks Brothers to properly suit him up.

Exeter gave John such a top-quality education that he obtained a full scholarship from Carlton College in Northfield where he earned his B.A. in art. All scholarship kids had to work at some job as part of the tuition-free contract, and John became a projectionist in the school's art auditorium, which gave him the opportunity to see classic European "art" films over and over again. John mused, "I loved movies but I never thought it could be a career—it seemed too remote, something people did in big cities on the coasts."

Hanson went on to postgraduate work in architecture at the Harvard Graduate School of Design while teaching art to inner-city kids through Boston's Milton Academy to pay the rent. But the call of film was too strong. Rob Nilsson and he were having a beer one day and Rob asked him, "What are you doing in architecture? Movies are where it's at." Then Nilsson put a crank 8mm camera in his hands.

Hanson took leave from Harvard to go to San Francisco, and worked with Francis Ford Coppola at American Zoetrope, after which he joined the Cine Manifest, a San Francisco film collective organized to produce independent features.

Hanson has presented his films at thirty film festivals in a dozen countries and more than a dozen states in the U.S. At the Sundance Festival Hanson (as part of his Minneapolis-based company, Executive Producer New Front films) won Grand Prizes for *Heat and Sunlight* and *Waiting for the Moon.*

A recent project was *Sisters: Portrait of a Benedictine Community* (2005). It was inspired by Sister Noemi, a person of deep faith but in many ways not a stereotypical nun. She was a noted photographer and won honors as a Kodak Woman of the Year. She started an artists' commune outside Duluth and she was known for her reckless scooter driving. She died, sad to note, before filming could take place.

Hanson recounted a story of filming one scene, in which a disabled sister is to duplicate Sister Noemi's seemingly reckless scooter driving. "We asked one of the disabled sisters to drive her battery-powered, three-wheeled scooter through the cemetery and toward the camera. On 'action' she sped down the hill past a row of gravestones, rounded a corner practically on two wheels and roared past the camera, her dog racing alongside. A stunt driver couldn't have done it better. We all laughed in amazement until we realized how close we came to disaster—if she had missed that turn and rolled over. As for the sister, she just waved and continued on back to the monastery."

When interviewed for *Independent Lens* on December 13, 2005, Hanson was asked why he chose public television to present his film. He replied, "While there are a growing number of venues for documentaries...public television, and especially Independent Lens, remains a prime showcase for unique, in-depth stories not to be seen elsewhere in the media."

His favorite films? *Raging Bull* (1980), *Tender Mercies* (1982), and *Unforgiven* (1993).

Asked why he has devoted his career to independent ventures when his success might have allowed him access to larger commercial pockets, he said simply, "To give voice to people who are ignored by the greater culture." This was the mission of the Cine Manifest that John, Rob, Judy and other "activist artists" signed onto when they joined the San Francisco collective—that they would make "socially-conscious entertainment films."

Yet at one time John did have an office in a George Lucas-owned building and another one at Warner Brothers Studio. He developed a film adaptation for Ole Rolvaag's novel, *Giants in the Earth* and formed a partnership among Norwegian, Danish, Canadian and American groups, but the financing fell apart at the eleventh hour when the American distributor pulled out..

"I had deals for a number of films," Hanson said, "but none finally went into production because of the usual Hollywood broken promises and last minute cold feet." So he left L.A. with no regrets.

Now that John is officially a senior citizen he is reaping other glories. He sits on the Wisconsin Humanities Council board, a previous benefactor for his work.

[Much of this biographical information is drawn from an article by Masarah Van Eyck in *Wisconsin People & Ideas*, Winter 2007.]

George Roy Hill

Born 20 December 1921, Minneapolis, MN
Died 27 December 2002, New York, NY

The Cooper Theatre in St. Louis Park was jammed past capacity for the première of George Roy Hill's *Slaughterhouse Five* one summer night in 1972. The movie had been largely shot on sites around the Twin Cities, especially at Lake Minnetonka. And Hill himself, whose previous film, *Butch Cassidy and the Sundance Kid*, had been a huge success, was a local boy, having grown up at 5121 Bryant Avenue South in Minneapolis. As the theater lights were dimming to black, a tall, thin man in khaki pants walked into the auditorium. It was George Roy Hill.

He didn't look flashy in his drab, casual dress and simple crew-cut, but you could feel his authority, his casual power. He delivered some self-effacing remarks about having been a mediocre student at Blake School in Hopkins, Class of 1939. Yet, he had earned a B. A. at Yale University before becoming a transport plane pilot for the U. S. Marine Corps in the South Pacific during World War II.

Hill's father, George Roy Hill, Sr., was Treasurer of the Minneapolis Automobile Club, and his mother, Helen Frances (Owens) Hill, was a homemaker. Of Irish ancestry, the Hills were Midwesterners with backgrounds in business and journalism. George Jr. was active in the Drama Club at Blake and acted in the school play, *Yes Means No,* taking the part of the secretary, Miss Collins. He also sang in the Glee Club at Blake and at Yale where he was a Whiffenpoof "gentleman songster" at Mory's Tavern in New Haven. His degree was in classical music, one of his two life-long passions.

Flying was the other one. As a boy he frequently saw the barnstorming pilots of the 1920s do aerial acrobatics at the State Fair grounds and the Cedar Avenue Airport. His favorite flyer was Charles "Speed" Holman who always flew upside down when cruising past the bandstand to greet the crowd. That really impressed young Hill. (The private airport east of downtown St. Paul today is named Holman Field.) His other favorites were stunt flyers Frank Clarke and Roy Wilson, and World War I aces Eddie Rickenbacker and Ernst Udet. Georgie could recite all their stats to anyone who cared to listen.

After the War he worked briefly for a newspaper in Texas, then went to Dublin, Ireland, to study music and literature at Trinity College on the G.I. Bill. He took a B.Litt degree from there in 1949. In Dublin he made his first professional stage appearance in Cyril Cusack's production of Shaw's *The Devil's Disciple.* He was in an Off-Broadway production of Strindberg's *The Creditors* in 1950 and also toured with Margaret Webster's Shakespearean Repertory Company. On April 7, 1951, he married Louisa Horton, a cast mate in the Webster Company. After the tour he landed a job on a radio soap opera, *John's Other Wife.* Then the Marine Corps called him up for another stint as a pilot.

The road to films began in TV and Broadway. Hill directed, wrote and produced *A Night to Remember* for Kraft Television Theater in 1954, which won him Emmy Awards for both writing and directing. *The Helen Morgan Story,* which he did for Playhouse 90 in 1954, also brought an Emmy nomination, as did *Judgment at Nuremberg* also for Playhouse 90, in 1957.

Hill's first job directing on Broadway was the adaptation of Thomas Wolfe's *Look Homeward, Angel* which won the New York Drama Critics Circle Award and the Pulitzer Prize. The play ran for seventeen months, 1957-59. In 1960 he directed *The Gang's All Here* about President Warren G. Harding, followed by Tennessee Williams play *Period of Adjustment*. Both plays ran for exactly 132 performances.

On the strength of his work on Broadway, Hill was invited to Hollywood to direct the film version of Williams's play. The reviews were good but not great, and the critical response to his next film, an adaptation of Lillian Hellman's play, *Toys in the Attic* (1963), was even more tepid. The third time was the charm with *The World of Henry Orient* (1964) starring Peter Sellers. The public and the critics loved the comedy with Sellers as a zany, Oscar Levant-styled concert pianist dealing with two teenage girls who follow him around and annoy him—early "groupies."

James Michener's hugely successful book, *Hawaii*, was Hill's next project, but the challenge of condensing the sprawling book down to a reasonable, not-too-complicated film story proved too daunting. It's not that they weren't trying. Dalton Trumbo wrote fifty versions of the script before one was finally approved. Max von Sydow played the stern Calvinist Missionary who pushes a bitter pill of repressive Christianity down the throats of the Hawaiians. Julie Harris plays his frail wife. As the budget went over the $14 million mark, Hill was replaced by Arthur Hiller but the large cast of Tahitians went on strike. One actress said, "We can and will perform only for our friend, Monsieur Hill." Hill returned. This actress, Joyce La Garde, weighed 418 pounds, and her physique was well-suited to the part of Queen Malama. Unfortunately she spoke French but no English, so Hill trained her phonetically.

Thoroughly Modern Millie (1967), Hill's next production, was also a bit long but was still a lively romp through the Jazz Age with Julie Andrews, Bea Lillie, and Mary Tyler Moore. *New York Times* critic Bosley Crowther wrote (March 23, 1967), "[It] is a thoroughly modern burlesque of the manners and styles of flaming youth in the jazzy 1920s, of movie melodramas in the silent days…. It is a joyously syncopated frolic…." The length of the film was an issue. In an unusual Hollywood dispute, Hill argued that a twenty-minute segment should be *cut* and Ross Hunter, the producer, fought to keep it. Hill was fired during the editing.

A second work of revisionist history, ***Butch Cassidy and the Sun-***

dance Kid (1969) was a blockbuster, with the magical pairing of Paul Newman with Robert Redford, who truly became a star with this film. Hill earned his first Oscar nomination for directing and the film was nominated for Best Picture. It did win Oscars for Conrad Hall's rich cinematography, Burt Bacharach's Musical Score, and the song "Raindrops Keep Fallin' on My Head."

Slaughterhouse Five (1972) though not his most popular film, may be the one closest to Hill's heart. It's based on Kurt Vonnegut's novel of a man's experiences in a German prisoner-of-war camp during World War II, which result in his becoming "unstuck in time." Both the book and the film are blackly comic and surreal, and some viewers were unconvinced by Hill's attempt to render the bizarre time-shifts involved.

Hill returned to familiar ground with *The Sting* (1973) which once again pairs Redford and Newman in the roles of likeable crooks, this time as Depression-era Chicago con-men out to swindle a major racketeer who has killed a friend of theirs. Marvin Hamlisch won an Oscar for his ragtime music score. Hill won for Best Director, the film won Best Picture and David S. Ward won for Best Screenplay with only his second script ever. At the time it ranked as the fourth biggest Hollywood moneymaker ever, exceeded only by *Gone with the Wind, The Godfather,* and *The Sound of Music.* (Today it's ranking is below 140.)

Though Hill was urged to pair Newman and Redford again, a suitable project never materialized. His next film, *The Great Waldo Pepper* (1975), starred Redford in a picture about barnstorming pilots of the twenties. Hill provided the story for the script from his own childhood scrapbooks and he also produced the film. William Goldman (who had written the *Butch Cassidy* script) wrote the screenplay.

Newman starred in Hill's next film, *Slap Shot* (1977) about a failing minor league hockey team. It's raunchy, violent and funny—a celebration of locker room humor—with Newman as the struggling manager. When it was released it was widely criticized for its ugly portrait of machismo behavior and its non-stop profanity, but it is now considered an insightful rendering of the sporting ethos and one of Newman's best roles.

As he was finishing *Slap Shot* as part of a new deal with Pan Arts, Hill directed the marvelous action movie, *Rescue at Entebee* (1977, TV), a true story of an Israeli rescue of its citizens captured at an airport in Uganda. In an entirely different vein, *A Little Romance* (1978) features Laurence Olivier in a Maurice Chevalier-type role of an old man encouraging two teenagers to run away to Venice, Italy, to honor their love.

Shifting gears once again, Hill made an attempt to bring John Irving's brilliantly facetious novel *The World According to Garp* (1982) to the screen, with mixed results. John Le Carré's book, *The Little Drummer Girl*, was his next film, with Diane Keaton starring as an actress who's recruited by Israeli agents to spy for them. He closed out his film career with *Funny Farm* (1988) with Chevy Chase in which old jokes get recycled slowly as Chevy plays a sports writer who moves to the country but has to adjust quite a bit to it.

Hill never lost his boyish looks and casual dress, preferring shaggy sweaters and jumpsuits to sharp, fashionable clothes. In fact, one of his hobbies was to shop at thrift stores and brag later about how little he spent for his togs. He has been described as shy and sweet-tempered, but also intense. Paul Newman said that Hill was "flexible – he listens." Redford said that Hill's style was a "scholarly approach combined with the military approach he learned in the Marine Corps." Katherine Ross, the female relief in *Butch Cassidy*, found him to be "rigid" while Valerie Perrine in *Slaughterhouse Five* said that he gave her "total support."

George and his wife Louisa raised two boys and two girls: George Roy III, John, Frances, and Owens. The children were only a year apart so at one point all four of them were in college at the same time. They had twelve grandchildren. Hill's years following his last film were spent teaching drama at Yale, but Parkinson's disease forced him into complete retirement.

For recreation he flew an antique, open-cockpit Waco, played the piano, and read a lot. He said, "Just as I play nothing but Bach for pleasure, so do I read nothing but history for pleasure." George and Louisa were living in a brownstone on East Seventy-eighth Street in Manhattan when he died in 2002.

Jerome Hill

Born 2 March 1905,
St. Paul, MN
Died 21 November 1972,
New York, NY

Jerome was an all-around artist. He was an accomplished painter, photographer, composer, and filmmaker. Over a forty-year period Jerome directed seven films, producing four of them and writing three. In 1957 his film about Dr. Albert Schweitzer, the great twentieth-century humanitarian, won an Oscar for Best Documentary.

Jerome was the son of Louis W. Hill and the grandson of James J. Hill, the builder/developer of the Great Northern Railroad, which traveled from St. Paul to Seattle, Washington. He attended Saint Paul Academy, class of 1923, and Yale College, graduating in 1927 with a degree in music.

But painting was the first discipline to capture his attention. He may have been inspired by his grandfather's collection of paintings by Corot, Delacroix, Rousseau and other masters that was hanging in the house just down the street on Summit Avenue. But he had soon added photography to the list of pursuits, and as a youth he worked with all kinds of cameras including motion picture cameras.

By the early 1930s Hill was making experimental films, among them *La Cartomancienne* (1932). An accomplished skier, he filmed European ski instructors demonstrating their techniques, the idea being to market the footage to American resorts. Much of the location shooting was done on Mount Rainier in Washington. The film is called *Ski Flight* (1938), and it was distributed by Warner Brothers.

Next came *The Seeing Eye* (1940), a documentary about training groups of dogs for the blind. He joined the army in 1941 and scripted two training films there: *Chow Hound* (1943) and *Poison Ivy* (1943). He worked in aerial photography and surveillance but also used his language skills interrogating prisoners of war. When he was discharged in 1944 he returned to his paintings.

In 1949 Hill combined his interests in painting and film to make his first really serious documentary, *Grandma Moses*. Moses was a woman who took up painting when in her sixties and made a great name for herself as an American Primitive. The film benefits from unusual camera effects and the narration of poet Archibald MacLeish.

It gained national attention and high praise from Twentieth Century and Universal Studio executives among many others.

Hill once again drew on the expertise of cinematographer Erica Anderson, who had worked with him on *Grandma Moses*, to shoot *Albert Schweitzer*, which won the Best Documentary Oscar for 1957. Schweitzer, of course, was one of the wonders of the age, a polymath who had earned doctorates in medicine, music, mathematics, and theology before dedicating himself to providing medical care to the poor people of the Congo. Cinematographer Anderson had grave misgivings about filming in Lambarene, Congo, where Schweitzer's hospital was located, because of the extreme variability of the weather, but the film was finally completed. Schweitzer had agreed to the project in 1951 after seeing *Grandma Moses*, and Carl Jung also had high praise for the earlier film. Schweitzer went on to collaborate with Hill on a small work, *Schweitzer and Bach*, filmed in his home town of Gunsbach, Switzerland, where he is seen playing several Bach compositions on the pipe organ in the town church.

What to do after hitting the jackpot? Hill was fascinated with Swiss psychologist Carl Jung and his theories on the subconscious mind. (Hill's cousin, Maud Oakes, had introduced Jung's ideas to him.) Casting aside a traditional documentary format, Hill used Jungian ideas allegorically as a young boy builds a sand castle on a beach attracting eccentric beachgoers. He created an elaborate stop-motion animation sequence at the end of the film revealing a new personal style for documentaries. The film, which premiered in 1961, was called *The Sand Castle*.

Open the Door and See All the People (1964) was based on Hill's unpublished book, *Peacock Feathers*. It touched on the creative process, eccentricity, a parent's role, and the social order, in the course of examining the lives of two aging sisters. The farcical tone and elliptical character development may reflect Hill's many years of exposure to European life and culture.

His final film is a personal memoir called *Film Portrait* (1973), a collection of many unreleased, short films which provide a great insight into Hill as an artist and a man.

Jerome did not live in St. Paul after reaching adulthood. He kept a house in Norden, California, near the Sugar Bowl ski resort. He lived in New York City for long periods and in Paris, too, but his spiritual home was Cassis, a French port town on the Mediterranean Sea, and that's where he spent most of the last forty years of his life.

An artist will try almost anything, perhaps, so...Jerome Hill did one spot of acting; he played Convict #1 in *Hallelujah the Hills* (1963).

Peter Markle

Born 24 September 1946,
Minneapolis, MN

Peter Markle grew up near Ferndale Road at 345 Highcroft Lane in Wayzata. He is the son of Thomas and Barbara Markle. During his high school years at Blake School he stood out as a hockey star, and he was also a fine football and baseball player. At Yale he played on the same team as goalie Mark Dayton, future Minnesota senator, and rubbed elbows with future film director Oliver Stone and future President George W. Bush. (Both Markle and Stone are mentioned in passing in Kitty Kelley's book about the Bush family, *The Family: The Truth about the Bush Dynasty*.) Peter eventually played with the U.S. Hockey Team, the pinnacle of accomplishment in American hockey.

Markle had written a screenplay about young people searching for love in the then latest mode—the "personals" columns of newspapers. While working for the Eberhardt Co. and living with wife, Melinda, at 2217 Humboldt Avenue South, Markle began to study filmmaking. He made some TV commercials and broke into the industrial film sector, meeting apprentice editor Stephen E. Rivkin in the process. (Rivkin edited Markle's first four features). Through his insurance agent he was reconnected with an old Blake hockey teammate, Pat Wells. Wells was familiar with the ins and outs of money-raising, and he agreed to act as Markle's executive producer and co-producer.

A cast was assembled that included Bill Shoppert and Karen Landry, alumni of the University of Minnesota's Theatre Arts Department, Chris Forth, and Michael Laskin. Film locations were scouted at Lake Calhoun, Lake Harriet, Lake of the Isles, Shoppert's apartment, Markle's house, and other sites. When shooting had been completed, Pat and Peter took their finished film, *The Personals*, to Los Angeles and found a distributor (New World Pictures). And eventually the film turned enough of a profit to encourage Peter and Pat to try again.

In an unusual move, the Cooper Theatre in St. Louis Park ran *The Personals* for three months straight. No doubt community pride was involved, though the exposure did help this local project to make it.

By the way, Peter wore four hats for this film: co-producer, director, screenwriter and cameraman. A hat trick?

Next came *Hot Dog...The Movie* (1984), an action comedy about a cute, teenage runaway girl who hitches a ride with a naïve but talented skier on his way to Squaw Valley, Idaho, to train for the World Cup. It has fine skiing scenes and some soft-porn. It cost $2.5 million to make and earned gross receipts of more than $20 million.

Markle and Wells co-wrote the story of *Youngblood* (1986), the romances of a star hockey player. Rob Lowe and Patrick Swayze led the cast. This film cost $5 million to make and brought in gross receipts worldwide of $25 million.

Gene Hackman starred in *Bat 21* (1988) playing a 53-year old Air Force missile intelligence expert shot down behind enemy lines. Danny Glover is the pilot who tries to rescue him. One critic called it an "effective and suspenseful drama of the muddle and moral experiences of war, based on a true story" by William C. Anderson who also wrote the screenplay.

Wagon's East! (1994) stars the rotund, comic actor John Candy in the last movie appearance before his untimely death. For better or worse, it has similarities to Mel Brooks' *Blazing Saddles* (1974). The tagline for the film is: "They came, they saw, they changed their minds." Other cast notables: Richard Lewis, Rodney A. Grant (*Dances with Wolves*) and Russell Means (*Last of the Mohicans*).

Markle's last feature film, *Virginia's Run* (2002), with Gabriel Byrne and Joanne Whaley, tells the story of a teenage girl trying to cope when her mother dies in a horse-riding accident. Markle once again wears several hats: co-producer, screenwriter and director.

Along the way Markle has also directed television episodes and made-for-TV movies, including *White Dwarf* (1995, Fox); *The Last Days of Frankie the Fly* (1997, HBO) starring Dennis Hopper and Darryl Hannah; and *Saving Jessica Lynch-The Rescue of an American Soldier* (2003, NBC). Among the many TV series in which he has directed episodes are *Without a Trace* (2002-2003, CBS); *The X-Files*, *ER*, and *L. A. Doctors*.

David Burton Morris

Born 1948, St. Paul, MN

In 1972-73, say, how much capital would you need to get started in the movie biz? If you asked David Burton Morris, he might toss off an answer, "Oh, about thirty grand, I guess." That just happens to be the amount he drummed up to produce *Loose Ends* in 1974. And it was a decent film. Its commercial possibilities encouraged him to stay in Los Angeles for the next eighteen years. Despite living there so long, he has directed four features in Minnesota: *Loose Ends* (1976), *Purple Haze* (1983), *Patti Rocks* (1988), and *Hometown Boy Makes Good* (1990, TV).

Raised in Highland Park Village, Morris lived first on Highland Parkway and later on Mt. Curve Blvd. a few blocks from River Road. He left town at eighteen to attend two well-known institutions: UCLA and the College of Hard Knocks. UCLA was easy and took only a few years. Hard Knocks took a lot longer.

Morris's debut film at UCLA, *Restless Sleep* (1975), was a 55-minute modern Western based on Jean-Paul Sartre's novel, *Nausea*. He followed this with a more ambitious work, *Loose Ends,* much of which was shot at Midway Chevrolet on University Avenue in St. Paul. It had script input from cast members Chris Mulkey, John and Linda Jenkins, and David's wife, Victoria Wozniak, who also co-directed. Other featured cast members are Irv Fink, Gerald Drake, Faye Gallos, and Chris Mulkey, Sr. The film was produced by American Eagle and Fat Chance Films, and distributed by Bauer International and UCLA.

TV film critic Roger Ebert lavished praise on *Loose Ends*, and David and Victoria were invited to film festivals around the world. Nor was Ebert alone in praising it. Vincent Canby of the *New York Times* called it "one of the most interesting American films I've seen in years," and Andrew Sarris of the *Village Voice* placed it in his Top Ten List for 1976. It was shown at the Museum of Modern Art and the Renoir Theatre in New York.

Eight years later *Purple Haze* was finally finished and distributed by Columbia Pictures through their art film division, Triumph Releasing. It follows the daily life of a young man who drops out of college in the late 60s, and returns home until drafted for Vietnam. The film ends as he is boarding the army bus for basic training camp.

Victoria was executive producer/co-writer for *Purple Haze*, which was shot in various Twin Cities' locations, including under the Ford Bridge where David had spent a lot of time as a kid, hanging out. *Purple Haze* won the Grand Prize for Best Feature Film at the Sundance Film Festival.

There is a reason for living in L.A. The closer you live to the studios, the more work you get. Studios don't call long distance unless you're a super special dude they just have to have. Well, one day the phone rang inviting Morris to direct *Volunteers* (1985). However, when Tom Hanks and John Candy joined the cast, the budget jumped from $7 to $12 million and Morris was bumped into second-unit directing. He was considered too green to trust with such a big budget.

Morris's career turned around in 1988. When bummed out, he reasoned, go home. He returned to St. Paul to direct *Patti Rocks* using the Ace Box Tavern as a backdrop (called The Club in the film). The film was a big hit, and suddenly, *Loose Ends*, which had some of the same cast, was considered the "prequel." Says David, "We shot *Patti Rocks* in December of 1986. Film Dallas Pictures was the first company I gave the script to and they immediately decided to finance the film. It was the easiest time I ever had raising money. We got greenlit in October and started shooting two months later."

The plot: A married man, Billy Regis (Chris Mulkey again) takes a long-lost buddy, Eddie Jenks (John Jenkins) on a long ride to the home of his pregnant girlfriend, Patti Rocks (Karen Landry). (Others in the cast are Joe Minjares and Buffy Sedlachek.) The man and his buddy are classic male chauvinist pigs and their conversation is full of locker-room language, yet clearly many viewers found genuine character development in this film.

Patti Rocks drew rave reviews around the world and played in one theatre in Paris for ten straight months. Initially, Rocks was rated "X" based on "the cumulative effect of the dialogue." On Morris's second appeal the court reversed itself and it was released as an "R." It was nominated for seven IFP Independent Spirit Awards and was in the main competition at Sundance Film Festival. *Ms* and *Cosmopolitan* magazines both gave the film rave reviews which shocked Morris, who had been leary of feminist reaction.

He had been committed to making films for theatrical release—but TV kept calling. "I resisted TV movies for a long time," he said. "I was stupid." Now they were his bread and butter. Morris had worked on the TV series, *China Beach* (1988) and on ***Vietnam War Story: The Last Days*** (1988) and it wasn't as humiliating as he'd anticipated. (This was Mulkey's third film for Morris.) Morris connected with HBO for whom he wrote and directed the episode "Three's a Crowd" for *Tales from the Crypt* in 1990.

On the heels of that he came home again to direct ***Hometown Boy Makes Good*** for HBO. This was also shot in the Ace Box Tavern in St. Paul (named Buck's in this film, inspired by a billboard ad for Berman Buckskin). Exterior scenes were shot in "old town" Hastings, (renamed Desmond) so that the Twin Cities can masquerade as a small town for the film. Other locations used were the Golden Valley Country Club and Dayton's Bluff in St. Paul.

Another HBO project was ***A Body To Die For*** starring Ben Affleck. David received an Emmy nomination for Best Director. Chris Mulkey once again appears, but Anthony Edwards stars as a geek named Boyd Geary. Peter Thoemke, who has appeared frequently on stage at the Guthrie and Chanhassen Dinner Theaters, plays an old high school nemesis with the look of a glazed zombie who bumps into Boyd at Buck's and delivers such endearing lines as: "Hey, I know you! I used to pay you to kiss things in grade school." Jeff Gadbois is also featured.

The story involves a small-town boy who has neglected to tell his mother that his career as a medical-student has ended in grief, and he now works as a waiter in San Franscisco. He travels home to tell his mom the truth, but the mayor makes him an offer to move his "practice" back home…"

A note on Chris Mulkey: Born in Viroqua, Wisconsin, he graduated in Theatre Arts from the University of Minnesota and was a company member of the Children's Theatre at the Minneapolis Institute of Arts before moving to Los Angeles. He has appeared in a hundred films and TV episodes. He is married to actress Karen Landry and they have two children. Ms. Landry has oodles of credits, too, and is a graduate of the U of M's Theatre Arts Department.

Morris's style of directing is modern. You might see him on the set in a faded blue-plaid shirt with blue jeans and cowboy boots, a can of coke in one hand and a cigarette in the other, not to mention the long hair. After adjusting lights here and there and speaking softly to actors between takes, he might say, "That looks excellent, everybody. Keep that energy up, people. Do we have a towel to clean up the floor so nobody slips?" After the next shot he says the magic words: "Great! Print it!" but will go on to shoot one more take just to be absolutely sure he has what he wants.

(This observation comes from Greg Cummins, his photographer and co-producer.)

Jersey Girl (1992), Morris's fifth theater-release feature, stars Jami Gertz and Dylan McDermott in a tale involving a high-powered Manahttan salesman who falls in love with the woman who has just crashed into his car. Unfortunately, Peter Guber, the head of production at Sony Entertainment, sold the film to Fox TV just as Morris and his stars were in the Twin Cities doing a promotion tour that cost as much as the entire *Loose Ends* budget—about $30,000.

The Price of Love was Morris's first Movie of the Week for Fox-TV, who wanted to produce an independent film on teenaged male prostitutes that traffic their bodies along Santa Monica Blvd. It was a critical hit, and led to other TV-directing offers.

Speaking of David's guidance of TV movies, he feels that network TV people treat directors like hired hands. However, he feels that the hurried pace and constant compromising which needs to be done have made him a better filmmaker. He has also been better able to meet young talent such as Keri Russell, who starred in his *The Babysitter's Seduction* (1995). Keri, an unknown then, has gone on to greater fame in *The Waitress* (2007) and other films.

In 1994 David and Victoria moved back to Minnesota, buying an old estate in Deephaven on Lake Minnetonka. He imagined that he would be home a lot, since it only takes three months to do a Movie of the Week, but feature filmmaking kept him away nearly all the time.

Morris's credits in the 90s range all over the map, from *And the Beat Goes On: The Sonny and Cher Story* (1999) to *Jackie Bouvier Kennedy Onassis* (2000) to *The Almost Perfect Bank Robbery* (1998) to *Come On, Get Happy: The Partridge Family Story* (1999) to *Still Holding On: The Legend of Cadillac Jack* (1998).

Jay Underwood, the actor portraying Sonny Bono in *And the Beat Goes On*, is another Minneapolis connection. He took acting classes in the Children's Theatre Company School in Minneapolis. While many TV producers might think that Morris ought to stay in L.A. to view pre- or post-production work instead of returning to the Twin Cities, Underwood views Morris's lifestyle choice as "the coolest thing. As a director or a performer, the business center is here in Los Angeles, and it's an insane city to live in. That he insists on keeping his family out of it is good for him."

In a millenium edition of the *St. Paul Pioneer Press*, Morris was listed as one of the hundred most influential Minnesotans of the century. He is a member of the WGA, DGA, the Academy of Motion Picture Arts & Sciences, a founding member of the IFP West along with his wife, Victoria, the first president of the organization. Together they created the Spirit Awards, now called Findies, which are nationally televized the Saturday afternoon before the Oscars.

Among Morris's current projects are *Assuming Room Temperature,* for the theatrical division of HBO. It's set in Duluth but will be shot mostly in the Twin Cities. He and David Eyre are also adapting Frederick Exley's cult novel, *A Fan's Notes,* to be produced by Pearl Pictures. Also in the works is *Full Cleveland* to be shot in New Mexico with Kevin Kline.

Gordon Parks

Born 30 November 1912,
Fort Scott, Kansas

Born one of fifteen children to upstanding Methodist farmers in Fort Scott, Kansas, Gordon Parks became a nationally prominent photographer and the first black film director to direct a film for a major studio, *The Learning Tree* (1969). In 1989 this film was chosen by the Library of Congress as one of twenty-five films to be preserved in the National Film Registry for all time.

Drawing on his childhood memories, Parks wrote *The Learning Tree* as a book before considering film as a suitable medium to tell the story. The main character, Marcus Savage, is a teenage boy in an oversized body with an undersized intellect. His mother is dead and his father is a drunk. Marcus himself lives in a reform school for boys. Along with writing the screenplay and directing *The Learning Tree,* Parks also composed the score.

Parks's mother, Sarah, died when he was sixteen, and his father sent him up to St. Paul to live with his older, married sister. His father said, "Just mind your mother's teaching and you'll make out all right." After two weeks his brother-in-law threw him out along with his cardboard suitcase, leaving him homeless and broke. He fought a skinny dog for the carcass of a pigeon and won, and roasted the bird over a paper fire.

Parks soon found work as a bus boy at the Minneapolis Club at 8th Street and 2nd Avenue South and later found a more lucrative job playing piano in a St. Paul bordello which closed rather abruptly after a fatal stabbing. He toured one season with a semi-professional basketball team, and later toured as a pianist with a big band. When he was stranded by the bandleader in New York after a gig, he became a delivery man for a dope dealer.

Parks enlisted in the Civilian Conservation Corps, where he met and married Sally Alvis in 1933. They came back to Minneapolis and Parks worked as a porter on the North Coast Limited. Thumbing through the magazines left in the seats, he was impressed and inspired by the photos of Walker Evans, Dorothea Lange, Ben Shahn, Jack Delano, John Vachon, and Carl Mydans. He bought a camera at a pawn shop—he called it his "choice of weapons"—and at that point his life began to improve.

Parks's photos attracted attention, and before long he was doing fashion shoots for Frank Murphy's department store in Saint Paul. On the strength of a photo essay on Chicago's South Side ghetto, he won a fellowship to take photos for the Farm Security Administration during the war. One thing led to another, and eventually Parks became a reporter and photographer for *Life Magazine*.

By the mid-1960s, Parks career was moving in new directions. He co-founded the magazine *Essence*, and become the first black man to direct a major motion picture with *Shaft* (1971), the film which inaugurated the Blaxploitation genre.

Shaft stars Richard Roundtree as the coolly composed detective, John Shaft, a tough, sexy, and violent man adored by white and black audiences alike. Isaac Hayes's title song and score added a good deal to the film's appeal. ***Shaft's Big Score*** (1972), with even more violence, also did well at the box office. Parks himself composed the score for this film. The comedy-drama ***The Super Cops*** (1974) in which two suspended cops carry on their own private war against crime, also did very well.

Parks's next film, ***Leadbelly*** (1976) relates the life and times of the famous black blues singer Huddie Leadbetter. He cast adopted Minnesotan Ernie Hudson in the title role. Hudson, born in Detroit, had moved to Minnesota to get his doctorate in Theatre Arts from the University of Minnesota. Hudson waited a long time for his next good part, as Winston Zeddemore in the mega-hit ***Ghostbusters*** (1984). (While at the U, Hudson starred as Jack Jefferson in *The Great White Hope* at Theatre-in-the-Round Players on the U's West Bank in 1975.)

After some years away from film making, Parks directed *The Odyssey of Solomon Northrup* (1984) and *Moments without Proper Names* (1986). He himself was the subject of a documentary narrated by Denzel Washington called *Half Past Autumn* (2000). *A Choice of Weapons* and *Voices in the Mirror* are perhaps, along with *The Learning Tree*, the best-known of his many books.

In 1997, the Corcoran Gallery of Art in Washington, D.C. mounted a career retrospective on Parks, "Half Past Autumn: The Art of Gordon Parks."

Parks was married three times. With Sally Alvis (married 1933-1961) he had three children including filmmaker, Gordon Parks, Jr. (*Superfly*, 1972). He also married Elizabeth Campbell (1962-1973), and Genevieve Young (1973-1979). Gordon is the Godfather of Quibilah Shabazz, the daughter of Malcolm X.

A critic for *Arts Magazine* once wrote, "After a hardscrabble life in the Depression, Gordon Parks picked up a camera instead of a gun. But as the massive retrospective of his work reveals, his sympathies have often remained with those who went the other way."

Charles F. Reisner

Born 14 March 1887,
Minneapolis, MN
Died 24 September 1962,
La Jolla, CA

Chuck Reisner had a hardscrabble childhood, and worked as a boy soprano, paperboy, and prize-fighter before finding work as a gag man with Mack Sennett. He moved on to acting and eventually became a director of comedy, working with Charlie Chaplin during the first seven years of his career, and later with Syd Chaplin, Buster Keaton and, finally, with one of the greatest film comediennes ever, Joan Davis.

Reisner's father was Austrian by birth and his mother Italian. He was one of eleven children, and the family was poor, though his parents nevertheless instilled in him an appreciation of music and the theater. At the age of six, while handing out programs at the Bijou Theatre, he met Gentleman Jim Corbett, the boxing champion of the world. He so adored this man that at the age of fourteen he too became a fighter, though he wisely hung on to his job at the Bijou, which stood at First Avenue North and Washington Avenue. There he graduated to assistant property man, then property man, and finallty he began to appear on stage in minor parts.

Reisner toured in vaudeville on the Keith-Orpheum Circuit for a few years, then joined a stock company in Salt Lake City where Willard Mack was leading man. Mack introduced Chuck to movie acting. By this time Chuck had become a "heavy." The two wrote their own stories, filmed them during the day, and watched the "rushes" between acts of the play at night.

Chuck found his way to Hollywood by 1916 and was picked up by Mack Sennett as a gag man. Every studio had one. When the director was stumped in some scene that needed humor, he would call out "Oh, Doctor" and the gag man came running. Some earned as much as a thousand dollars a week. Many gag men dreamed of becoming a director but Charles Reisner was one of the few who actually did. (Mervyn LeRoy was another.)

After thinking up gags for two years Chuck moved to the other side of the camera, taking bit parts in movies starring Charlie Chaplin. Ever observing and learning, Chuck was trained to direct and became a "second unit (assistant) director" as well as actor for Chaplin's films *A Dog's Life* (1918), *A Day's Pleasure* (1919), *The Kid* (1921, their first full-length film) and *The Pilgrim* (1923). He assistant-directed only on four others plus the Chaplin masterpiece, *The Gold Rush* (1925). On all nine films Charlie himself was director, writer, and producer.

By the mid-1920s Reisner was working with Chaplin's half-bother Syd, writing the scripts and directing him in *The Better Ole* (1926), *The Missing Link* (1927), and three others. At the time *The Gold Rush* and *The Better Ole* were the only comedies considered worthy to be shown at Grauman's Egyptian Theatre.

Chuck made these observations about the two Chaplins. "Charlie has a mysterious personality. You're always trying to solve him, and you never do. He is almost feminine in his moods and the elusive quality of his personality. One morning he speaks warmly to you. The next he says nothing at all. He is an artist and temperamental. Now Syd is more masculine. He is a great character actor. He can so change his personality in a scene that I can't recognize him. It is almost uncanny. Where Charlie's pictures are dramas, Syd's are melodramas. The two are exactly opposite, and it is the finest experience in the world working with them." Syd retired in 1928 at the age of forty-three.

From apprentice directing with Chaplin, Chuck went to Warner Brothers as a full-fledged writer-director in May of 1925. After all, he had studied with the master. Because he had worked with both Mack Sennett and Chaplin, he was pigeon-holed as a comic director, but he yearned to do dramas. "I don't care if it's only a program picture and I don't care what the story is or who works with me but I want to start directing dramas," he said in late 1926. "I know I can do it. I have always felt that I could and if I go on much longer I will be forever branded as a comedy director and will never get a chance at anything else." Every comedian, it is said, wants to play Hamlet but never gets the chance.

A major milestone in Chuck's career was directing the Great Stone Face, Buster Keaton, in his classic *Steamboat Bill* (1928). At Warners he worked with comedy director Brian Foy, son of the great Vaudevillian, Eddie Foy. Chuck had met "Brynie" at the Bijou in Minneapolis when Eddie Foy and the Seven Little Foys had played there in the 1890s. Brian, like Chuck, was a musician and had composed the signature song for Gallagher and Shean. Chuck won some musical fame, too, with his World War I hit, "Good-bye Broadway, Hello France," which was recorded with Leo Feist Music, Inc., a major music publishing house then. He composed it while touring the country on a recruiting drive.

In 1929 he joined M-G-M and stayed there for seventeen years as a producer, writer, and director. He directed *Everybody Dance* (1936), the only time his son, Chuck Reisner, Jr. appeared in one of his films. His son, Dean F., later became a writer.

Chuck directed the Marx Brothers in *The Big Store* (1941). In 1946 he re-joined Brian Foy at the Eagle-Lion Studio where he directed his last three pictures, ending his career in 1950 with *The Traveling Saleswoman* starring St. Paulite Joan Davis. A heart attack that year sent him into retirement at age sixty-three, and he died twelve years later.

Chuck met his first wife, Miriam Hope, while they both were appearing in the Irving Berlin musical, *Stop, Look and Listen*. Miriam died in 1947. He also starred in the musical *Queen of the Movies*. He directed sixty-one films in all, acted in twenty-three, wrote eighteen, and produced three. This man of many talents also wrote two novels, a children's book, and the TV series, *Night Watchman*. Chuck was survived by his second wife, Irene, and son Dean. He was given a requiem mass at the All Hallows Catholic Church at La Jolla and buried at the Eternal Hills Cemetery, Oceanside. He never did direct Hamlet but he made us laugh.

Ali Selim

Born 30 April 1961,
Minneapolis, MN

Ali Mohamed Selim became a film director after an apprenticeship producing TV ads for national companies. In 1991 he won a Gold Lion at the Cannes Film Festival for a YMCA ad he produced for Clarity Cloverdale, a Minneapolis agency.

Ali's father came to the United States from Egypt in 1953, fleeing from the repressive regime of Gamal Abdel Nasser, whose stingy policy for emigrants allowed Selim to bring all of $52 with him. He eventually settled in Minneapolis, studied economics at the University of Minnesota, and upon graduation found a teaching job at St. Thomas College. Then he found time to marry Evelyn Neimeier, who at the time was a commercial illustrator at Dayton's. Ali was their first born, followed by his brother, Ramy, and lastly, by his sister, Mond. Ali attended Fulton Elementary and Burroughs Elementary Schools. From seventh grade through high school he attended St. Thomas Academy. He was an English major at St. Thomas College.

At eighteen Ali went to Egypt to meet his father's brother who gave him a tour of the old neighborhood where his father grew up. The uncle added, "If you don't know where you've come from, you can't possibly know where you're going." This experience undoubtedly contributed to the interest Selim took in the multi-generational element latent in the story that became his breakthrough film *Sweet Land.*

Once her three children were in school, Evelyn became a docent at the Minneapolis Institute of Art, leading visitors of the MIA on a room-to-room tour of the great works of art in the permanent collection. She did that for twenty years, all the while instilling in her children an appreciation of art. This influence was also a guiding force leading Ali to film directing.

Professor Selim retired in 2006 after almost fifty years of instructing students. A colleague at the University was asked once, "Who on campus best exemplifies the Christian values we attempt to inspire in our students?" He replied, "That Muslim in the Economics Department." In line with this thinking of high-minded values, Mohamed

Ali Selim is credited with creating the program of free-of-charge education for senior citizens at St. Thomas.

After graduating from St. Thomas University in 1983, Ali got a brief taste of feature film production as an assistant editor on *Blood Hook* (1985). Hook was a Minnesota film made mostly in Wisconsin. His high school alma mater invited him to direct a recruiting film for which he earned several awards. Ali then went professional as a commercial producer, and later as a director, with his own production company, Departure Films. It was an instant success, and Ali was off and running, making one hundred ad spots a year. Since 1989 he has done over 850 TV ads and *Ad Week Magazine* lists him in the top 1% of most sought after directors in the country.

Winning the Gold Lion, advertizing's most coveted award, brought Selim national attention, and he joined a prestigious New York firm, Giraldi/Suarez. After two years there he joined The Story Companies, based in Chicago. There he bolstered his credits with commercials for Coke, Miller Life, McDonald's, Citibank, Blockbuster Video, and Reebok. Some of his ads have found a home in the permanent collection of the Museum of Modern Art in New York City.

In 1990 Selim read Will Weaver's short story, "A Gravestone Made of Wheat," in the *Star Tribune Picture Magazine*, and it occurred to him that it would make a good feature film. He purchased the film rights in 1994. (Will Weaver is a professor at Bemidji State College and the author of several works—see his bio in this book.) He was finally convinced he had a winner on his hands when he read that Weaver himself had cried upon completing the story.

While the project that eventually became *Sweetland* was percolating in his brain, Ali plunged into his first serious feature film work, directing and writing the screenplay for *Emperor of the Air* (1996). In this film local acting star Paul Boesing plays the Old Teacher who performs strange antics in order to keep a certain tree from being cut down. (Boesing with his ex-wife, Martha, were founders of The Fire House Theatre in South Minneapolis in the 1960s. He has performed his one-man-show on Walt Whitman at Park Square Theatre in Saint Paul and around the U.S.).

It was not until 2004, however, that Selim mustered the time and resources to begin shooting the Will Weaver story. After an extensive search, Montevideo, Minnesota, was chosen for location filming, and it was a busy town for a month, as sixty members of cast and crew assembled to get the job done. The production schedule called for work six days a week, twelve hours a day. Nearby Dawson provided additional background sites.

Sweet Land (2005) is the story of a Norwegian immigrant farmer and his German mail-order bride who struggle to find love and overcome anti-German prejudice in rural Minnesota after World War I. Their plight is made more difficult because Inge lacks the papers required to perform the marriage ceremony. The scenes flash back and forth from generation to generation, and an undercurrent of socialist activism occasionally rises into view, but the heart of the film's success lies in it's portrayal of friendship, community spirit, and budding romance.

The film captures the majestic landscape of western Minnesota effectively. Montevideo's Heritage Hill, an antique farm machinery organization, provided the steam-powered threshing machine, and it came to life right on cue for live threshing duty and performed with flying colors. The town's Northern Pacific Depot served as a backdrop for some shots and its Pioneer Village for others. David Tumblety deserves special credit for his cinematography, which richly fills the screen during the moments of silence that often punctuate the Scandinavian work day.

Elizabeth Reaser anchors the cast as the newly-arrived beauty Inge, Tim Guinee plays the rather naive and inarticulate Olaf, and a well-seasoned cast of veterans including Ned Beatty, John Heard, Alex Kingston, Alan Cumming, and Lois Smith round out the cast. Also making an appearance are Guthrie actor Stephen Pelinski, James Cada, Jodie Markell, Karen Landry, Paul Sand, Jim Westcott, Stephen Yoakam, Barbara Kingsley, Tony Pappenfuss, Wayne A. Evenson, John Paul Gamoke, Stephen D'Ambrose, Tom Gilroy, and the author, Will Weaver himself. This independent film had a budget of just over $1 million.

Sweet Land's world premiere was at the thirteenth annual Hamptons International Film Festival where it won the Audience Acclaim Award for the Best Narrative Feature Film. Elizabeth Reaser was named a Rising Star by the Festival. The *Minneapolis Star-Tribune* named Selim the Minnesota Artist of the Year in 2006. *Sweet Land* was named one of the Ten Best Films of 2006 by over a dozen critics including the *Los Angeles Times* and *Entertainment Weekly*. It went on to win the 2007 Independent Spirit Award for Best First Feature.

Jack Smight

*Born 9 March 1925,
Minneapolis, MN
Died 1 September 2003,
Los Angeles, CA*

Jack Smight grew up in South Minneapolis at 3841 12th Avenue South, though during his high school years he commuted by bus every day to Cretin School in St. Paul, where he graduated in 1943. Graduating in the middle of World War II, Smight professed in his high school yearbook that his chief ambition was to "earning my wings." The wings we are grateful for are the directorial ones he earned in TV and film after the war.

Music was Jack's first passion and First Lieutenant Smight was in Glee Club '43 and the Choral Society '42-'43 at Cretin. He also formed a fifteen-piece dance band outside of school which he conducted from the piano bench.. He met saxophone player Peter Aurness (Peter Graves) in this combo. He and Graves also did summer stock theater and a community play together.

Upon graduation Jack joined the Army Air Corps and flew missions in the Pacific until the end of World War II. Then he entered the University of Minnesota, majoring in theatre. So did his old pal, Peter Graves. In fact, Jack was dating Joan Endress before she met, swooned for, and later married Pete. Both men graduated from the U in 1949 and went to Hollywood against the advice of Pete's older brother, James Arness. Peter recalled, "We got a room together with kitchen privileges for six bucks a week (another source says $7.50) and started scouring the *Hollywood Reporter* and *Daily Variety* for auditions." Jack's first job was as a carhop in a drive-in, while Peter was hired to drive a taxi. Peter knew the L. A. layout a bit from earlier family vacations taken there.

The girlfriends came out to join them. When Pete was secure enough with steady jobs and regular paychecks, he married Joan on

December 16, 1950, while Jack had to wait until 1951 before he could marry actress Joyce Cunning. By then he was a floor director for TV's *The Colgate Comedy Hour*. Pete said, "We both married Minnesota girls." Jack added, "The irony is that I used to date his wife and he used to date mine."

Smight gave up acting nearly as soon as he arrived in California. Pete said that "Jack was smart, so he got promotions. *The Colgate Comedy Hour* was tremendous training ground for him." Smight stayed in TV and Graves worked mostly at movies. By 1953 Jack and Joyce moved to New York to direct live dramas like the Kraft and Philco Theater dramas, the *U. S. Steel Hour*, and *Armstrong Circle Theater*. The first filmed TV drama he directed was *Eddie* starring Mickey Rooney. He won an Emmy for his work.

From the 1950s through the 1970s Smight directed episodes for many TV series, but he spent much of his time directing feature films starting with *I'd Rather Be Rich* (1964), a comedy starring Maurice Chevalier and Sandra Dee; *The Third Day* (1965); and *Harper* (1966), the first of two films he did with Paul Newman. *Harper* was Jack's breakthrough film, hugely popular at the box office and pleasing to critics.

In *Harper*, Newman plays a Los Angeles private eye hired to find Lauren Bacall's missing husband. In 1966 Jack was interviewed regarding the film. "I just wanted to make a straight movie, with straight cuts and no dissolves, no tricks, no optical effects." In the comedy *The Secret War of Harry Frigg* (1967), Newman plays a private who succeeds in rescuing five captured generals.

In *Kaleidoscope* (1966) Warren Beatty stars as a crooked playboy gambler in a comedy-thriller set in London. Rod Steiger stars in Smight's next two films. In *No Way to Treat a Lady* (1968) with detective George Segal on the trail of serial killer, Steiger plays seven roles, showing great comic flair. In *The Illustrated Man* (1969), science fiction film based loosely on three Ray Bradbury short stories, he searches for the witch who put tattoos on his body that foretell world events. It was produced by Minneapolis movie house owner Ted Mann.

Smight said in a 1968 interview with the *Los Angeles Times* while filming *The Illustrated Man*, "I love movies with a surprise around every corner. With all the technicians and equipment at your disposal, it's such a temptation to indulge yourself. You've got to be careful not to be like a woman putting on too much jewelry." This film is entered in the Guinness Book of Movie Facts and Feats as the longest ever make-up job as it took two days to apply the tattoos on Steiger's body.

Jack lost his professional "cool" and disowned his filming of John Updike's novel, *Rabbit, Run* (1970) dismayed by how it had been edited. The public didn't like the picture much either. *The Traveling Executioner* (1970) is Smight's own favorite among his films, a black comedy in which Stacy Keach carries an electric wheelchair all around Alabama but falls in love with a condemned woman. Jack produced this film as well as directed it. It was his first film with M-G-M after being with Warner Bros. throughout the Sixties.

A great surprise to some critics was Smight's sensitivity in handling the made-for-TV film, *Frankenstein: The True Story* (1973) starring James Mason, John Gielgud, Ralph Richardson, Margaret Leighton, Agnes Morehead, and Michael Sazzarin, which brought out aspects of the monster's character that had never before been seen in films. Unfortunately, most of these touches were removed from the theatrical version, which had been reduced by half-an-hour, and it was given a lukewarm reception. Film historian Leonard Maltin calls it "the thinking man's horror movie."

M inneapolis-raised Robert Vaughn played the young Harry Truman in *The Man from Independence* (1974), a made-for-TV retelling of the early years of Truman's political career. Another suspense-filled romp is *Airport 1975* (1974) starring Charlton Heston. Karen Black does very well as the stewardess who guides a 747-jumbo jet plane to a safe landing after the Captain and his cabin crew are killed or injured in a mid-air collision. It has a large, star-filled cast— a Smight trademark, it seems. Gloria Swanson makes her final film appearance in this film, and another oldie, former Queen of Hollywood Myrna Loy, plays an alcoholic on this bumpy flight.

Jack directed one of the biggest, finest casts ever assembled on the screen in *Midway* (1976), though most of them had very small parts. In Smight's second-to-last feature film he is reunited with Peter Graves for *Number One with a Bullet* (1986). Jack retired after forty years of directing in 1989.

Jack's wife of fifty-one years, Joyce, died in 2002. He was survived by sons, Tim and Alec, an editor.

Smight was better known by film industry people than by the fans, though studio bosses liked him because he always brought in a solid film, on time and on budget. When he died the *Liverpool Daily Post* wrote, "He was a lover of the macabre, the unexpected, the tragic, the horrific and the mysterious, harnessing all these qualities to a glittering cast..." Add some comedy (or black comedy)... and we have a perfect Jack Smight movie.

Stephen Sommers

Born 20 March 1958,
Indianapolis, IN

It's hard to categorize Stephen Som-mers as just a director (12 films) because he's done just as many filmed screenplays and produced nearly as many films (9). He has inherited the mantle of the horror interpreter of the twenty-first century, redoing *The Mummy, The Mummy Returns* and *Van Helsing,* but he's also done the Mark Twain classics *The Adventures of Huck Finn* and *Tom and Huck,* Charles Dickens' *Oliver Twist* and Rudyard Kipling's *The Jungle Book.* He is now doing sci-fi films and redoing the early rocket classic of *Flash Gordon.*

Stephen is the oldest of five children of Dr. Stephen Sommers, a pediatrician, and his wife Mary. He grew up in St. Cloud, (the family lived at 2000 Pandolfo Place) attended St. Paul's Primary School, and graduated from Apollo High in 1976. He graduated from St. John's University in Collegeville (Spanish and English Major) in 1980 and went to Spain to study at the University of Seville for a year. He spent the next two years in Dublin, London, Paris, and Amsterdam, acting in a street theater group and managing a rock band, The Horizontal Dancers. Then he moved to Los Angeles to attend USC's School of Cinema-Television for three years earning his master's degree in 1988.

To earn his master's degree he wrote and directed an award-winning twenty minute film, *Perfect Alibi.* This was all the encouragement he needed to scrape up $800,000 for his first real feature, a teen movie, *Catch Me If You Can* (1989), written and directed by Sommers and filmed in St. Cloud during the autumn of 1988. Its national première was at the Parkwood 8 in Waite Park, which devoted four screens to the event. Most school scenes were shot at Cathedral High but some were done at Apollo and Technical High Schools. Close to two-thousand St. Cloud residents appear as extras in the film, the first professional film shot in St. Cloud.

The story focuses on the efforts of a group of students to raise money for their school by means of illegal car racing. The woman who is class president and the guy racing the cars fall in love. Mayor Sam Huston and Tom Moore of the Chamber of Commerce were in the film. The Zapp Bank hosted a reception for film goers afterward. (The film itself eventually grossed more that six million.)

Disney Studios produced and distributed Steve's next two films: updated versions of *The Adventures of Huck Finn* (1993) and *The Jungle Book* (1994). Stephen said, "I always loved *The Adventures of Huckleberry Finn* as a kid and, hell, I grew up on the Mississippi River." Regarding *Jungle Book*, "I wanted real animals interacting with real humans. It was tough but I couldn't be happier with the movie." *Jungle Book* grossed $28 million in its first three weeks. It was filmed in India in 110 degree heat with 300 lions, tigers, bears, panthers and orangutans. His next Disney assignment was to write and produce *Tom and Huck* (1995).

Sommers changed hats for writing and directing the B-budget action film *Gunmen* (1994) and the suspense-thriller *Deep Rising* (1998), starring Treat Williams as one of two survivors of a sinking ocean liner attacked by a strange sea creature. This was the first film where Stephen really flexed his special effects muscles, and he loved the result. He continued down the special effects road and never looked back.

The film that really put Sommers' name on the map was *The Mummy* (1999). Brendan Fraser stars in this imaginative thrills-and-spills adventure, produced by Universal, the grandfather studio of horror movies. Sommers talked studio executives into raising the budget from $17 to $75 million and giving him free rein, and they were not disappointed with the result. The special effects are wildly entertaining without obscuring the film's considerable comic and dramatic charms. The box office receipts in the U.S. alone were $155 million.

The sequel, *The Mummy Returns* (2001) is loaded with dazzling special effects, too. The film cost $100 million to make of which $30 million went into special effects. It grossed $425 million world-wide. The film was shot in Egypt, Israel, and Jordan. Wrestling star, Dwayne Thompson, aka The Rock, appears as the Scorpion King. The Rock reprised his role in *The Scorpion King* (2002) with his head is affixed to a twenty-eight-foot computer-generated scorpion. A second sequel to *The Mummy*, *Revenge of the Mummy: The Ride* (2004) has had the same blockbuster success. Sommers evidently knows what people want and gives it to them In *Van Helsing* (2004) a monster hunter tracks to "kill" the Dracula AND the Wolfman.

Rumor has it that Industrial Light & Magic, the special effects arm of Lucasfilms, has jokingly created the 'Stephen Sommers Scale' to measure the extent of digital effects used in a given movie scene. The four parts of the scale, from lowest to the highest, are: 1) What The Shot Needs, 2)What The Computers Can Handle, 3) Oh My God, The Computers Are About To Crash, and finally, 4) What Stephen Wants.

Sommers married Jana Hydusik, a Pennsylvania native with a Master's Degree in Psychotherapy, on July 24, 1993, in St. Paul's Catholic Church in St. Cloud. There were no celebrities among the 230 guests, no paparazzi hounding the couple with questions. Many old friends from school days there as well as Stephen's siblings David, Michael, Jane, and Kathleen.

At the wedding a reporter from the *St. Cloud Times* asked Sommers if Hollywood had changed him at all. He replied, "I still drive an old car, an '81 Toyota Celica. I just have a small house. I don't have a pinky ring. I still go back to Minnesota for Christmas." How did the two meet? Don Shane, producer of *Catch Me If You Can*, introduced them during the filming in St. Cloud. They did not marry until Stephen finished work on *The Adventures of Huck Finn* four years later. The couple did move to Woodland Hills, then to Pacific Palisades, and on to Santa Barbara.

As a youth Stephen had the reputation as a "teacher's nightmare," and his mother feared that he would never be allowed into high school. He had the "attention span of a fruit fly" and a hyperactive imagination. Today his condition would be diagnosed as ADHD, Attention Deficit Hyperactive Disorder. Yet, he has used this condition to his advantage in filmmaking and he thrives on a fast pace. He's not a slacker but is very self-driven and can focus for days on end without a pause, partly because he fears that the days are numbered for most writers and directors.

Stephen Sommers gave the keynote address to the St. John's University 1995 graduating class. He told the graduates to "Take risks, seek your dreams and don't worry about becoming Ward Cleaver overnight." He told of his chasing after Forest Gump director, Robert Zemeckis, in a parking lot to ask if he would succeed in movie making and Zemeckis said, "If you want something bad enough, and work at it hard enough, you will get it. Somehow." He also advised the graduates not to "feel compelled to quickly find a career, marry, have children and sign on to huge mortgages. If they do, they will be living the expectation of a bygone generation." He considered himself as on the edge of Generation X.

In 2003 Sommers donated a digital film studio featuring Apple Computers to St. John's University where its students can learn basic skills in filmmaking, video art, broadcasting graphics and Web publishing.

Not only does he come home for Christmas but other times, too, for a visit to the Southside Boys & Girls Club, where they watched a short movie about the making of *The Mummy Returns*. The kids asked lots of questions and got autographs. People from around the world know that Stephen will be in Minnesota at Christmas so that's where Monty Python's John Cleese, a family favorite, finds him to wish him holiday greetings. Sam Neill from *The Jungle Book* has made the same call.

What's your guess, dear reader, as what classic film director would be Stephen's favorite? Here's a clue: he directed *Captain Blood*, *The Adventures of Robin Hood*, *The Seahawk* and *Casablanca*. This master of action films, filled with romance and drama is...Michael Curtiz, a longtime director at Warner Brothers Studio.

John Griffith Wray

Born 1881-82,
Minneapolis, MN
Died 12 July 1929,
Los Angeles, CA

John Griffin Wray graduated from the American Academy of Dramatic Arts in New York City and stayed there to make his way in the theater. He acted on the New York stage and toured the United States and Asia for eighteen years. He eventually formed his own stock company in San Diego. In 1920 Wray decided to study the motion picture business. Veteran film director and producer Thomas H. Ince took Wray under his wing and promptly made him a director. Through Ince he also met veteran scenarist, editor, and screen writer C. Gardner Sullivan, a native of Stillwater, Minnesota. Sullivan, dubbed the "Dean of the Silent Screen Writers," wrote six screenplays for Wray including *Hail the Woman* (1921); *Soul of the Beast* (1923); *Human Wreckage* (1923); and *The Marriage Cheat*

(1924). Besides becoming a director, Wray became general manager for Ince's film studio.

Ince was a master of the Western who understood better than any other director how to make a picture move, or so said master director John Ford. Ince's star cowboy, and Hollywood's number one cowboy star from the mid-teens to the early 1920s, was Minnesotan William S. Hart. Hart retired from movie making in 1925, the year after Ince died mysteriously in a boating incident.

On March 11, 1922, Wray was quoted in *Moving Picture World* as saying that movies need surface thoughts and simple emotions, "no intellectual stuff. The producer who is wise will woo his public on the solid ground of fundamental and therefore universal emotions. He will forgo these artistic heights and depths which flower in the regions of the intellect." Wray did admit at the same time that the public deserved better films.

After Ince's death Wray assumed the position of General Manager at Universal Pictures, but resigned in March of 1925 to join Fox Studios as a movie director. His first film for Fox was *The Winding Stair* (1925).

Wray moved on to direct films for M-G-M Studios. In 1928 he returned to Universal Pictures as Production Manager. A week before his death he had completed his last film, *A Most Immoral Lady* (1929), starring Leatrice Joy, an actress from his San Diego Stock Theatre Company.

Wray was married at least twice. He was married to Virginia Brissac with whom he managed the San Diego Stock Company. Brissac, a stock and repertory stage actress, divorced Wray on May 11, 1927. He married Miss Bradley King, a scenarist at M-G-M, on October 7, 1928. He was a director at M-G-M when they met. Apparently, the Wray newlyweds had grand plans for a large new home as John had recently bought a thirty-three acre orange orchard in the Canoga Hills near Ventura Blvd in a $100,000 cash transaction. The Wrays were going to build an Indian-styled house on knolls that look out over the San Fernando Valley, but in the summer of 1929 Wray died from complications following an appendectomy.

Screenwriters

Houston Branch

William Houston Branch
Born 5 March 1899,
St. Paul, MN
Died 27 January 1968,
Los Angeles, CA

To have written eighty screenplays and stories, as Houston Branch did, plus novels and plays, and to have more than half of your log book actually make it to the screen, is quite an accomplishment.

Branch's ancestors settled in St. Paul (Pig's Eye) before Minnesota had become a state. His parents were Dr. Uriah and Hannah (Swanson) Branch. Their older child was Charles and they lived at 1205 Churchill Street. Uriah died on July 15, 1902. In 1912 Hannah and the boys lived at 1150 Argyll Avenue according to the City Directory.

As Houston grew up he spent summer vacations working as a farm hand in North Dakota. He showed a flair for writing as a student, graduating from St. Paul Central High School in 1917. He attended the University of Minnesota in 1918 for half a year while doing night shift duty as a crime and police reporter for the *St. Paul Pioneer Press*. Then he left town.

Branch's restlessness took him first to San Antonio, Texas, where in 1920 he met Tex O'Reilly, who exposed him to the inner circles of a Mexican revolutionary junta. Houston later wrote a play, *Donna Maria*, about that experience. The play flopped but the theater bug had bit him. He became a theatrical agent, handling transcontinental tours of John Philip Sousa's Band, the San Carlo Opera Company, and a circus.

By 1924 he was working for the *San Antonio Express*, where he was Political Editor. In 1925 he became associate editor of *Western Magazine*. Later he became editor of the *Sportsman Handbook*.

When Hollywood began to take a serious interest in his short stories in 1926, Branch moved there, though his first jobs on the coast were as a tool dresser in the Tampico oil fields and as tuna fisherman. Little by little the writing started to pay. His credited debut is *Once and Forever* (1927) for which he wrote the story and the screenplay. His second film, *The Showdown* (1928) was based on his play, *Wild Cat* (1928).

From 1939 to 1947 Branch was editor-in-chief of *National Surveys*. Yet, he was able to piggy-back work for the U. S. Army Signal Corps (1942-1943) during World War II into consulting on propaganda and training films. Plus, he was a respected public relations man for the film industry and was consulted often by major industrial corporations.

He was the Founder and Director of the American Library Foundation during the 1940s where he was a strong advocate for federal funding for rural libraries. The ALF published a number of his booklets, including "Two Gifts of Books;" "Give Rural Youth an Equal Chance;" and "The Story of Horace Mann".

Two of Branch's popular novels were co-written with Frank Walters: *River Lady* (1942) and *Diamond Head* (1948). *River Lady* was made into a film in 1948 starring Yvonne de Carlo as Sequin, owner of a Mississippi gambling boat. She has several lumbermen friends who develop river towns at her request by rafting Minnesota lumber to the building sites.

Diamond Head is a historical romance involving a Confederate naval officer who falls in love with a whaling captain's daughter. He takes the Confederate ship Shenandoah into New England's waters to raid the whaling fleet, unfortunately unaware that Lee has already surrendered to Grant at Appomattox.

Branch wrote the stories for *Mr. Wong, Detective* (1938) second in a series of a Chinese detective starring, quite surprisingly, Boris Karloff; *Women in Bondage* (1943) with Gail Patrick, is a story of how Nazis treated their women; *Belle of the Yukon* (1944), an Oscar-nominated musical with Gypsy Rose Lee and Randolph Scott; *Block Busters* (1944), an East Side Kids comedy starring Leo Gorcey, Huntz Hall and jazz clarinetist Jimmy Noone; *Wild Harvest* (1947) with Alan Ladd and Dorothy Lamour; and *Untamed Frontier* (1952) a Western with Joseph Cotton and Shelley Winters.

A nice piece of trivia is Houston's writing *Klondike Kate* (1943) as this has been part of the St. Paul Winter Carnival festivities for many years now. Each year a new Klondike Kate is crowned and she is nearly as important as Miss Minnesota. She must sing in a naughty, bold, and brassy style blending Mae West and Sophie Tucker. Mae West's *Klondike Annie* (1936) was probably Branch's inspiration. Oh, yes, the Kates must be buxom—in the Mae West mode.

From 1959 to 1963 Houston edited technical publications for the Marquardt Corp; from 1963 to 1968 he was Executive Director of the Academy of Applied Sciences. He was a member of the Authors League of America, the Academy of Motion Picture Arts and Sciences, the Screen Writers Guild, and the American Rocket Society.

Houston's first marriage was to Mildred Eugenia Clark on January 13, 1942, but that ended in divorce. They had a daughter: Victoria Elaine. Mildred died in July of 1957. His second wife was radio actress Mary Raymond.

Sidney Buchman

Born 27 March 1902,
Brainerd, MN
Died 23 August 1975,
Cannes, France

Duluth is not only one of the world's largest inland harbors. It has also harbored great artistic talents such as singer/song writer Bob Dylan; singer-dancer Jane Frazee; Marguerite de la Motte, the leading lady for five of Douglas Fairbanks' films of the 1920s; and Carol Dempster, the discovery and esteemed love of D. W. Griffith. It was also the home of Oscar-winning screenwriter Sidney Buchman.

Robert Buchman, manager of The Golden Rule Store, and Sarah Zalk had five children: three boys and two girls. Both Sidney and Harold became screenwriters and rose to the top in Hollywood. Sidney was born in Brainerd but was raised mostly in Duluth, where the family moved in 1903. They lived at 421 First Avenue West, moving in 1909 to 120 East Fourth Street. In 1910 the family returned to Brainerd, where Robert managed the Buckman Mercantile Co. at 301 S. Broadway. The family lived at 523 Holly Street, where Harold was born in 1912.

In 1914 the family returned to their old haunts at 421 First Avenue West in Duluth. Sidney attended Jackson Elementary School though possibly went to the newly built Nettleton Elementary School. Sidney had two sisters, Dorothy and Marian.

Sid graduated from Duluth Central High in 1919. He was vice president of his class, excelled in athletics, served as sports editor for the school paper, and was business manager of the class play, among many other accomplishments. At graduation he gave the commencement oration.

In 1919 Sidney moved down to Minneapolis to attend the University of Minnesota. After a year he moved with his family to New York City and received his B.A. from Columbia University three years later. Then he "went up" to Oxford University in England, but the class consciousness of the place irked him and he dropped out after a few weeks to tour France and Italy by bicycle.

He had grown up in a melting pot of Irish, Scandinavians, Poles, Yugoslavs, and Jews, and later reflected, "As a matter of fact, I was altogether too unconscious of the benefits I received in my early days from the race harmony prevailing in Minnesota. It wasn't until years later, when I was reaping dividends from it in my writing, that I realized I had grown up in one of the real melting pots of the world. Today, when the whole world is being drawn into democratic unity, it is easier to understand what Duluth had to offer."

During his year of touring Europe Sidney became convinced that he would be a writer with an emphasis on the theater. Back in England, he hung around London's Old Vic to observe and study it.

He returned to New York to write plays and stayed there eight years. He had two plays produced on Broadway, one of which was *This One Man* starring Paul Muni. The other was *Storm Song* with Francine Larrimore. In 1930 he moved to Hollywood. At first he contributed to script dialogue and worked with a team of other writers at Paramount Studios. In 1932 he contributed to the scripts for four productions, including *If I Had a Million* with W. C. Fields and Charles Laughton and *Sign of the Cross* directed and produced by Cecil B. De Mille, starring Claudette Colbert, Charles Laughton and Fredric March. In *Million* Sidney was part of a team of eighteen writers and seven directors. De Mille gave Buchman his first serious credit, quite a plum for such a newcomer.

Buchman went on to write *From Hell to Heaven* (1933) for Carole Lombard and Jack Oakie; and *All of Me* (1934) with Fredric March and Miriam Hopkins. Then he took a trip back to the old stomping grounds of Duluth and spent a week visiting his cohorts on the school yearbook, *The Zenith*, including the yearbook advisor and English teacher, Miss Mira Southworth. He walked a bit around town waxing sentimental, especially at the corner of Lake Avenue and Third Street, formerly a candy store where, as a youth, he would spend all the money he made delivering newspapers. The city itself shocked him at first. After living in New York, London, and Los Angeles, Duluth seemed to have shrunk.

Buchman returned to Hollywood to assume a new position as vice president and executive producer at the Columbia Studios, where Harry Cohn was boss. Right away he was teamed up with the brilliant director Frank Capra for *Broadway Bill* (1934) though Sidney is uncredited. It starred Warner Baxter and Myrna Loy. The great and witty writer, Robert Riskin, who wrote several scripts for Capra, got the credit. Sidney would soon get his turn with Capra. His fifteenth film was *Love Me Forever* (1935) with Grace Moore and Leo Carrillo. Sidney got sole screen writing credit for *She Married Her Boss* (1935) with Claudette Colbert and Melvyn Douglas. He did another operetta starring Grace Moore and Franchot Tone in *The King Steps Out* (1936), directed by Josef von Sternberg; then *Adventure in Manhattan* (1936) with Joel McCrea and Jean Arthur. Greater glory came with the hit *Theodora Goes Wild* (1936) starring Irene Dunne and Melvyn Douglas. This is a crazy comedy wherein a small town girl writes a titillating bestseller. The stars do some zany antics.

Sidney made only minor contributions to the classic *Lost Horizon* (1937) and went uncredited. The film stars Ronald Colman, Jane Wyatt, Thomas Mitchell, Edward Everett Horton, H. B. Warner, and Sam Jaffe in the story of survivors of a plane crash who stumble upon Shangri-la in the snow-covered Himalayas. This peace-loving civilization is governed by a very old monk who wants to leave the minikingdom to Ronald Colman.

The Awful Truth (1937) follows with Irene Dunne and Cary Grant. Once again Sidney is not credited. Next is *Holiday* (1938) with Katharine Hepburn, Cary Grant, and Lew Ayres. Sidney's work on *Mr. Smith Goes to Washington* (1939) earned him an Oscar nomination. In this very popular film Stewart plays the honest, plain-speaking Jefferson Smith, who eventually becomes a senator. His next screenplay *The Howards of Virginia* (1940) was another vehicle for Cary Grant with Martha Scott and Albert Lea-born Richard Carlson.

Buchman finally took home the Oscar for Best Screenplay for *Here Comes Mr. Jordan* (1941), which explores the dilemma of a prizefighter who dies in a plane crash and goes to heaven—by mistake. He was slated to live another forty years. He returns to earth only to find that his body has been cremated, so he has to find another one. And so on.

Sid shared the Oscar with his writing partner, Seton I. Miller. The film itself was nominated for Best Picture, Best Director, Best Actor, Best Supporting Actor, and Best Cinematography, seven nominations in all! Other stand-out films that year included *Citizen Kane*, *The Maltese Falcon*, *The Little Foxes*, and *How Green Was My Valley*.

Buchman served as president of the Screen Writers Guild that year, but he also found time to write *Talk of the Town* (1942), another hit (and Oscar nomination) starring Ronald Colman, Cary Grant, and Jean Arthur, in which comedy and melodrama find an easy balance.

Still on a roll, he scripted and also produced *A Song to Remember*, a film about Chopin with Cornel Wilde as the great composer/pianist. He then adapted Ruth Gordon's play *Over Twenty-One* into film (1945). (Minneapolis audiences may remember Gordon as Maude in *Harold and Maude* (1971) which had a very long run at Edina's Westgate Theatre.)

Buchman struck paydirt again with the hugely popular *The Jolson Story* (1946) with Larry Parks doing a great job as Al Jolson, Broadway's greatest singer-entertainer ever. Sid was only involved in a small way with the script but he was hired to reprise the film in *Jolson Sings Again* (1950) for which he received his fourth Oscar nomination as well as a Writer's Guild nomination.

After the release of *Jolson Sings Again*, Buchman returned to Duluth to be honored with "Buchman Day" on February 1, 1950. His visit opened with a press-radio session and breakfast reception at the Hotel Duluth. The visit was planned to coincide with the opening of *Jolson Sings Again* at the Granada Theatre where he made a personal appearance. He also gave a speech to the Duluth Chamber of Commerce, "The Outlook for the Coming Year in the Entertainment Industry." He met with old classmates at an informal reception at the Athletic Club and was feted at the Central High auditorium where he gave a speech.

Saturday's Hero (1951) starring John Derek was the last writing and producing project he completed before politics reared its ugly head. He testified to the House Un-American Activities Committee that he had been a communist from 1938 to 1948. He was fined $150 and given a one year suspended prison sentence. Nevertheless, the Writer's Guild nominated *Saturday's Hero* as Best Screenplay that year.

But Buchman would not name the names of his "fellow travelers" to HUAC. He was therefore blacklisted for the next ten years. During that time he wrote under the name of Milton Holmes.(Woody Allen's film, *The Front* (1976) deals with this issue quite well.)

By the end of the 1950s the witch hunt furor had died down and nearly everyone came back to work with their proper names. Sidney was lured back to America from France by Twentieth Century Fox to write and produce *The Mark* (1961) with Rod Steiger, Maria Schell and Stuart Whitman. He joined his old colleague Joe Mankiewicz as one of the main writers for Liz Taylor's *Cleopatra* (1963). He also wrote and produced *The Group* (1966), a film based on Mary McCarthy's novel directed by Sidney Lumet. In 1965 the Writer's Guild of America gave him the Laurel Award.

Sidney Buchman was married twice, the first time to Beatrice Rosenthal, with whom he had a daughter, Susan. He spent the last ten years of his life in France, and his brother Harold joined him there. Though less celebrated than his brother, Harold did write the scripts for thirty-four films. He retired in 1974 and died in 1990, also in Cannes. Their sister Marian Lamm lived in Minneapolis.

Buchman's final film was *The Deadly Trap* (1971) starring Faye Dunaway in a mystery thriller about an American couple's two children kidnapped in Paris.

Vincent T. Bugliosi

Born 18 August 1934,
Hibbing, MN

Vince is the author of *Helter Skelter: The True Story of the Manson Murders*, a sensational best-seller that chronicled the forty-one week trial of the Charles Manson murder cult. He also co-wrote the screenplay for two TV versions of the book (1976 & 2004). His nine other published works include another blockbuster best-seller and two novels made into TV movies, yet Vincent claims he is happiest in a courtroom as a prosecuting attorney.

Vincent's grandfather was an Italian immigrant who came to the Iron Range of northern Minnesota to work in the mines. His father was a Hibbing grocer. Vince was a top student and also a state tennis champion. He graduated from the University of Miami, Florida, with a B.B.A. in 1956 and from UCLA (University of California-Los Angeles) with an L.L.B. in 1964. He paid his way through college with a tennis scholarship and also worked as an assistant tennis pro part-time. That's how he met his wife, Gail Talluto. They married in 1956 and have two children, Wendy and Vince, Jr.; they live in a Los Angeles suburb, and Vincent has a law practice in Beverly Hills.

Bugliosi's connection with the film world revolves around the events of August 9, 1969, when a killing spree orchestrated by cult-leader Charles Manson took place. Among the victims were Sharon Tate, wife of Polish film director Roman Polanski, and supermarket chain owner Leno LaBianca and his wife. Vincent was the Assistant District Attorney for Los Angeles County in this macabre, high-profile case. At the time Bugliosi had won 105 of 106 cases he prosecuted as Deputy D.A. and he had never lost a murder trial. Because of this trial his legal work caught public attention, of course, but his book on the trial established him as one of the finest legal minds in America. In fact, renowned trial lawyer F. Lee Bailey called Bugliosi "the quintessential prosecutor."

Later Bugliosi wrote the novel, *Till Death Do Us Part* (1978), based on a second murder trial. It won the Edgar Award from the Mystery Writers of America in 1979. (*Helter Skelter* had won an Edgar in 1975 in the Best Fact Crime category.)

Till Death Do Us Part (1992) became a made-for-TV movie as did another of Bugliosi's books, *And the Sea Will Tell* (1991).

In his book *With Outrage: The Five Reasons Why O.J. Simpson Got away with Murder* (1996) Bugliosi shows how the prosecution muffed the "Trial of the Century." Not shy about dealing with big stories, Bugliosi's other books include *Drugs in America: The Case for Victory* (1991); *The Phoenix Solution: Getting Serious about Winning America's Drug War* (1996); *No Island of Sanity: Paula Jones v. Bill Clinton: The Supreme Court on Trial* (1998); *The Betrayal of America: How the Supreme Court Undermined the Constitution and Chose Our President* (2001); and *Lullaby and Good Night: A Novel Inspired by the True Story of Vivian Gordon* (1987).

Bugliosi was the Democratic candidate for district attorney, Los Angeles County, in 1972, and for California Attorney General in 1974. He was professor of criminal law in Beverly Hills School of Law, 1968-1974. He served in the U.S. Army in 1957 attaining the rank of captain. He has been a member of the California Bar Association since 1964. Among his recent publications is *Reclaiming History: The Assassination of President John F. Kennedy*, a lengthy tome dedicated to establishing beyond all doubt that Lee Harvey Oswald acted alone. This time the film has already been made, however…and it doesn't end that way.

Joel & Ethan Coen

Born 29 November 1954, & 21 September 1957, St. Louis Park, MN

"Now, boys," asked Ted Kuller, "you want me to give you money to make a film? Why are you asking me to help you when I know nothing about movies except whether I like them or not. I know about making gloves, not movies. I know I will sell the gloves I make because this is Minnesota and people will buy gloves to keep their hands warm in winter. I've met your father, a nice man, who teaches economics at the university. Has he taught you two to understand money? Do you know how to manage money? Because you know, you're talking about lots and lots of money?" Kuller loaned them $25,000 then shook his head and muttered to himself that he had thrown the money away.

The Coens went virtually door to door, scrounging the capital they needed to fund *Blood Simple* (1983). At the end of a year they had collected $750,000 from several dozen investors, few of whom had ever before even considered invested in a movie. For every twenty people they talked to, one invested. Architects, lawyers, real-estate agents, and beauty salon owners were among the ranks of investors. Joel said, "We were selling air and confidence as we had no track record." Ted Kuller laughs now; he got his money back—with some interest.

Professor Edward Coen, long retired now from the University of Minnesota's Economics Department, did infuse the boys with some smarts about money, it seems. Each film they have made has turned a tidy profit. Their mother, Rena, deceased, was a professor of art history at St. Cloud State College. She observed that Joel was a highly social boy with friends at their house every day after school. "It was wall-to-wall kids in the house," she said. Joel was very "social and gregarious."

Ethan was the opposite. He "was really very quiet, very reticent" and "could be content with just a book." Yet, in movie-making they work together hand-in-glove on every phase of production.

They learned how to manage money and respect it. They are serious pre-planners of every step of film production. They write the screenplays together and discuss some aspects with seeming telepathy, such is the closeness of these brothers. Because of this zealous planning and pre-planning, they have shown a talent for saving money. "If we didn't pre-plan it," Joel said, "I don't think we'd be able to handle the pressure. I couldn't walk out there without knowing just what I was after. I'd flounder, and the movie would get away from me and I'd face the horror of watching it veer off into the ditch." Responsible? Yes!

The Coen brothers grew up in St. Louis Park, a western suburb of Minneapolis. As pre-teens the boys published a newspaper, *The Flag Avenue Sentinel* and sold copies for two cents apiece. Joel was eight when he began to take a serious interest in movies and bought a Super-8 camera with money he had earned mowing lawns. He and Ethan did remakes of their favorite movies like *Advise and Consent* and *Naked Prey* and they also made original films like *Henry Kissinger – Man on the Go*. Most of the movies they saw growing up, with Bob Hope or Doris Day in the leading roles, they considered "kitschy."

They attended the local schools until high school age when they transferred to Simon's Rock College, a place in the Berkshire Mountains of New Hampshire for bright, restless kids who didn't want to finish regular high school and were eligible for early college placement. Later Joel transferred to New York University's Film School, from which he earned his B.A. Ethan gained his B.A. from Princeton in philosophy, 1980.

Joel told *New York Times* reporter Judy Klemesrud that at NYU he "sat in the back of the room with an insane grin on his face." He found his work editing low-budget horror flicks for directors like Sam Raimi to be more valuable than four years of college study. He studied film briefly at the University of Texas at Austin before returning to New York City.

In 1980 the Coens began writing their first film. Ethan had just moved to New York and he took a job at Macy's as a statistical typist. Sometimes they would go to Central Park and have screenwriting contests with each other, taking just ten minutes to pen a plot and some dialogue for what might be a ten-minute movie.

Blood Simple (1983) is a variation of *The Postman Always Rings Twice* wherein a Texas bar owner knows his wife is cheating on him so he hires a hit man to kill her and her lover. Frances McDormand, Joel's real-life wife, plays the naughty lady. It is considered a good film, and parts of it are very good. It is full of misunderstandings and plot twists. At this time the brothers were impressed with James M. Cain's novels, and they strove to create a cinematic equivalent for the thriller tension to be found in Cain's work. Dashiell Hammett was also an inspiration.

Major Studios refused to distribute *Blood Simple*, however. They deemed it to be too "arty" for the blood-and-gore audience yet too gory for the art audience, so it was distributed independently by Circle Releasing Co. Some critics thought it was a *comédie noire* and others did not know how to take it. Others thought it was fresh and exhilarating. Whatever the reason, it became a surprise hit at the 1984 New York Film Festival, and the brothers won a Grand Jury Prize at the United States Film Festival.

Their next project, *Crimewaves*, was a collaboration with Sam Raimi. It is a farce about rat exterminators who become people exterminators. It had limited release in 1985. The brothers are credited with co-screenwriting only in this film. Raimi said, "Writing with them was like watching a badminton game. Joel would mention a line of dialogue, and Ethan would finish the sentence. Then Joel would say the punch line and Ethan would type it up."

By this time the brothers had developed a reputation for murderous cynicism that many critics found hard to take, and their next venture took people by surprise. *Raising Arizona* (1987) was the Coen's first attempt at mainstream moviemaking. Nicolas Cage is addicted to robbing convenience stores though he is always unarmed. The police officer who books him after one failed attempt is a woman (Holly Hunter), and the two fall in love. Unable to have their own children, they kidnap quintuplets belonging to the local "furniture king" store owner. The silliness goes on and on, and the entire escapade is caste in a very stylized and facetious light.

As a result of this somewhat dumbed-down stylization, the Coens have been accused of stifling the creative spirit of the actors they work with. Nicholas Cage once remarked, "Joel and Ethan have a very strong vision and I've learned how difficult it is for them to accept another artist's vision. They have an autocratic nature."

Most critics raved about this movie though the *Los Angeles Times* critic Sheila Benson thought it was "deeply condescending." Though Hunter and Cage are likeable they are very dull-witted and Benson questioned whether such flagrant law-breaking people could ever be good parents. (Well, Charlie Chaplin's little tramp was hardly a model of bourgeois propriety either, yet millions have found both humor and meaning in his behavior.)

The Coens are reminiscent of Ruth Gordon and Garson Kanin, in their script writing. Joel-Garson paces and smokes while Ethan-Ruth operates the typewriter. Sometimes they laugh hysterically at their own stuff and Joel seems to care only about pleasing Ethan. Critics especially praised the script. The budget of the film was six million dollars, a fraction of the cost of the average Hollywood movie. Joel was director.

The Coen's next film, *Miller's Crossing*, was released in 1990. It starred Gabriel Byrne, Marcia Gay Harden, John Turturro, and Albert Finney in a solidly-made period piece, in which a corrupt, powerful politician's aide is gunned down in crossfire between two rival gangs perpetually battling for more turf. Joel directed again.

The Coens won a triple prize at the Cannes Film Festival with *Barton Fink* (1991), a dark satire on the film industry. A left wing playwright (ala Clifford Odets) goes to Hollywood to write a film story for Wallace Beery as a wrestler in the 1940s. They won for Best Director (Joel Coen), Best Actor (John Turturro) and the Palm d'Or for Best Film. No other film had won three prizes in the forty-four years of the Cannes Festival. Yet the film's originality and black humor all but undermined it's box-office appeal. As usual, some viewers loved it, others hated it.

The Hudsucker Proxy (1994), a Warner Brothers production (after three films in a row distributed by Twentieth Century-Fox), stars Tim Robbins, Jennifer Jason Leigh, Paul Newman, and Charles Durning. It's a frantic comedy about a bright but gullible young business-school graduate in the 1950s who jumps from the mail room to the presidency of his firm due to the nasty politics among the board of directors. Once again, the reaction was very mixed. Some critics found it empty and too silly, while Halliwell says, "Clever and enjoyable pastiche of Hollywood comedies of the 40s, close in spirit to Preston Sturges with an ending straight out of Frank Capra. It is stylized, stylish and civilized entertainment."

But with *Fargo* (1996) the Coen brothers made a film that *almost* everyone liked. They took home an Oscar for Best Screenwriting and Frances McDormand won as Best Actress. Joel was nominated for Best Director; the film for Best Picture; William H. Macy for Best Supporting Actor; Roger Deakins for Best Cinematography, and Roderick Jaynes (Joel and Ethan Coen) for Best Editing; - seven nominations in all and two winners. What a coup for the Coens and non-mainstream filmmakers generally!

The Big Lebowski (1998) stars Jeff Bridges (as the Dude), John Goodman, Julianne Moore, Steve Buscemi, John Turturro, Ben Gazzara and Sam Elliott in a story of Bridges' dope-smoking his way through a haze of misunderstandings. He happens to have the same name as a millionaire whose porno-actress wife has been kidnapped, and complications ensue. It's a strange ride, and many felt that after their big success with *Fargo* the Coens were just messing around. But the film does have one classic line: "The Dude abides."

On the other hand, with **O Brother, Where Art Thou?** (2000), a period piece set in the Deep South during the 1930s Depression, the Coens produced a remarkably entertaining comedy which also draws strength from its fine country and bluegrass musical score. Three convicts escape from a chain gang, rob a bank, cut a record, participate in a gubernatorial election campaign, and disrupt a Ku Klux Klan meeting—though not necessarily in that order. (The most Coen-esque scene is also the worst: Baby Face Nelson shoots an innocent cow.) The Coens claimed to have drawn inspiration from Homer, Bonnie and Clyde, and The Beverly Hillbillies, but it's clear that in pulling such disparate influences together their own story-telling gifts and bizarre sense of humor had finally coalesced. The film has a rhythm and a whimsy all of its own, "part ditty and part Delta ballad," (as Adina Hoffman reports in *American Prospect*) and George Clooney, John Turturro, and Tim Blake Nelson do some very fine comic ensemble work.

The Coen's tenth screenwriting film (Joel's ninth film as the director) is *The Man Who Wasn't There* (2001). Chain-smoking Billy Bob Thornton portrays a lazy barber who is blackmailing his wife's boss/lover so he can invest in a dry cleaning shop. Frances McDormand is the naughty lady again. It's a love-letter to film noir, which some viewers found empty at the core, while others were fascinated by the lighting.

Intolerable Cruelty (2003), with Clooney and Catherine Zeta-Jones, is one of those films that actually remind us of the screwball comedies of the forties that aren't really good enough to rave about, but remain entertaining from start to finish. *The Ladykillers* (2004), on the other hand, was an actual remake, and also a flop.

The originality of the Coen Brothers vision puts them in that select group of film-makers—Robert Altman and Woody Allen have been other recent examples—for whom actors want to work...at least once. They do not write, direct, or produce for mainstream America. In fact, the average film-goer often finds their work distasteful, and with good reason. A Coen-brothers film can be mannered, feverish, grotesque, and thoroughly adolescent in its approach to violence and obscenity. Yet nearly all critics agree that their style is intriguing, whether the film happens to be a comedy or a genre suspense thriller. There is, perhaps, more that one masterpiece to be found within their oeuvre—it's just that no one can agree on which ones they are.

F. Scott Fitzgerald

Francis Scott Key Fitzgerald Born 24 September 1896, St. Paul, MN Died 21 December 1940, Hollywood, CA.

F. Scott Fitzgerald's book, *The Great Gatsby* (1925) frequently appears atop the lists of the most significant American novels of the twentieth century. The book figures into the history of movies because it has been filmed four times. The first version was filmed in 1926, while the ink was still wet on the pages. In 1949 it was taken up again with Alan Ladd in the lead. In 1974 we got the version with Robert Redford and Mia Farrow; and in 2000 and television version was aired with Toby Stephens and Mira Sorvino in the leading roles.

Several of Fitzgerald's other books were also made into films. And during the later part of his ultimately sad career Fitzgerald himself worked on screenplays in Hollywood.

Scott grew up in Saint Paul, near the Commodore Hotel-University Club area of Western and Summit Avenues. While living in Saint Paul he patronized the Commodore Hotel and the University Club, where he is supposed to have carved his initials (yet unfound) into the downstairs bar. Among the homes the Fitzgeralds lived in during Scott's youth were at 294 Laurel Avenue and the Frank Kellogg house at 626 Goodrich in the Crocus Hill area. His main summertime hangout was the White Bear Yacht Club on White Bear Lake. His parents,

Mary (Molly) and Edward Fitzgerald, were also active in the Cotillion Club. Scott had a sister, Anabel, five years younger than he.

Scott attended Saint Paul Academy from 1908 to 1911 and Newman School in New York, also a private "prep" school, until he went off to Princeton in 1913. He was a mediocre student, and he left Princeton without a degree in 1917 to join the army, where he was commissioned as a second lieutenant. While at Camp Sheridan near Montgomery, Alabama, he met Zelda Sayre, a lovely Southern belle from Montgomery. Inspired by her beauty and Southern charm Fitzgerald returned to his family's brownstone flat at 599 Summit Avenue to complete a novel he had begun in college. It eventually became *This Side of Paradise* (1920). (The event is marked today by a brass plate near the front door of the house.)

This debut novel, though considered "immature" today, sold twenty thousand copies in its first week of issue. (How many writers can claim such success?) Its popularity allowed Fitzgerald to marry Zelda and it also opened the door to the lucrative markets offered by prestigious weekly magazines such as *Collier's* and the *Saturday Evening Post*. Scotty's second book, *The Beautiful and the Damned* (1922), also penned in St. Paul, was markedly better than the first, and it was a big seller, too (43,000 the first year). It was made into a film in 1922 with Kenneth Harlan as Anthony Patch and Marie Prevost as Gloria, directed by William A. Seiter, later husband of Minnesota actress Marian Nixon. Both works depict the adventures and mischances of wealthy and handsome young "society" men and their equally well-heeled girlfriends during the early years of what came to be known as the Jazz Age.

Scott and Zelda moved to France, and it was in Paris that he finished *The Great Gatsby* in 1924. Though sales were lukewarm, with time the book has come to be seen as Fitzgerald's masterpiece. He and Zelda hobnobbed in Paris with Gertrude Stein, who introduced them to Ernest Hemingway and other American writers. Hemingway looked up to Fitzgerald as an established, and gifted, professional writer, but he also chided Fitzgerald for neglecting his novels to write short stories for fashionable magazines. Yet Fitzgerald made $4,000 per story in his heyday from such publications, and he needed the money to maintain the lavish lifestyle to which he and Zelda had become accustomed. Unfortunately, by the time Fitzgerald finished his next novel, *Tender Is the Night* (1934), ten years had passed, the Great Depression was in full swing, and few wanted to read about the lives of rich expatriates on the French Riviera.

Meanwhile, *The Great Gatsby* opened as a play on Feb. 2, 1926 at the Ambassador Theatre in New York City, in an adaptation by

Owen Davis. George Cukor directed, and James Rennie and Florence Eldridge starred. (Incidently, a second authorized play script was staged in July, 2006, at the opening of the new Guthrie Theatre in Minneapolis. Eleven days after the Guthrie's production closed, "Gatz" opened at the Walker Art Center in Minneapolis. This production used the full text of the book and took six hours to perform.)

Fitzgerald made his first trip to Hollywood in 1927 in search of paying work. John Considine, a United Artists Producer, offered him $3,500 to write a screenplay for *Lipstick*. If the work was actually filmed he would receive $12,000 more. At. M-G-M he was teamed with novelist-turned-screenwriter Budd Schulberg at $1,500 per week. In eight weeks he made $12,000, matching four years of royalty income from the sale of 50,000 copies of his debut book. Though Scott was reluctant to jump on the Hollywood boat, he couldn't resist the lure of the big money.

He made several other trips to Hollywood, the last one extending from 1937 to 1940. He was under contract to M-G-M from 1937 to 1939, and worked on such films as his fellow-Minnesotan John Monk Saunders's script of *A Yank at Oxford* (1938), *Marie Antoinette* (1938), *Gone with the Wind* (1939), *The Women* (1939), *Madame Curie* (1943), and others, but his material was never used. He received his one screenwriting credit for *Three Comrades* (1938). Yet such are the ways of Hollywood that for screen-writing work on just six films (2,400 pages) at M-G-M, in eighteen months, he earned $88,500.

Fitzgerald had developed a drinking problem during his college years, and it got worse as both his career and his personal life floundered. Budd Schulberg wrote a novel, *The Disenchanted* about his trip with Fitzgerald to Dartmouth College to research college life, and Fitzgerald is portrayed as being drunk during the entire trip. His marriage had long since sunk into disrepair and in 1930 Zelda was diagnosed as schizophrenic and institutionalized.

Fitzgerald died of a heart attack in Hollywood in 1940 at the age of 44. The drinking, smoking, and wild living had finally taken their toll on the golden boy of the Lost Generation.

In the following years Fitzgerald's reputation reached its nadir, but during the 1950s there was a revival of interest. For example, the film *The Last Time I Saw Paris* (1954) with Elizabeth Taylor, Van Johnson, and Walter Pidgeon, draws upon material from Fitzgerald's story "Babylon Revisited." And in 1959 *Beloved Infidel,* the story of Fitzgerald's years of dissipation in Hollywood, was filmed with Gregory Peck, Gloria Graham, and Minneapolis-born actress Karin Booth. Scott's novel *Tender is the Night* was filmed in 1961 with Jason

Robards, Jr., Jennifer Jones, Tom Ewell, and Joan Fontaine; and again in 1985 in a marvelous BBC-20th Century Fox TV production with Peter Strauss and Mary Steenbergen. Fitzgerald's last unfinished novel, *The Last Tycoon*, was brought to the screen in 1976 by Elia Kazan with a star-studded cast that included Robert Mitchum, Robert DeNiro, Jack Nicholson, Tony Curtis, and Jeanne Moreau.

The St. Paul World Theater, 110 Exchange St, was renamed The Fitzgerald in 1990 to honor St. Paul's most famous writer. The theater serves as the base for Garrison Keillor's popular live weekly radio show, "The Prairie Home Companion."

Al Franken

Born 21 May 1951,
New York City, NY

A star writer for TV's *Saturday Night Live*, Alan Stuart Franken grew up in the Minneapolis area, graduating from Blake School in Hopkins in 1969. At Blake he was a National Merit Scholarship Semi-Finalist; he scored an 800 (perfect score) on his English SAT; he won the sophomore Declamation Contest; he was a member of the Chess Club; Library Club; Science Club; soccer and wrestling teams, and was vice president of his class.

As if warming up for *Saturday Night Live*, he wrote *The Blakely Barb* with subtle humor as well as drawing the cartoons. He was a pep fest leader and known for his grin. Tom Davis (Blake '70) became his partner as "Franken and Davis" in writing comedy skits and doing improvs around the Twin Cities in clubs like Dudley Riggs' ETC at Seven Corners (Washington & Cedar Avenues) and Dudley's Brave New Workshop at 26th and Hennepin Avenue South. Franken eventually hit the big time on *Saturday Night Live* where he wrote and appeared for fifteen years. And he has done some movies along the way, written books and been a dinner guest at the Clinton White House.

Al's parents, Joe and Phoebe Franken, were active for some twenty-five years at Theatre-in-the-Round Players, a community theater of near professional quality in Minneapolis. His dad introduced

Al to "live" theater. At the time they lived at 7931 W. 25th St. in St. Louis Park. He and his brother, Owen, shared a private phone line while in school. Joe was a printing salesman and Phoebe a real estate agent. Al graduated from Harvard in 1973 with a degree in behavioral sciences. He has been married to Franni since 1976 and they have two grown kids.

His parents enjoyed forays into community theater but never thought of theater as a possible career for themselves or their kids. However, Al Franken feels his roots in satire go back to grade school when he and the boys in his class parodied a play performed by the girls.

Some of his *Saturday Night Live* sketches, which number in the 100s, include "Daily Affirmations with Stuart Smalley" and "The Final Days," a comic piece describing President Nixon's last days in the White House. This paved the way for Al's first best-selling book, *I'm Good Enough, I'm Smart Enough, and Doggone It, People Like Me* (1992), a collection of Stuart Smalley's aphorisms.

Al became a noted political commentator-satirist when he produced and starred in the NBC sitcom *Lateline*. He wrote *Rush Limbaugh Is a Big Fat Idiot*, a book he also recorded and for which he won a Grammy Award in 1997 for Best Comedy Spoken Album. The first printing of the book sold out in just a few weeks and it eventually sold more than a million copies. He left SNL as a writer and regular cast member in 1995. He wanted to be the Weekend Update news anchor but his request was denied. For his work on SNL Franken was honored with five Emmys, four for writing and one for producing.

Franken has appeared often on *The Late, Late Show* with host, Craig Kilborn, who hails from Minnesota. He has also revisited SNL and appeared on *Third Rock from the Sun*. While Al has been predominantly a writer/producer/actor for TV, he has also appeared in five movies: *Tunnel Vision* (1976, as Al); *Trading Places* (1983, as Baggage Handler #1); *One More Saturday Night Live* (1986, as Paul Flum); *Stuart Saves His Family* (1995, as Stuart Smalley) for which he also did the screenplay; and *The Definite Maybe* (1997, as Vagabond). Al was the co-screenwriter and executive producer for *When a Man Loves a Woman* (1994) a film about alcoholism starring Meg Ryan and Andy Garcia.

Franken has in recent years become more deeply involved as a political commentator. He has done well facing off against Arianna Huffington, a fiercely right-wing Republican, on Comedy Central. He commands large fees for public speaking engagements but, he confided to Richard Blow of the *Village Voice*, "I speak for free to the Democrats and charge the Republicans." The lecture circuit provides some good fall-out for Franken. Speaking to a political group is better than stand-up comedy, he says, in that "the audience isn't drunk."

In 1998 he anchored *Lateline* for a year, a parody of *Nightline*. His latest book is *Why Not Me? The Making and Unmaking of the Franken Presidency* (1999). He and Stuart Smalley may appear in film form yet again because his brains, mirth pangs, and talent know no bounds. Evaluating his career thus far, Franken told Mark Shapiro of *Salon* (on-line) in a February, 1996, interview, "I consider myself foremost a comedian. I'm a comedian who pays a lot of attention to politics, because I'm a citizen. But I don't know if I want to commit my career to politics." Many people clearly see that the two are very linked together.

Al Franken is currently running for the U.S. Senate in the state of Minnesota.

Eleanore Griffin

Born 29 April 1904,
St. Paul, MN
Died 25 July 1995,
Woodland Hills, CA

Eleanore Griffin did not limit herself in her dreams for accomplishment and she didn't want others to do it either. Her mother, Nellie (Mrs. Patrick J. Griffin), raised her to think that way. She also believed in the inherent goodness of people. She wanted to put her writing talent to use to inspire people to think more lofty thoughts, behave better, and make this world a better place to live. Her movie stories reflect this spiritual striving.

Eleanore grew up at 1040 Mississippi Street and she attended Johnson High School, Class of 1922. She did not excel as a student by her own admission but she did as an audience member of every film that came through St. Paul, and she dreamed of being a movie actress. When the family moved to Hollywood in 1923 after her sister, Alice's, high school graduation, she believed her dream would really come true. She did get a few jobs as an extra but she soon realized it would take more than a pretty face with a great desire to accomplish the goal of Hollywood stardom.

It was through writing rather than acting that Eleanore made her way in Hollywood. She sold short stories to several magazines, including *Pictorial Review, McCall's, Good Housekeeping, Woman's Home Companion*, and *Delineator*. Life got more complicated in 1935 when she collaborated with William Rankin on a short story for *Pictorial Review*. The two fell in love and a year later they ran off to Tijuana for a quickie marriage. One year later Eleanore sued for divorce, only to discover she had never been legally married. Mexican marriage laws required a certain length of residency and Mexican witnesses had to know the marrying couple for at least three years. Eleanore could not remember the name of their Mexican witness though the other witness was a friend of Rankin's. Judge Charles S. Burnell told them, "First you have to prove there is a marriage before you can get a divorce." On the advice of the court, she sued for annulment instead.

Though the marriage had been a bust, Griffin and Rankin continued to work together, and collaborated on six films between 1936 and 1945. Their best script together was *The Harvey Girls* (1946), an MGM musical featuring Minnesota's Judy Garland, who sang the film's Oscar-winning song for 1946, "On the Atchison, Topeka and the Sante Fe."

Griffin plunged into story production with *When Love Is Young* (1937) when she turned her McCall's Magazine article, "Class Prophecy," into a film plot. Minnesota-born Virginia Bruce is a Broadway star who returns home to marry the beau she left behind, only to find that he isn't quite what she remembered him to be.

Thoroughbreds Don't Cry (1937), her third film story, starred Judy Garland and Mickey Rooney in their first pairing together in a feature film (They had done a couple of Andy Hardy short films earlier). J. Walter Ruben, who married Virginia Bruce in 1937, was her writing partner for that one, along with Lawrence Hazard. Rooney is a jockey who wins a chance to ride a top-notch English horse in this MGM production.

Eleanore hit the bullseye in her fourth film, winning an Oscar for Best Story for *Boys Town* (1938) starring Mickey Rooney and Spencer Tracy in a film about Father Flanagan, who founded a home and school for juvenile delinquents. Dore Schary co-wrote the story and shared the Oscar with Griffin. Tracy won the Oscar for Best Actor. This MGM film was also nominated for Best Picture and for Best Director (Norman Taurog).

Eleanore switched over to Paramount Studios for *St. Louis Blues* (1939) and for *Street of Missing Men* (1939) then to Columbia for *Only Angels Have Wings* (1939) with Cary Grant, Jean Arthur and Rita Hayworth, directed by Howard Hawks. Eleanor made suggestions to the story but did not write it. All three of these films are collaborations with William Rankin.

She wrote the story *I Wanted Wings* (1941) for Paramount, starring Ray Milland, William Holden, and Brian Donlevy as three recruits in the American Air Force. Critics thought it was a good film. She made a comedy in *Blondie in Society* (1941) based on the comic strip, starring Penny Singleton and Arthur Lake. *Hi, Beautiful* (1944) was another team effort with Rankin. She produced another fine story, *Nob Hill* (1945), with George Raft and Joan Bennett, for Twentieth Century-Fox Studios, about a saloon owner in San Francisco trying to break into society with an eligible young lady in the1890s.

The Harvey Girls (1946) is based on history whereby a wealthy town-building man wanted clean cut young women of virtue to work in his chain of restaurants in the Old West. Judy Garland is a singing–dancing waitress as are all the other girls. Ray Bolger co-stars among a fine cast. Margaret O'Brien and Angela Lansbury star in *Tenth Avenue Angel* (1948) in which a little girl of poor parents loses her faith in life.

Meanwhile, Eleanore kept writing stories for magazines, for which there was a steady market in those pre-television days. She also dabbled in TV when it arrived, penning "An Episode of Sparrows" (1954) for *Climax Mystery Theatre*.

Returning to an inspirational theme, Eleanore wrote a film biography of Scottish clergyman Peter Marshall, who became chaplain to the United States Senate in *A Man Called Peter* (1955). English actor Richard Todd starred along with Jean Peters. Her next film, *Good Morning, Miss Dove* (1955) was a tear-jerker starring Jennifer Jones, Robert Stack, and Duluth-born-and-raised Peggy Knudsen. Knudsen and Jones became very good friends during the making of this film, and because Eleanore did the screenplay (rather than just the storyline), it brought her closer to the real workings of film production.

Eleanore did the screenplay for the remake of *Imitation of Life* (1959) starring Lana Turner, and also adapted James Ramsey Ullman's novel, *Banner in the Sky*, for the screen. Disney produced this film, made in Great Britain, about a Swiss man's obsession with conquering a local mountain.

Eleanore worked on a remake of *Back Street* (1961), produced by Ross Hunter, and had John Bloch for a partner writing the screenplay for her last film, *One Man's Way* (1964) starring Don Murray as Norman Vincent Peale, with Diana Hyland and William Windom, whose grandfather was honored by having a Minnesota city named after him.

Griffin spent the last thirty years of her life in retirement—she lived to be ninety-one.

Frank Gruber

Born 2 February 1904,
Jorvontal, Austria-Hungary
Died 9 December 1969,
Santa Monica, CA.

Elmer, Minnesota, was the adopted home of prolific writer Frank Gruber. Gruber is best known as a writer of Westerns, but he also wrote detective stories, science fiction, and romances. All told, he is credited with more than sixty novels, two-hundred-odd screenplays and TV teleplays, and more than three hundred short stories. No wonder he is among those writers who are sometimes referred to as a "King of Pulp Fiction."

You may ask, where is Elmer, Minnesota? Most Minnesotans wouldn't be able to tell you. However, this town does exist and can be found in Saint Louis County about midway between Duluth and Hibbing.

Frank was the younger son of Josef and Susanna Gruber who came from Austria-Hungary to Winnipeg, Canada, in 1906. Six years later they ventured south to Chicago, and finally applied for the Petition for Naturalization on July 18, 1918. Josef took his Oath of Allegiance on March 5, 1920.

The Gruber family arrived in Minnesota in September, 1918. Josef was a laborer; his first son, Frank's his older brother Anton, was born August 25, 1902. Frank says he grew up on the family farm in Elmer which is slightly true. Their address was P. O. Meadowlands Box 144. As there was no school nearby, Anton and Frank rented rooms with the Henry and Elizabeth Krier family at 1705 Dayton St. in Chicago. After high school he did a stint in the U. S. Army. Then Frank worked as a bellhop and ticket-taker for a movie house.

His first published works were for agricultural trade magazines. In 1934 he moved to New York to become a full-time writer. Times were tough and he soon had a wife, Lois Mahood, and a young son to support, but he eventually broke into the detective genre writing "quickies" for the pulps. As he honed his skills Gruber's work began to appear even in *Black Mask*, considered the most prestigious pulp of the time.

Gruber wrote several stories about a smooth-talking crime solver and encyclopedia salesman named Oliver Quade which were collected in a book called *Brass Knuckle*. The success of this volume encouraged Gruber to write longer stories, and novels were not far behind.

With time Gruber became best known for his dozens of Western novels, and he also wrote a fine biography of the master Western writer Zane Grey. His stories often centered on a specific thing such as a dog show or antique furniture, and readers enjoyed learning about a particular subject as the story unfolded. Yet the tales themselves were also gripping, with heroes such as con-man Johnny Fletcher and his side-kick, strong man Sam Gragg. The private eye Simon Lash was also popular. *The Accomplice* (1946) was based on a Lash novel.

In the detective genre Frank's first film experience came when his Oliver Quade story, "Death of a Champion" from the short story "Dog Show Murder," was filmed in 1939. His second film, *The Kansan* (1943), based on his novel, *Peace Marshall*, starred St. Paul's Richard Dix, Jane Wyatt, and Victor Jory. Dix plays a wandering marksman who stops off in a frontier town just long enough to become sheriff. His famous line is, "I'll make this town keep the peace—if I have to blow it to pieces!"

Northern Pursuit (1943) was only Gruber's third film, yet he was given sole credit for screenplay. Such was the respect that came with him into the film world. Errol Flynn starred in this action adventure ably directed by Raoul Walsh. *The Mask of Dimitrios* (1944) was his next screenplay, based on an Eric Ambler thriller. The film is a show-case for secondary principals including Sidney Greenstreet, Peter Lorre, Victor Francen, and Zachary Scott, who sustain the mood of international intrigue throughout the film.

A Gruber novel was the basis for *The Oregon Trail* (1945) with Fred MacMurray as a New York reporter sent west to cover the great western migration. The next year he adapted another of his novels, *The French Key* (1946) for the screen.

Gruber wrote the screenplays for two Sherlock Holmes films distributed by Universal Studios: *Terror by Night* (1946) and *Dressed to Kill* (1946) with Rathbone in the lead; then wrote ***Bulldog Drummond at Bay*** (1947) followed by ***The Challenge*** (1948), starring Tom Conway (aka The Falcon).

Regarding Minnesota connections, Gruber was one of three screenwriters for ***Johnny Angel*** (1945) starring George Raft, Claire Trevor, Hoagy Carmichael, and St. Paul's Lowell Gilmore. ***Hurricane Smith*** (1952) starred John Ireland and St. Paul's Richard Arlen.

Gruber wore three hats in ***Twenty Plus Two*** (1961) as he wrote the novel and the screenplay and also produced the film. This Allied Artists film was also called ***It Started in Tokyo***.

When television came he wrote teleplays for the TV series *Tales of Wells Fargo*, (1957, as story consultant and series creator), *The Lawman* (1958), *Shotgun Slade* (also creator), *Zane Grey Theater*, and *77 Sunset Strip*, among others.

In 1967 Frank wrote *Pulp Jungle*, a collection of memories of his thirty plus years of writing for the pulps. He recalled that on his arrival in New York he lived on home-made tomato soup from automat restaurants. He would get hot tea water and add the free ketchup and toss in the cookie given with the tea. He knew other writers in similar plights in the Depression Days.

Frank Gruber died at age sixty-five, fairly young by modern standards. Yet his career spanned forty-five years, with thirty of them in the movie biz. He appeared in one film, ***Town Tamer*** (1965), as a hotel clerk. He apparently did not have a contract with any special studio yet seemed to be welcome in all studios as Warner Bros, United Artists, Twentieth Century-Fox. Universal, RKO, Paramount and Republic were the producing/distributing studios for his first eight films.

Judith Guest

Born 29 March 1936,
Detroit, MI

Like a comet blazing across the sky, Judith Guest's novel *Ordinary People* blazed into best-seller status from the get-go in 1976. This was the first unsolicited work published by Viking Press in twenty-six years. It was selected by four book clubs and serialized in *Redbook*, and the paperback rights were sold to Ballantine Publishers for $635,000.

Guest graduated from the University of Michigan with an education degree in 1958, and in that same year she married her college sweetheart and took a job teaching school. She and husband Larry eventually had three sons, Larry, John, and Richard. She quit teaching after three years, and when her youngest son began school in 1972, she began writing seriously. She says her writing became "my escape, my terror, my compulsion, my life."

Contrary to custom, Judith sent her manuscript to Viking Press without a preceding letter of inquiry, without an outline, and without a plot synopsis. Luckily, an editorial assistant read the manuscript and sent Guest an encouraging note.

Eight months passed (not to mention the four years it had taken to write the book). Judith and her husband, Larry, were in the process of moving to Minnesota from Michigan in the summer of 1975 when she received word that Viking would be honored to publish her book. Cinderella became a princess and went to the ball.

The story centers on seventeen year-old Conrad Jarrett, who survives a boating accident in which his brother dies. Gradually a depression engulfs him, leading him to a suicide attempt to which his parents have difficulty adjusting. *Newsweek*'s Walter Clemons said, "The feelings in the book are true and unforced. Guest has the valuable gift of making us like her characters; she has the rarer ability to move a toughened reviewer to tears."

Irma Pascal Heldman of the *Village Voice* praised the novel, "Guest conveys with sensitivity a most private sense of life's personal experiences while respecting the reader's imagination and nurturing an aura of mystery."

The film *Ordinary People* (1980) won Oscars for Best Picture, Best Director (Robert Redford), Best Screenplay (Alvin Sargent) and Best Supporting Actor (Timothy Hutton) while Mary Tyler Moore was nominated for Best Actress and Judd Hirsch for Best Supporting Actor. Donald Sutherland played Moore's husband.

Guest had nothing but praise for Mary Tyler Moore, who played the enigmatic role of Beth Jarrett, the mother of the troubled son. "[MTM] just knocks me out. She's a terrific actress, a very complex person and she brought a complexity to the character that I wish I'd gotten into the book." (from an interview with John Blades of the *Chicago Tribune*). Guest was very pleased with the editing of the film, which left the story even more open-ended than the book.

Judith wrote the screenplay for *Rachel River* (1987) from three short stories by Minnesota writer Carol Bly. The film deals with a everyday happenings among the townsfolk in a Northern Minnesota town. Pamela Reed, Craig T. Nelson, and Viveca Lindfors are its stars.

Guest's second novel, *Second Heaven,* appeared in 1982. She co-wrote *Killing Time in St. Cloud* (1988) with Rebecca Hill; and *Errands* (1997).

Mark Steven Johnson

Born 30 October 1964, Hastings, MN

Mark's career got its first big boost in the fourth grade at Pinecrest Elementary School in Hastings, where he confided to his teacher, Arloa Ironside, that he wanted to be a writer. Without a hint of surprise she encouraged him to pursue that ambition. He never forgot her supportive response, and credited her with being his first inspiration at a luncheon talk he delivered to the Knights of Columbus in Hastings twenty-one years later.

It was not until the sixth grade, however, that Mark knew he was going to make movies. He went to every film that passed through town, and his mother took him to the Riviera Theatre in South Minneapolis to see *Jaws*. Watching that film convinced him that he would write for the movies. In high school he sent away for movie scripts and studied them carefully, later completed a college program with a degree in journalism, and headed for Hollywood.

Arriving in Los Angeles Johnson found a secretarial job at Orion Pictures, which went bankrupt not long afterward (no connection). Having nothing to occupy his time now, he wrote a script in four weeks but had no one to show it to. His wife, Susie, heard of someone through a work connection who had once been an agent. The agent took a look at it, considered throwing it away, took a second look, and showed it to a producer friend at Warner Brothers. The man bought it. The script became *Grumpy Old Men* (1993). Mark collected a salary of $300,000 for the script. Not bad?...

Mark wrote *Grumpy Old Men* with Jack Lemmon and Walter Matthau in mind for the old guys. However, Warners thought of other possibilities first. Kirk Douglas was suggested to play opposite George C. Scott; then a reunion between Jerry Lewis and Dean Martin was suggested. Mark suffered lots of anxiety during such moments but the sad reality was that there was nothing he could about it. And to think it was memories of his grandfather that had really triggered writing this script.

While he was writing the script Mark imagined that oldsters would be its prime audience. He had know idea that the 18-25 group would love it best. And because test audiences were so enthusiastic, the studio moved the release date up from mid-winter to Christmas Day. It opened in more than 1,300 screens, nearly as many as Robin Williams' *Mrs. Doubtfire*. People from the South, East and West loved it as much as Minnesotans.

Johnson later admitted, "I never expected this. To be honest, at best I thought this would be a good writing sample that would help get me work in Hollywood. It's not going to win an Academy Award," he added. "There are other, superior films out there. But the bottom line is that people walk out feeling better than when they walked in, and that's enough for me."

Johnson attended a test audience screening in Los Angeles. "There was this buzz going on in the audience," he said. "I kept thinking, 'What are we into?' Then I realized that the opening scene has a snowplow in it, and the audience was fascinated with that."

Initially, the film was going to be made outside of Minnesota. "They looked at Ohio, they looked at Illinois, they even looked at Aspen, for Pete's sake, which looks nothing like Minnesota," he said.

"They kept thinking that snow is snow. I had to push pretty hard, but I finally got them to look at Minnesota. [Director] Donald [Petrie] became fascinated with the people. He told me that he stopped in a bar in Red Wing to get a feel for the area. He asked the bartender, 'Is there a lot of partying that goes on around here?' She said, 'Not a lot of partying, just a lot of drinking.' He was charmed." In the end, much of the film was shot in Faribault and Wabasha.

Comments from its stars: Says Matthau, "I wasn't that cuckoo about the script. Then a year later, Lemmon calls and says, 'I read this script called *Grumpy Old Men* and I think we should do it.' And I said, 'You actually liked it?' so I went back and read it. It had improved." All the actors and everybody on the set were allowed input into the script and it did improve. The movie grossed over $150 million and a sequel followed, *Grumpier Old Men* (1995).

In the sequel Sophia Loren was added to the cast as Matthau's love interest, to balance Lemmon's pairing with Ann-Margaret. Burgess Meredith reprises his role as Lemmon's father. Others in the cast of both films include Kevin Pollak, Daryl Hannah, and Minnesota-born Ann Morgan Guilbert in the role of Sophia Loren's very Italian mother.

Johnson's next film was *Big Bully* (1996) with Tom Arnold and Rick Moranis playing two men who cannot resist reverting to the patterns of behavior they established as enemies back in grade school. There's plenty of slapstick involved, but the effect is more often moronic than inspired.

Flushed with success Mark wrote and also directed *Simon Birch* (1998), which he adapted from a John Irving novel, *A Prayer for Owen Meany*. Big time stuff, though the reaction from critics was mixed, with many finding it too maudlin and contrived. It sported a strong cast that included Ashley Judd, David Strathairn, Joseph Mazzello, and Jim Carrey, but Johnson's career as a director was stopped in its tracks by all the bad reviews.

Screenplay number four was *Jack Frost* (1998) starring Michael Keaton as a dead rock singer who comes back to life in the snowman built by his twelve-year old son. The film is described as "gruesomely sentimental" though it might also be said that Mark has a big heart, especially for disadvantaged kids such as those who have lost a parent.

Mark returned to the director's chair with his next project, *Daredevil* (2003), based on a comicbook hero. He wrote the screenplay, and seemed to know so much more about the film than other candidates that the producers had no choice but to assign him to direct.

Daredevil cost $100 million to make, only half the cost of making *Titanic* but very sizeable nonetheless. Special effects swallowed much of the budget, though they sometimes fell flat. At times Mark ripped out several pages of the relevant comic book and pasted them on a wall for all to view closely, so that a similar effect would be conveyed to the viewer.

Mark's most recent efforts are *Elektra* (2005) for which he is uncredited and *Ghost Rider* (2007).

Jerome Odlum

Born 26 August 1905,
Minneapolis, MN
Died 2 March 1954,
Los Angeles, CA

This former Managing Editor of the *Minneapolis Shopping News* (1934-37) also penned some novels and movie scripts, cutting his movie teeth on two James Cagney films: *The Oklahoma Kid* (1939) and *Each Dawn I Die* (1939, aka *Killer Meets Killer*). Four of his first seven film credits come from novels he wrote. His books dealt mainly with crime and political racketeering.

Warner Brothers Studio bought *Each Dawn I Die* for Cagney and that is how Odlum entered Hollywood, on rather a high note, I should say. Warners also bought his novel, *Dust Be My Destiny*, for John Garfield; *Nine Lives Are Not Enough* for Ronald Reagan; and *Once I Saw the Sun*, which was never filmed.

Both the Cagney and Garfield films came out in 1939, Reagan's in 1941. Odlum was hot stuff. *Dust Be My Destiny* had Humphrey Bogart in second billing. (He did not become a star until 1941 in *High Sierra*.) The final scene shows the murder of three men. Whew! Dust was such a well-made, successful, social melodrama that it was filmed again three years later as *I Was Framed*.

At the time all studios kept an eye on hot new books and Broadway plays, of course, just as they do today. Republic Studios outbid Warners for Odlum's *The Morgue Is Always Open*, published by Scribners in 1944 a year *after* it was filmed under the title, *A Scream in the Dark* (1943). Odlum was one of many writers who were in almost daily contact with studio agents, which is why this film preceded the published book.

In time Jerome also developed a knack for writing screenplays and penned *Strange Affair* (1944), *Cover-Up* (1949) and *Highway Dragnet* (1954). He also wrote stories for *Marine Raiders* (1944), *In Old Sacramento* (1946), *Last Frontier Uprising* (1947) and *Song of India* (1949). He also could adapt other's work such as *Crime Doctor* (1943), a radio series starring Walter Greaza that was later turned into a popular film series starring Warner Baxter.

Jesse Lasky, a co-founder of Paramount Studios, worked with Odlum on the scenario for *Never Trust a Gambler* (1951); from that collaboration Jerome wrote the story. Other Odlum novels on crime and political racketeering are *Mirabilis Diamond* and *Lady Sourdough*. The Mirabilis hero is John Steele, a private detective in the cocky Sam Spade mode. There is a beautiful blond in the story, which leaves a trail of corpses from Yucatan to Hollywood. There is also the very loyal office secretary ala "Effie" in Bogart's *Maltese Falcon* and Steele himself has rippling muscles and sports a close-cropped bluish-black beard.

In his youth Odlum's family lived at 624 E. 17th St. He attended Minneapolis Central High School, graduating in 1923, and worked as a clerk for the Soo Line Railroad after graduation. His parents were George and Maude A. Odlum and he had an older brother, George, born in 1901. George, the papa, died in 1917; Maude died in 1939; and brother George in 1945.

Jerome and his first wife, Mildred P., lived at 5714 14th Avenue until they moved to California in 1938. They divorced. He was survived by his second wife, Shirley, and their daughter, Nan. He and Shirley lived at 1919 Argyle Avenue in Los Angeles.

Pat Proft

Born 3 April 1947,
Columbia Heights, MN

This Minneapolis-bred actor and writer came "from the stage," specifically from Dudley Riggs' Brave New Workshop at 26th and South Hennepin Avenue in Minneapolis. He went on to explore the further depths of broad comedy in such modern classic series as **Police Academy**, **Naked Gun**, and **Hot Shots**.

Dudley's workshop was an innovative comedy club, anticipating many of the elements and effects that later made TV's *Saturday Night Live* so appealing. Some of Pat's peers at Riggs were Anita Anderson, Irv Letofsky, Michael Anthony, Tom Sherohman, Ruth Williams, and Mike McManus. Jim Wallace directed. Letofsky did most of the writing; Pat studied it as he performed there from 1965 to 1968.

Who were Pat's movie favorites growing up? Laurel and Hardy, of course, and the Marx Brothers and the Road pictures of Bob Hope and Bing Crosby. In short, he had an early love of slapstick and physical humor, and often made up comedies using toy soldiers or cowboys. "I had no thought of being a fireman or a policeman or a cowboy. It was always to be in movies somehow." Being the class clown in a Catholic school (Immaculate Conception) where the nuns were "punchers and hitters" also helped him develop his skills in comedy. He was entertainment chairman at pep rallies at Columbia Heights High School. He wrote and directed hilarious skits back then.

Proft broke into TV in 1972 as an actor in the ABC pilot, "Madhouse 90," a parody on the high quality 1950s dramatic show, *Playhouse 90*. He won a spot as a regular on *The Burns and Schreiber Comedy Hour* in 1973. Before settling in as a writer, he also appeared in the CBS pilot, "Joey & Dad" and "Van Dyke and Company" both in 1975, then became a writer and script consultant for the 1975 series *When Things Were Rotten* aka *The French Dis-connection*.

At this point the writing took over. Suddenly Pat was everywhere at once on the TV comedy map: *The Smothers Brothers Show* (1975); *Cher* (1975-76); *Welcome Back Cotter* (1975-79); *Bob Hope's Christmas Party* (1975); *Van Dyke and Company* (1976, winning him an Emmy nomination for writing); *The Redd Foxx Comedy Hour* (1977-78); *The*

Star Wars Holiday Special (1978); *The Mary Tyler Moore Comedy Hour* (1979); *The Roy Clarke Special* (1979); and *All Commercials: A Steve Martin Special* (1980).

Pat wore his producer hat and did a little bit of everything in *Airplane* (1980) , a spoof of the film *Airport* (1970) starring Minneapolis-born Peter Graves and an all-star cast. Actually, Pat had met the Zucker Bros, producers of *Airplane*, and Jim Abrahams in 1972 when they joined forces for the Kentucky Fried Theatre Revue. Writing for Steve Martin brought him into executive-producing also for *Twilight Theatre II* (1982, TV); exec-prod for *Moving Violations* (1985); wrote/exec-prod *Hot Shots* (1991); *Hot Shots, Part Deux* (1993); and wrote/produced, directed and appeared in *Wrongfully Accused* (1998).

During the 1980s Pat worked on several TV pilots. Meanwhile, the film *Police Academy* (1984) was a huge success and spawned seven sequels into 2007. Pat wrote the story and first screenplay but just the characters' dialogue on the sequels: Police Academy 2: Their First Assignment (1985); *Moving Violations* (1985); *Police Academy 4: Citizens on Patrol* (1987); *Police Academy 5: Assignment: Miami Beach* (1988); *Police Academy 6: City under Siege* (1989); *Police Academy: Mission to Moscow* (1994); and *Police Academy* (2007). Today, you can buy a special boxed set of seven discs (DVDs) of the Police Academy series—great party stuff!

In the same vein is *The Naked Gun: From the Files of Police Squad!* (1988) and its progeny: *Naked Gun 2½: The Smell of Fear* (1991); *Naked Gun 33 1/3: The Final Insult* (1994); and *Wrongfully Accused* (1998) all of which star Leslie Nielsen, formerly a deadly serious actor in police action films and TV series. In this last film a smattering of Minnesota is sprinkled into all the characters' names: Lt. Fergus Falls (Richard Crenna), Dr. Fridley (Sandra Bernhard), Sgt. Orono (Ben Ratner), Lauren Goodhue and Hibbing Goodhue (Kelly Le Brock and Michael York). Pat directed, produced, wrote and also appeared in the film. In *Hot Shots* he wore all the hats except a director's.

His next project, *Mr. Magoo* (1997) was produced by Disney Pictures' Buena Vista Films. It also stars Leslie Nielsen and Minnesota-actress Kelly Lynch as Luanne Leseur, while Minnesota-educated Ernie Hudson plays Agent Gus Anders. Magoo, very near-sighted and depending on his dog, Angus, to clear the way for him, stumbles into trouble anyway,

Is Pat Proft trying to be offensive in writing a scene for *Scary Movie 3* (2003) showing Mother Teresa bobbleheads? Was he when he had the Secret Service blow a hole through a wall-sized picture of her so that a confused U. S. President could escape from the White House.

Answer: "I'm never out to offend anybody. It's just that it sounded funny to me—to blow a hole through the face of the woman who is for peace and love," said Proft, an alumnus of Catholic education.

Proft's other notable films: *Brain Donors* (1992), *High School High* (1996), and *Scary Movie 4* (2006). His proud parents are Bob and Marguerite Proft. Pat's first wife was Connie and they had a son, Patrick. Actress Karen Philipp is wife number two; she appeared in *Moving Violations*.

Allen (Erwin) Rivkin

*Born 20 November 1903,
Hayward, WI
Died 17 February 1990,
West Hollywood, CA*

A llen Rivkin was born and raised in Hayward, Wisconsin, famous even today for its annual lumberjack celebration, its internationally-certified Birkebeiner cross-country ski race, and its world-class fishing museum, which allows you to view the town from the mouth of an enormous fiberglass muskellunge. During his formative years Allen developed a taste for the rustic charms of Scandinavian-American culture which a B.A. in Journalism from the University of Minnesota could not entirely erase. Rivkin eventually wandered from newspaper work into the more alluring world of film, and he drew upon his small-town upbringing to write (with Laura Kerr) his most memorable film, *The Farmer's Daughter* (1947). It introduced Minnesotan James Arness to film audiences in a minor role, and Loretta Young won the Oscar for Best Actress as the Swedish maid who counsels the Minnesota Congressman (Joseph Cotton) about the finer points of public service.

The critics loved all aspects of this film, from the script and the camera work to the directing and acting. "Patricians, politicians, even peasants are portrayed with unusual perception and wit," said critic James Agee. Another described it as a "well-made Cinderella story with a touch of asperity and top notch production values and cast."

Ethel Barrymore, Charles Bickford (nominated for Best Supporting Actor) and Harry Davenport round out a fine cast.

Rivkin's papa, Samuel Richard Rivkin, was a merchant; his mama, Rose (Rosenberg) Rivkin was a homemaker. After college days Allen worked as a newspaper reporter, a publicity man and later as an advertising man. *Radio Patrol* (1932) was his debut script—the first of five that he wrote 1932, with four more the following year. In all at least fifty-three of Rivkin's screenplays were produced, many of them for major studios, and along the way he picked up a special moniker: "the clean up man." This is another way of saying that he was a "script doctor."

He married Laura Hornickel ("pen name" is Laura Kerr), with whom he co-wrote *The Farmer's Daughter*, on November 8, 1952. Politically, Allen was a life-long Democrat. He was a co-founder of the International Writers Guild, and a member of the Dramatists Guild, the Academy of Motion Picture Arts and Sciences, and other organizations, including the West Side Riding and Asthma Club. Rivkin was a joiner.

Socio-political causes often played a part in Rivkin's screenplays, and he also took an active part in several campaigns. "Few have helped the community of screenwriters in Hollywood as much as Allen Rivkin." Stephen O. Lesser once remarked. But Rivkin's activism took him far beyond the issues of his own guild. He was the director of the "Hollywood for Roosevelt" campaign, 1936-44; "Hollywood for Truman, 1948;" "Hollywood for Stevenson, 1952-56;" and "Hollywood for Kennedy, 1960. He was the National Director of the Democratic National Convention, 1960.

Rivkin did wartime service for the U. S. War Department as head motion picture officer in the Special Services Division (1942-44). He was founder and president of the Motion Picture Industry Council, director of Jewish Film Advisory Committee from 1963 to 1986, and served as treasurer of the Writers Guild Foundation (1966-1990) among many other positions.

He wrote an anonymous autobiography, *I Wasn't Born Yesterday* with Leonard Spigelgass (1935); and near the end of his career he and his wife wrote *Hello Hollywood: A Book about the Movies and the People Who Make Them* (1962). He edited *Who Wrote the Movie... And What Else Did He Write?* (1970).

In 1954 he won the Books and Authors 7th Annual Award for *Timberjack* which was made into a film the next year; the Valentine Davies Award from the Writers Guild of America, 1963, for community service; and the Morgan Cox Award from the Writers Guild of America, 1972, for guild service. Rivkin wore many hats—and he wore them all well.

His other notable films include *70,000 Witnesses* (1932); *The Devil Is Driving* (1932) starring St. Paul's Richard Dix; *The Picture Snatcher* (1933) starring James Cagney; *Melody Cruise* (1933); *Meet the Baron* (1934) Jack Pearl, Jimmy Durante; *Dancing Lady* (1934) with Joan Crawford, Clark Gable, and Fred Astaire; *Cheating Cheaters* (1934) with Fay Wray; *Our Little Girl* (1935) with Shirley Temple and Joel McCrea; *Love under Fire* (1937) with Loretta Young; *This Is My Affair* (1937); *Straight, Place and Show* (1938): *The Ritz Brothers*; *It Could Happen to You* (1939); *Let Us Live* (1939) with Henry Fonda and Maureen O'Sullivan; *Typhoon* (1940) with Dorothy Lamour; *Joe Smith, American* (1942) with Robert Young; *The Thrill of Brazil* (1946) with Evelyn Keyes; *Till the End of Time* (1946) with Dorothy McGuire; *Dead Reckoning* (1947) with Humphrey Bogart; *The Guilt of Janet Ames* (1947) with Rosalind Russell; *My Dream Is Yours* (1948) with Doris Day; *The Strip* (1951) with Mickey Rooney and William Demarest; *It's a Big Country* (1952) with Ethel Barrymore; *Prisoner of War* (1954) Ronald Reagan; and *The Eternal Sea* (1954) Sterling Hayden.

John Monk Saunders

Born 22 November 1895 or 1897,
Hinckley, MN
Died 11 March 1940,
Ft. Myers's, FL

John's father Robert, a lawyer born in Virginia about 1865, arrived in Hinckley in 1891. The huge Hinckley Forest Fire of 1894 destroyed the town and the forests in Pine County and many survivors never went back, but Robert did return, found the object of his affection, Nancy Monk, and married her in early 1895.

John was the second oldest of eight children. The family later moved to Seattle, Washington, and John eventually enrolled in the University of Washington. With war raging in Europe, he dropped out during his senior year to enlist in Officers Training School and graduated from the U. S. School of Military Aeronautics at Berkeley, CA. in 1917, as a second lieutenant in the U. S. Air Corps.

After the War John moved back to Seattle to join his parents. He re-enrolled in UW and graduated with a B. A. in 1919. He won a Rhodes Scholarship to Magdalen College at Oxford University from which he took an English B. A. in 1921 and an M.A. in 1923 (probably via correspondence). He married Avis Hughes in January, 1922, and they had a son.

John joined the editorial staff of the *Los Angeles Times* in 1922, moved on to the *New York Tribune* in 1923, and became an associate editor of *American* magazine in 1924. During these years he also contributed stories to *Cosmopolitan* and *Liberty* magazines among many others.

Like many other aspiring artists, John wandered into Hollywood in 1925 and landed a job writing two scripts that were produced that year, *Too Many Kisses* and *The Shock Punch*. His third try was the charm, as they say, as he drew on his experience as a pilot to write the story for *Wings* (1927) starring Richard Arlen, Charles "Buddy" Rogers, and super-star-to-be Gary Cooper. The film won the first Best Picture Oscar. In its inaugural year the awards were presented in the ballroom of the Hollywood Roosevelt Hotel on West Hollywood Boulevard. The emcee for the evening was Douglas Fairbanks, Sr. who took all of three and a half minutes to announce the winners. Times have changed!

John's career was no longer in doubt. He received $12,000 to write the story for *The Legion of the Condemned* (1928), a sequel with the stars from *Wings* plus Fay Wray, a newcomer. Oozing with self-confidence, and recently divorced, he proposed to Wray on the set and they married June 15th, 1927. Fay once said of John, "He was one of the most handsome men in Hollywood and, with the additional assets of athletic prowess and a superior education, infinitely attractive." It was Saunders's second marriage; he and Fay had one child, a daughter, Susan Cary. Fay became famous for portraying the love object of *King Kong* in 1933. This was followed by *The Docks of New York* (1928) and *She Goes to War* (1929).

Saunders continued to milk his experience as a pilot, and in 1930 he won an Oscar for Best Original Story for *Dawn Patrol* (1930) with Douglas Fairbanks, Jr., Richard Barthelmess and Neil Hamilton, directed Howard Hawks. (Most viewers are more familiar with the 1938 version, one of the few remakes that's actually superior to the original, though the new version draws upon much of the original aerial footage of "dog fights" and aerial acrobatics of loops, half loops and roll-outs. The remake starred Errol Flynn, Basil Rathbone, David Niven and Donald Crisp, and was directed by Edmund Goulding.)

When you're newly married, still in love and the world still heaps praise on you, what do you do? You write another story for your love. *The Finger Points* (1931) stars Fay Wray, Clark Gable, Richard Barthelmess in a story about a crime reporter who succumbs to pressures of the underworld. Back to flying themes again, Saunders wrote *The Last Flight* (1931) with Richard Barthelmess, Helen Chandler, Elliott Nugent, and future cowboy star John Mack Brown. It's about four flyers who opt to stay in Paris after World War I to calm their broken physical and emotional states. Saunders captures their cynical view of the recent war and its false post-war hopes with some brilliant scripting, which is enhanced by William Dieterle's direction. Critic Tom Milne wrote, "A narrative as tight and spare as a Racine tragedy....unique in Hollywood at that time in its persistent, calculated understatement." The original magazine title was "Nikki and Her War Birds" but the novel's title was *Single Lady*.

Saunders drew *The Eagle and the Hawk* (1933) with Fredric March, Carole Lombard and Cary Grant, from his story, "Death in the Morning." In Paris, 1918, two American flyers hate each other but come together just before one of them dies. The echos of Dawn Patrol are unmistakable.

Saunders had jumped Warners' ship by this time and was working with Paramount Studios. He moved to RKO for *Ace of Aces* (1933) in which an American sculptor is branded a coward for refusing to enlist but later becomes a hero in France, albeit with a bitter taste in his mouth.

James Cagney stars in *Devil Dogs of the Air* (1935, Warners) with fine support provided by Pat O'Brien, Frank McHugh (the Irish Rat Pack), Ward Bond, and Margaret Lindsay. The film offers a comic slant on war-time flying, with rough-housing, romance, and rivalry in the U.S. Marines. *West Point of the Air* (1935) though seen as a "routine sentimental flag-waver," boasts a fine cast that includes Wallace Beery, Robert Young, Maureen O'Sullivan, Lewis Stone, Rosalind Russell, and Robert Taylor. An army sergeant father proudly pushes his air cadet son into fame.

With *I Found Stella Parish* (1935) Saunders's explores a new vein in a story about an actress attempting to prevent a blackmailer from exposing her sordid past to her daughter. He returned to flying with *Conquest of the Air* (1936). And then Saunders took a break.

Two years later John completed the scenario for *A Yank at Oxford* (1938) using notes from his own stay there just after World War I. It starred Robert Taylor, Maureen O'Sullivan, Vivien Leigh, and Lionel Barrymore, and it was a huge pre-World War II success. But Saunders seemed to have trouble finishing the script to the producer's satisfaction. It's reported that thirty-one writers worked on it without credit.

And then, for some reason, this bright, highly-educated, athletic, charming, handsome man took his own life in 1940. He and Fay Wray had divorced the year before, his output was diminishing, and his final film, *Star of the Circus* (1938, aka *The Hidden Menace*) was a bomb. Evidently the future had begun to look black and unlivable.

Jack Sher

Born 16 March 1913,
Minneapolis, MN
Died 23 August 1988,
Beverly Hills, CA

Like many Hollywood writers, Jack Sher began as a journalist, specifically as a columnist syndicated in over forty newspapers. He then became an author. Then his career path merged with the entertainment business and he plied his trade as a playwright, a screenplay writer then as a producer and director of movies. His first major film credit was co-scripting for Bob Hope and Hedy Lamarr in *My Favorite Spy* (1951).

Jack was the oldest of five children of Polish-born Jacob J. Scher and Iowa-born Blanche (Hewitt) Scher. He had three sisters, Natalie, Betty, and Barbara, and one brother, George. The Scher family lived at 206 W. Franklin Avenue, Apt. 4, when Jack was born. They lived at 3033 Portland Avenue in 1917 as Jacob worked as a salesman for the Bureau of Engraving. When Jack started school in 1918, they lived at 4143 Garfield Avenue and Jacob was a department manager at the Bureau of Engraving. In 1920 Jacob worked for Federal Schools, Inc. as the advertising manager. They were doing well enough to have a live-in servant. It is curious that Jack's father went by the American name of John for some years, then switched to his birth name of Jacob, and then switched back to John. Jack's mother Blanche died in 1926 and John, after a few months, married Vella H. By 1929 John was vice president at the Bureau of Engraving and they moved to 4410 Colfax Avenue South, a very nice, swanky neighborhood in those days.

Jack finished high school in 1931 and attended the University of Minnesota for several years before dropping out, perhaps due to financial constraints brought on by the Depression. But we soon find him writing a column for the *New York Reporter* and doing free-lance work on the side for the *Saturday Evening Post, Esquire, Redbook, Reader's Digest,* and *Colliers.* (Remember, folks, there was no TV in the 1930s and 40s and everyone read magazines and/or listened to the radio.) In later years he was the author of *The Cold Companion, Twelve Sports Immortals, Twelve More Sports Immortals,* and *Beach Pad.* He wrote a Broadway play, *The Perfect Set-up* (1962). His TV script, "Goodbye, Raggedy Ann" was nominated for an Emmy Award for 1971-72 (Sher also produced it). He wrote the TV series *Bewitched* (1964), *Holmes and Yoyo* (1976) among others.

The most distinguished film for which Jack received a credit was the classic Western *Shane* (1953)—he wrote additional dialogue. Loyal Griggs won the Oscar for Best Cinematography, and *Shane* also received nominations for Best Picture, Best Director, Best Screenplay, and two nominations for Best Supporting Actor (Brandon de Wilde and Jack Palance).

Yet Sher is best remembered today as screenwriter of *Paris Blues* (1961) for Paul Newman and Joanne Woodward. He also wrote *Move Over Darling* (1963) with Doris Day and James Garner; and a slew of Audie Murphy films (most of them Westerns) including *World in My Corner* (1956); *Walk the Proud Land* (1956); *Joe Butterfly* (1957), and *Wild and the Innocent* (1959) Sher wrote and also directed *Kathy O* (1958), and brought his film career to a close with *The 3 Worlds of Gulliver* (1960) and *Critic's Choice* (1963) starring Bob Hope and Lucille Ball.

Sher married Madeline Thompson in 1942 but they divorced. Their children are Stephen and Deborah. He married Moira Stanley in 1965. He earned a Bronze Star in World War II, serving in the U.S. Army from 1942 to 1945, in the Pacific Theater of Operations.

Max Shulman

Born 14 March 1919,
St. Paul, MN
Died 28 August 1988,
Los Angeles, CA

Max Shulman was born to be a writer, and his talent was recognized as an undergraduate at the University of Minnesota. "Campus humor" was his acknowledged expertise. Novels, magazine stories, Broadway plays, films and television scripts awaited the ticklish stroke of his pen. And he delivered well in each medium.

His father Abraham was a house painter. He and wife Bessie (Karchmer) had two children. Max and sister Esther grew up at 701 Selby Avenue, and they attended St. Paul's Central High School. Max graduated in 1936 and entered the U as a journalism major. He edited the *Sky-U-Mah*, a campus humor magazine with a staff of Thomas Heggen, Bud Nye, Ted Peterson, Norman Katkov, and Harry Reasoner, the "bush league version of the Algonquin Club." Max also wrote a column "Sauce for the Gander" in the *Minnesota Daily.*

Brimming with self-confidence, Shulman showed his writing to Nobel Prize-winner Sinclair Lewis, who advised him to get a job in a grocery store. Max had already done that, so he proceeded with his writing. He wrote a hundred stories for such magazines as *Collier's, Cosmopolitan,* and the *Saturday Evening Post.* An editor from Doubleday, Doran & Co. encouraged Max to write a book, which he did, and Doubleday published *Barefoot Boy With Cheek* (1943) a lampoon of college life that sold more than 250,000 copies.

Meanwhile, Max entered the Army Air Force in June of 1942 following college graduation. He said, "The only time I ever got emotional was when I went into the Army. I just knew I'd be killed, and I ended up writing training manuals for the air forces." *The Feather Merchants* (1944) was also published while Max was in the Army. This satiric look at civilian life on the home front sold 200,000 copies.

The Zebra Derby (1946) continued the adventures of Asa Hearthrug, who had been the hero of his first novel. Home from the army, Asa enter the "brave new plastic world" of post-war get-rich-quick schemes. Chip Boutell of the *New York Post* said, "It is absolutely impossible to describe the effect that Max Shulman has achieved. There are laughs on every page. Among the subjects dealt with are reconversion… door-to-door selling, new cars, Communism, surplus war materials, the press, and the GI's return to college. There are absurd and completely delightful fables tossed off in passing…. He is, perhaps, closest to S. J. Perelman. Nothing is sacred to either of these humorists, nothing impossible, nothing ever very probable. They both like puns, funny names… and both are satirists of no mean ability." The title, Max said, came from a hot flash in the night.

Also notable in the book is that there are twenty-four characters named Max. No wonder he was considered "a cultured Perelman," "a satiric genius," and "a master of undergraduate humor."

Max collaborated with producer George Abbott to turn *Barefoot Boy With Cheek* into a Broadway musical. It opened on April 3, 1947, and ran to July 5, 1949. Billy Redfield played Asa Hearthrug; torn between Yetta Samovar, a campus leftist (played by Nancy Walker) and Noblesse Oblige, a sorority girl. Red Buttons appeared as Shyster Fiscal. Shulman said that he rewrote the play nine times, "Every time I watch a player cross the stage, I think of a funnier line to put in his mouth. It's driving Mr. Abbott crazy."

He teamed up with Robert Paul Smith on writing the Broadway comedy *The Tender Trap*, starring Robert Preston as a New York bachelor with lots of love troubles, among them Kim Hunter. It opened October 13, 1954, running 102 shows. (Preston was the perfect Music Man six years later and Hunter went on to star as Stella in *A Streetcar Named Desire* on Broadway. She later reprised the role in film, winning an Oscar in 1951 for Best Supporting Actress.)

The film version of *The Tender Trap* was released the next year with Frank Sinatra and Debby Reynolds in the starring roles.

In 1957 Doubleday published Shulman's next novel, *Rally Round the Flag, Boys*. It deals with how the citizens of a fictitious town in Connecticut's Fairfield County react when the United States Army installs a guided missile station there. It sold 100,000 copies and became a Twentieth Century-Fox film starring Paul Newman and Joanne Woodward.

Shulman had a weekly humor column, "On Campus," appearing in 350 college newspapers and it advertised Marlboro Cigarettes. (Get 'em when they're young) He borrowed from economics jargon to describe that he was in the "durable joke business."

CBS-TV announced in the spring of 1959 that it would produce a comedy series based on a book of Shulman's short stories, *The Many Loves of Dobie Gillis* (1951), and a more recent novel, *I Was A Teen-Age Dwarf* (1959). The shory story collection had already been made into a film, *The Affairs of Dobie Gillis* (1953) starring Debby Reynolds. The series reverted to the original title, *The Many Loves of Dobie Gillis*, with Dwayne Hickman as Dobie, Bob Denver as Maynard G. Krebs, and Tuesday Weld as the unattainable Thalia Menninger. It ran from 1959 to 1963, and the reruns kept it in view for many years after that. Marlo Thomas, Warren Beatty, Michael J. Pollard, and Ryan O'Neal were a few of the many stars appeared on the show. Maynard, the archetypical beatnik, shuddered every time he heard the word, "work." Dobie just floated around life not really knowing what he wanted even though he posed in each show under the statue of Rodin's "The Thinker."

Twenty years later Max returned to films with a screenplay for *House Calls* (1978), which he co-wrote with Julius Epstein and two others. It stars Walter Matthau as a middle-aged doctor, recently widowed, who seeks a new mate. Glenda Jackson, Art Carney and Richard Benjamin also star. This became a TV series in 1979. His last scripting was for the TV movie *Help Wanted: Male* (1982).

Max was a small man at 5' 6", and he weighed 145 pounds. He thought of himself as squat and moon-faced. He always voted Democrat and was a member of the Authors Guild, the Dramatists Guild and the Writers Guild of America. He liked to play croquet and snooker pool but felt that strenuous exercise was "bad for the tissues." He spent so much time playing snooker that he graduated from college in six years instead of four. He married Carol Rees on December 21, 1941, and they had two children, Daniel and Max, Jr. They lived in Westport, Connecticut, on two acres of land and 100,000 moles. His second wife was Mary Gordon and they lived in Beverly Hills. Their children were Peter and Marsha.

In 1958 Max was one of six Minnesotans honored to have a Minnesota lake named after them. He liked Lake Shulman, as it was small and round like its namesake. He appeared on *What's My Line* on August 30, 1959.

When asked about his writing habits, Max answered that his first draft was written in sand with a pointed stick and that *Rally Round the Flag, Boys* was six and a half miles long. His advice to young writers was: marry money.

Regarding his "rivalry" with Thomas Heggen, his colleague on the college humor magazine *Sky-U-Mah*, they both broke into Broadway in 1947 with long-running hits. Heggen's ran four years to Shulman's two. Shulman won hands down in the book department, with three published before his play and three afterward. Meanwhile, Harry

Reasoner, another colleague on *Sky-U-Mah*, became a TV newsman/ journalist. You've probably seen him on *60 Minutes* which has run for decades every Sunday night.

Max was interviewed by Nina Shepherd of the Minnesota Alumni Association Magazine for the September/October issue of 1982, forty years after his graduation. He told her that Friday was his favorite day of the week as a boy because the library would let each kid take four books home instead of three. In 1982 he was worried that the future for reading looked bleak, as TV had taken over the time given to reading. Funny novels had disappeared in favor of situation comedies on TV and writers were so well paid to write for TV that there was no reason to write funny books.

"I am very happy that I went to the University of Minnesota," Max told her. "I would have been an entirely different kind of writer had I grown up in the East. I came out of Minnesota very innocent, and it has served me well." Max admitted to learning more about writing from his time spent on *Ski-U-Mah* than in the journalism classroom. By the way, Sigma Delta Chi started this magazine in 1921, then in the 1930s it was taken over by the student body.

Where did Max really spend most of his time? In Coffman Union, because that's where the pool tables were. He would take on all comers in snooker 'til the day he died.

C. Gardner Sullivan

Charles Gardner Sullivan
Born 18 September 1884,
Stillwater, MN
Died 5 September 1965,
Los Angeles, CA.

Mr. Sullivan's obituary in *Variety* referred to him as the "dean of silent screen-writing." He wrote 375 scenarios that appeared on film beginning in 1911. This is certainly a record among Minnesota writers and perhaps a national one. It's unlikely to be broken now that films typically run well over two hours.

Charles lived with his parents, Franklin and Addie, at 218 Maple Street in Stillwater until he completed fourth grade. In the summer of 1894 the family moved to St. Paul and lived at 889 Fuller Avenue. He graduated from Central High in St. Paul and took a job as a cub reporter for the *St. Paul Daily News* in 1902. Two years later he enrolled at the University of Minnesota, but in 1907 he dropped out to return to the *Daily News*. He later moved to Cleveland and finally to New York City where he made a few film connections.

At first he sold story sketches to vaudeville shows as a sideline while working for the *New York Evening Journal*. Then he met Thomas Alva Edison, the inventor of the Kinetoscope, an early movie projector built to hold 35 mm film with sprocket holes on the edges. Edison bought the script for ***Her Polished Family*** (1911). He later bought several more Sullivan stories for his one-reel films.

Not long afterward Sullivan met Thomas W. Ince, the head of production at the New York Picture Company. A strong bond developed between the men and when Ince decided to move the studio to California in 1914 he offered Sullivan a lucrative job as his head writer. C. Gardner moved to Santa Monica, where he churned out story after story in an effort to keep pace with Ince's high-speed production schedule. After all, he had been a journalist who was used to short deadlines and was skilled at seizing the human interest angle in current topics. He was flexible enough to deliver nice, predictable domestic tales as well as big-budget extravaganzas.

At the time William S. Hart, another Minnesotan, was the top cowboy star in film. Hart often worked for Ince. Sullivan's first story for Hart was ***Two-Gun Hicks*** (1914). C. Gardner continued to write nearly every Hart scenario/script through Hart's last major film, ***Tumbleweeds*** (1925).

In 1915 the New York Picture Company merged with the Triangle Corporation, and C. Gardner was promoted to the head of the scenario department, where he began writing for five-reel films, though in his new position he spent more time supervising and editing others' works than writing his own.

In 1917 Sullivan moved with Thomas Ince to Famous Players-Lasky (Paramount Studios) where he developed close working relationships with respected film directors such as Fred Niblo and Minnesota-born John Griffith Wray. These associations became useful in 1919 when Sullivan left Paramount to write as a freelancer. Because of his close relationship with Ince and his actors, he was able to sell such scripts as ***Human Wreckage*** (1923), ***Wandering Husbands*** (1924) and ***Dynamite Smith*** (1924) to Ince. But when Ince suddenly and mysteriously died in 1924, Sullivan's future career began to look more problematic.

Sullivan first took a stab at collaborating with producer Joseph M. Schenck in adapting Broadway shows to film. In 1926 he met Cecil B. De Mille, an independent producer who maintained high production standards. For De Mille, Sullivan adapted and co-wrote *Three Faces East* (1926), *Corporal Kate* (1926) *Vanity* (1927), *The Yankee Clipper* (1927), and *Turkish Delight* (1927). Perhaps the peak of his career came in 1928 with his last two silent films, *Sadie Thompson* with Gloria Swanson, who was nominated for an Oscar for Best Actress, and *Tempest* starring John Barrymore.

Sullivan's first script for a sound film was *The Woman Disputed* (1928) directed by Henry King, which was followed by *The Locked Door* (1929) with producer Joseph Kennedy, who was Gloria Swanson's lover. He also wrote the first sound gangster film, *The Alibi* (1929). Sullivan teamed up with De Mille and Paramount Studios for *Father Brown, Detective* (1935), directed by Edward Sedgwick, *The Buccaneer* (1938), *Union Pacific* (1939) and *Northwest Mounted Police* (1940).

Sullivan felt no special threat to his script-writing when sound came in. The studios, however, were all struggling to establish what kind of scripting fit sound films. Out of natural insecurity the studios often filmed Broadway plays, which already had plenty of both dialog and action. Sullivan also filmed a few plays, as the pressures of the time dictated, the most important being Eugene O'Neill's *Strange Interlude* (1932). After years as a free-lance writer, Sullivan became script supervisor for Universal Studio in 1931, and did the same job later with M-G-M, while crafting the screenplays for the films mentioned above.

Sullivan retired for good in 1942 after three decades in movies. He was able to enjoy twenty-five years in retirement, though the grind of turning out hundreds of stories must have taken its toll.

Editors

John Stag Hanson

Born 14 August 1943,
Minneapolis, MN

Among the many unsung heroes in Hollywood's movie-making machine—costumers, art directors, cinematographers, directors, producers, composers, and editors—the editors are probably furthest from the limelight. John Stag Hanson has been an editor for a long time, and he is just now stepping out into that limelight a little.

John grew up at 101 Hawthorne Road in Hopkins, a block from Saint Louis Park's Meadowbrook Golf Course where he sledded and skated in winter. He lived two blocks south of Excelsior Boulevard and seven blocks east of his school, Blake, so it was convenient for classmates such as Eric Canton, Ralph Read, and Dave Kittams to stop over after school to shoot some pool in his basement and pet his furry white Samoyed, Nikki, before heading home for dinner and homework.

John's extra-curricular activities at Blake included Glee Club, wrestling, and dramatics, becoming student director his senior year. His favorite quote was "Neither rhyme nor reason" from Shakespeare. In his junior year he played Benny Southstreet in the Blake-Northrop production of *Guys and Dolls* and a townsperson in *Finians's Rainbow* his senior year.

He subscribed to *Variety Magazine* from the age of fourteen onward and often read about films. On Saturdays he would occasionally go downtown to see as many as four films. This is perhaps not really surprising behavior from someone who purchased a movie projector and a copy of *The Lost World* (1925) at the age of ten.

Upon his graduation from Blake in 1961, Hanson sped off for California, stopping at Stockton long enough to earn a B.A. in drama from the University of the Pacific before moving to Hollywood to attend USC's (University of Southern California) Graduate Cinema School for editing. He studied under professor Verna Fields with whom he worked on *American Graffiti* and *Jaws*. John's apartment was in the Watts Riot Zone, a very unsafe and unsavory neighborhood that later garnered a few national headlines.

At USC John became the campus projectionist as well as a film critic and features writer for Cinema and Movies International where he worked with future directors Peter Bogdanovich (*The Last Picture Show*) and Curtis Hanson (*L. A. Confidential*). He interviewed and became a close friend of Merian C. Cooper, producer and writer of the classic *King Kong*. "Coop" ran the RKO Studios after the Kong success; he produced many John Ford-John Wayne films; and told John tales of Hollywood's golden years.

Needing a paying job John applied to MGM Studios. After all, they had produced most of the Hollywood musicals. Each week he would appear with flowers for the personnel director of the editing union as he diligently sought a movie job. The flowers worked. He was hired to do a variety of odd jobs until he was finally accepted into the film editing school at MGM, a seven-year program.

With a year to kill before that program started, John and some college friends went to Europe to make a travelogue/docudrama, The *Gypsy Boys*, in the mode of *Easy Rider* (1969) which appeared the following year. Upon their return John shopped all the studios except Columbia looking for a producer-distributor but found no takers. Ironically, it was Columbia that released *Easy Rider* in 1969, and it found a large cult following.

The first two years of the editorship program focused on mastering mechanics. The second phase consisted of on-the-job training. John's first assignment was in the NBC Documentary unit where he met and worked with a young reporter named Tom Brokaw. He then worked on *Kelly's Heroes* (1969) starring Clint Eastwood and *The Out-of-Towners* (1970) directed by Billy Wilder, starring Jack Lemmon and Shirley MacLaine.

His next project was *Ryan's Daughter* (1970) directed by David Lean, who had started in the film trade as an editor and never lost his eye for detail. Lean was considered the best editor in Britain in the 1940s. John so admired him as they worked side-by-side that he named his first son David. *Ryan's Daughter* won two Oscars, one for John Mills as Best Supporting Actor and for Frederick A. Young for Cinematography.

David Lean deserves a special mention here because of his acknowledged genius in filmmaking. He won Oscars for Best Directing in 1957 for *The Bridge on the River Kwai* (which John saw at the old Radio City Music Hall at 9th and LaSalle in Minneapolis for four showings one Saturday in 1957) and in 1962 for *Lawrence of Arabia*. He was nominated for Best Director in 1965 for *Dr. Zhivago*, in 1946 for *Great Expectations* and *Brief Encounter* and in 1984 for *A Passage to India*, for which Lean was also nominated for Screenwriting and Editing.

John next joined the editing staff of *The Sting* (1973) directed by George Roy Hill. There was a lot of enthusiasm at first because of the great success Hill had had teaming Paul Newman up with Robert Redford in *Butch Cassidy and the Sundance Kid* (1970), but as the film editing drew to a close a vague sense of gloom could be felt among the staff of junior editors. One of them spoke up, "Bill (Reynolds), we're afraid there is too much dead time in the early scenes and we'll lose the audience because there's almost no dialogue and no great visuals to grab them." Reynolds responded, "Just wait til I lay in the audio track." That track was "The Entertainer" by Marvin Hamlisch, who blended parts of Scott Joplin's ragtime music into a marvelous score that took the Oscar that year for Best Music Composition. There was no need to worry. *Sting* won Best Picture, Best Director for Hill and Best Screenplay for David S. Ward.

Hanson rolled right into *American Graffiti* (1973), an acknowledged classic with a breakout performance by Richard Dreyfuss. John had the privilege of working for senior editor Verna Fields as well as the famous Conrad Hall on the lights and cameras.

Hanson's next assignment came as a bit of a letdown. The sequel to *The Godfather* (1972) made everyone skittish because sequels so often bombed. This one was different. *Godfather II* (1974) broke the sequel jinx and won Oscars for Best Picture; Best Director (Francis Ford Coppola); Best Screenplay (Coppola and Mario Puzo),Best Supporting Actor (Robert De Niro); and Best Musical Score (Nino Rota and Carmine Coppola).

The next winner was *Jaws* (1975) directed by Steven Spielberg and starring Richard Dreyfuss, Roy Scheider, and Robert Shaw. Verna Fields won the Oscar for Best Editing.

Following this remarkable apprenticeship in editing, Hanson's budding career suffered something of a setback when MGM dissolved its assets and reinvested everything into its new hotel, the MGM Grand, in Las Vegas. After fifty years as the top studio in Hollywood, MGM closed its doors, so to speak, with two goodbye films, *That's Entertainment I* (1974) and *That's Entertainment II* (1976). John still had one year to go in his program, but there was no program.

*B*aker's Hawk (1976) was his next editing job. This well-received Western starred big Clint Walker and Diane Baker and it was a critical success. John finally became a senior editor for the TV mini-series of Herman Wouk's *War in Remembrance* (1984). Officially, he was Post Production Coordinator of seventeen hours of film for this mini-series shot from 1979-1983. He also edited on TV for *Trapper John, M. D.* and *Wonder Woman*.

John Stag Hanson's other interests include food: He developed a healthy cereal, "Outrageous Fruit and Grains," in the 1980s and had some success marketing it with financial help from Minneapolis banker Carl Pohlad. He has been teaching English and film studies in high schools since 1995. He has married three times and has three children.

Stephen E. Rivkin

Born MN

Who says you have to leave town or go to where the action is in order to find success? Stephen Rivkin began his string of successes with the made-in-Minnesota film, *The Personals*, and he wound that string up into a large ball in Hollywood.

His true debut was *Ain't We Having Fun?* (1976) but it was teaming up with film director Peter Markle that got the ball rolling. He had worked with Markle in making TV commercials and industrial movies. When it appeared that Markle's light, romantic story *The Personals* had commercial possibilities, he signed on as editor. Markle wrote, directed, and did his own cinematography as well as co-produced but he needed a good editor. The film was shot entirely in the Twin Cities. Eventually, it made a profit and this encouraged Pat Wells, the co-producer, Markle and Rivkin, an associate producer for the movie, to go to Hollywood to try another film. The male lead, Bill Shoppert, was also an associate producer. Karen Landry co-starred as did Shoppert's real life girlfriend, Chris Forth, and Michael Laskin. Minneapolis's intercity lakes—Calhoun, Harriet and Isles—were featured film sites, really stamping Minnesota onto the film

The next film was *Hot Dog...The Movie* (1984), about a cute, teenage, runaway girl who hitches a ride with a naïve skier training for the World Cup in Squaw Valley, Idaho. The film has some nice skiing scenes and soft porn and it made some money, too. It cost $2.5

million to make and brought in receipts of $20 million worldwide. Rivkin's next was *Youngblood* (1986), about the romances of a hockey star, starring Rob Lowe and Patrick Swayze, and what do ya know but that made some money, too, as it cost $5 million to make and took in $25 million worldwide.

Stephen, ever keen on opportunities now, got wind of a film project, *Band of the Hand* (1986) for which Bob Dylan wrote a song and sang another, and worked on that. He edited *Stranded* (1987) and did his last film with Markle in *Bat 21* (1988), starring Gene Hackman as a 53-year-old missile intelligence expert downed behind enemy lines.

At this point Rivkin began to edit bigger films, including the fine comedies *My Cousin Vinny* (1992) and Mel Brooks's *Robin Hood: Men in Tights* (1993). The next year he edited one of the best romantic comedies of the era, *Only You* (1994), with Marisa Tomei and Robert Downy, Jr. Location filming was done in Italy and the USA.

Stephen edited the made-in–Minnesota film, *The Wooly Boys* (2001) starring Peter Fonda and Kris Kristopherson. He edited the biopic *Ali* (2001) starring Will Smith as boxer Muhammed Ali. And most recently Stephen has edited all three of the enormously popular *Pirates of the Caribbean* (2003, 2006, 2007) films, each of which has seemed longer the last. But who's complaining? The three films, considered in aggregate, are approaching 3 billion dollars in gross receipts.

Composers

Bob Dylan

*Robert Allen Zimmerman
Born 24 May 1941,
Duluth, MN*

This man of music has also dabbled in movies, and even won an Oscar for Best Song in the 2000 Academy Awards. The song is "Things Have Changed" from **Wonder Boys** (2000). All in all, this cultural icon has garnered thirty-five film credits, mostly as a song writer.

Dylan was born in Duluth and lived with his family until age six at 517-519 N. 3rd Avenue East in the Central Hillside neighborhood. The Zimmerman family then moved to 2425 7th Avenue in Hibbing. Bob graduated from Hibbing High School in 1959. His school yearbook states that he wanted "to join Little Richard." He formed several bands in school: The Golden Chords, Elston Gunn and His Rock Boppers. His father, Abe, worked in the auto parts department for a Standard Oil station and later was a furniture and appliance salesman. Beatrice (Beatty) Stone Zimmerman was a homemaker. He has a younger brother, Richard.

Bob wrote his first poems at the age of ten. While in high school he taught himself the rudiments of guitar, piano, and harmonica. His taste in music included country western as well as rock 'n roll, especially Elvis Presley, Hank Williams, Little Richard, and Jerry Lee Lewis.

During his time at the University of Minnesota Bob distinguished himself less as a student—he seldom went to classes—than as a singer and guitar player at the Ten O'Clock Scholar, a coffeehouse in Dinkytown. Bob Sharky, an historian on Dinkytown, said he was having coffee with Ron Smith one evening in the fall of 1959 when Dylan came in, unsnapped his guitar case, took out the guitar and began to play. The owner, Dave Lee, chased him out with epithets flowing.

Dylan would also sing and play in the living room of the Kappa Alpha Theta Sorority House, though most of the girls ignored him. Bob also played at the Purple Onion Pizza Parlor in St. Paul. (Dave Lee, by the way, sold the Scholar to Bob Fishman and Art Bathos and bought the Holland Bar, which became Caesar's Bar, 4th & Cedar Avenue, on the University's West Bank.)

Bob Zimmerman was living in a campus frat house in 1959 when he met Spider John Koerner, who taught him much of his guitar technique. (Koerner, along with Dave "Snaker" Ray and Tony "Little Sun" Glover, played frequently at the Triangle Bar off Riverside Avenue on the West Bank in those days, and also recorded several landmark albums of American folk music.)

In 1960 Bob started using the name Dylan and that same year he moved to New York City. He settled in Greenwich Village, where he performed occasionally in folk clubs, though he also spent time in the hospital room of his ailing hero, Woody Guthrie. In late 1961 he caught the attention of music maven Lou Levy, who made introductions for him and helped launch his career. Levy managed the Andrews Sisters and was married to middle sister, Maxene. But it was the legendary talent scout John H. Hammond who signed him to a recording contract with Columbia Records, after listening to him at a session where he had been invited as a harmonica player. The next year they released his first record, *Bob Dylan*, a rather stark collection of folk standards that also contained two original songs. Dylan's next album, *The Freewheelin' Bob Dylan*, included such classics as "Blowin' in the Wind" and "Don't Think Twice, It's All Right." His third album contained "The Times They Are A-Changin.'"

More albums and tours followed, and more classic songs, from "It Ain't Me Baby" to "Mr. Tambourine Man" to "Like a Rolling Stone."

Bob Dylan's film debut was in *Don't Look Back* (1966) a documentary of his and Joan Baez's singing tour in England the previous year. This is a cinematic mess, but also a cult favorite, as the footage shows the couple's innocence and teasing and jamming, along with plenty of music in performance. By the time it was released Bob and Joan were finished as a couple, however, and Bob later married Sara Lowndes.

On July 29, 1966, Bob Dylan was nearly killed in a motorcycle accident. When he returned to the music scene three years later he had turned toward country music. In the midst of these stylistic and spiritual convolutions, Dylan was awarded an honorary doctorate from Princeton University in June of 1970, and recorded his first number one album, *Planet Waves* (1974).

Five years later Dylan returned to films, writing music for *Little*

Fauss and Big Halsy (1970) and for *Jud* (1971) which presented the song "One Too Many Mornings." Director Sam Peckinpah asked Dylan to compose music for *Pat Garrett and Billy the Kid* (1973) and he also appears briefly in that film as an outlaw assassin named Alias. The film is no masterpiece, but one of the songs Dylan wrote for it, "Knockin' on Heaven's Door" has been covered by a wide array of groups from The Grateful Dead and Wyclef Jean to Television and Guided by Voices.

Dylan got into films in a big way with *Renaldo and Clara* (1978). He wrote the film's screenplay and also directed and edited it. He appears as a major character and co-composed the score. Unfortunately the film is far too long and full of self-indulgent touches, and Dylan himself comes across as a Las Vegas lounge performer trying to demythologize himself. As he was making *Renaldo*, Dylan divorced Sara, with whom he had had four children—Jesse Byron, Samuel, Anna and Jakob, who later formed the band The Wallflowers. A later film, *The Band of the Hand* (1986), was also a bust.

In early 1979 Dylan surprised many of his fans by becoming a fundementalist Christian. While full of this "born-again" spirit, he released his seventeenth album, "Slow Train Coming," a cut from which won a Grammy—Dylan's first.

Dylan continued to tour and cut recordings, and in 1988 he was inducted into the Rock and Roll Hall of Fame. At the induction ceremony Bruce Sringsteen remarked, "Bob freed the mind the way Elvis freed the body. He showed us that because the music was innately physical it did not mean that it was anti-intellectual.... He invented a new way a pop singer could sound, broke through the limitations of what a recording artist could achieve, and changed the face of rock and roll forever."

In 1990 the French awarded him their highest cultural award, the Commandeur dans l'Ordre des Arts et Lettres. In 1991 Dylan accepted a Lifetime Achievement Award at the Grammies Annual Awards Ceremony. In September of 1997 he had an audience with the Pope ... at the Pope's request! In December of 1997 Dylan received a medal for artistic excellence at the Kennedy Center for the Performing Arts in Washington, D.C. In 2000 he was awarded the Polar Music Prize, the Royal Swedish Academy of Music Award. In an October, 1997, interview with *Newsweek*'s David Gates, Dylan said about his career, "Some days I get up and it just makes me sick that I'm doing what I'm doing. Because basically—I mean, you're one cut above a pimp. That's what everybody who's a performer is. I have this voice in my head saying, 'just be done with it.'"

But Bob could not be done with it. He continues to add to his *oeuvre*, and his music has long since caught the imagination of an entirely new generation of listeners. His 1997 album, *Time Out of Mind*, and his 2001 album, *Love and Theft*, both won the Album of the Year in the *Village Voice*'s annual critics' poll. And returning to film in 2000, he won an Oscar for his soundtrack recording of "Things Have Changed" for *Wonder Boys*.

A more complete list of Dylan's film appearances would include *Don't Look Back* (1967); *Eat the Document* (1972); *Johnny Cash: The Man, His world, His Music* (1969); *Pat Garrett and Billy the Kid* (1973); *Concert for Bangladesh* (1972); *Rolling Thunder* (1977); *Renaldo and Clara* (1978); *The Last Waltz* (1978); *Hearts of Fire* (1987); *A Vision Shared: A Tribute to Woody Guthrie and Leadbelly* (1988); and *Imagine: John Lennon* (1988). Martin Scorcese's documentary for PBS, *No Direction Home* (2005), draws footage from many sources to tell the compelling story of Dylan's early years. Dylan's own recent commentary on his life and music, drawn from twenty hours of interviews, adds to the interest.

Yes, Bob Dylan is a true original, and some of his creativity made its way into films. Every year in Hibbing a festival is held to coincinde with Bob's May 24th birthday, and a surprising number of fans from all over the world show up to listen to music, swap memoribilia, watch a film or two, and have fun. A contest is held to see who can sound the most like Bob Dylan, and the rumor circulates annually that Dylan himself will finally make an appearance.

"Jimmy Jam" Harris

James Samuel Harris III
Born 6 June 1959,
Minneapolis, MN

Terry Lewis

Born 24 November 1956, Omaha, NE

Jimmy Jam is a songwriter, musician, record producer, and entrepreneur. He and partner Terry Lewis have written and/or produced more than one hundred albums and singles that have reached gold, platinum or multi-platinum sales, including twenty-five number 1 R&B singles and fourteen number 1 pop hits. They've been nominated for a Grammy Award six times in the Producer of the Year category for songs they have written for Janet Jackson, Mariah Carey and Shaggy. They've received the NAACP Image Award; a star on the Hollywood Walk of Fame; Writer of the Year honors at ASCAP's Rhythm & Soul and Pop Awards Dinners several times AND they've been nominated for an Academy Award for How Stella Got Her Groove Back (1998) and nominated for a Golden Globe for The Emperor's New Groove (2001) among some twenty film credits. Harris and Lewis appeared as themselves in Prince's film, *Graffiti Bridge* (1990).

It all began at Minneapolis's North High in the mid-70s. That's where Harris met Lewis and formed the band, Flyte Time, and it's where Harris and Lewis met Morris Day and the great Prince. In 1981 Morris Day joined them and they toured with Prince as Morris Day & The Time.

On one occasion a blizzard prevented Harris and Lewis from re-joining the band for a scheduled play-date so Prince fired them. Shortly thereafter they produced the SOS Band that scored gold with "Just Be Good to Me," a sensation that saved the hide of Harris and Lewis—so much for the power of the Prince. The song was set into their debut film, *Richard Pryor Here and Now* (1983).

Some of their pop hits: "On Bended Knee," "Miss You Much," "Escapade," "That's the Way Love Goes," "What Have You Done for Me Lately," "Just Be Good to Me," "Diamonds" and "4 Seasons of Loneliness." Only George Martin, the Beatles' producer, has more number 1 hits than Harris and Lewis.

Disney Touchstone Films produced their next film venture, *Tough Guys* (1986), with Burt Lancaster and Kirk Douglas teaming together (for the seventh time) as old train robbers just released from prison. The theme is appropriately called "Nasty," sung by Janet Jackson. "Just the Facts" sets the theme for *Dragnet* (1987) a comic caper starring Dan Aykroyd and Tom Hanks. The film also contains "Helplessly in Love."

The hit song in Eddie Murphy's *Raw* (1987) is "What Have You Done for Me Lately;" *Casual Sex* (1988) starring Rochester-born Lea Thompson, features "I Didn't Mean to Turn You On;" Janet Jackson sang the title song in *Rhythm Nation 1814* (1989); "Miss You Much" for *Ghost Dad* (1990); and "Money Can't Buy You Love," "Mo' Money Groove," "Ice Cream Dream," and several other tunes from *Mo' Money* (1992). The lead song for *Poetic Justice* (1993) is "Again." "What Have

You Done for Me Lately" was reprised for *Sister Act 2: Back in the Habit* (1993) starring Whoopi Goldberg again.

Harris and Lewis wrote "History" for *Michael Jackson: HIStory on Film - Volume II* (1997), a video; "Oh, Yeah, It Feels So Good" for *Metro* (1997); "I Will Get There (a cappella)" for the animated movie, *Prince of Egypt* (1998); and these songs for the Oscar-nominated film, *How Stella Got Her Groove Back* (1998): "Free Again," "Make My Body Hot," "The Art of Seduction," "Dance for Me," "Beautiful," "Luv Me Luv Me (contains 'Impeach the President')," "Never Say Never Again," "Your Home Is in My Heart (Stella's Love Theme)."

They wrote "Come On" for *Snake Eyes* (1998); "The Best Man Quartet" for *The Best Man* (1999); "Just Be Good to Me" for *Ten Things I Hate about You* (1999); "What Have You Done for Me Lately" reprised for *Duets* (2000); "Doesn't Really Matter" for *Nutty Professor II: The Klumps* (2000); "Free" for *Bait* (2000); "Would You Mind" for *How High* (2001); "Lillie's Blue Twister," "Tell Me If You Still Care," "Want You" and several other tunes for *Glitter* (2001); and songs for *The Emperor's New Groove* performed by Sting.

The list goes on: "No More Drama" for *Honey* (2003); executive Music producer for *The Fighting Temptations* (2003); "Sweet Kind of Life" for *Shark Tale* (2004); "Come On" reprised for *Melinda and Melinda* (2005); "Love's Dance" for *Robots* (2005); and "Definition of Love" for *Akeelah and the Bee* (2006).

Terry Lewis is married to Karyn White. Lewis also did "Eyes of the Heart" (Radio's Song) for the film, *Radio* (2003).

All that great music coming out of North Minneapolis and Edina! Sad to say but in the spring of 2004, Harris, Lewis and Flyte Tyme Studios relocated to Los Angeles to be closer to the music scene. After twenty years in Pentagon Park in Edina, Flyte Tyme said goodbye to Minnesota. Their new address is 8750 Wilshire Blvd in Beverly Hills (where they accept vocal demos).

S. L. Rothafel

Samuel Lionel Rothapfel
Born 9 July 1882,
Stillwater, MN
Died 13 January 1936,
New York, NY

Samuel Lionel Rothapfel grew up in Stillwater, which had once teemed with lumber mills, and perhaps the spirit of enterprise and construction sank in. At any rate, he conceived a dream and followed through on it, to build the best and biggest theaters in the biggest, most important city in America—the Roxy Theater and the Radio City Music Hall in New York City. Along the way he visited the world of film-making, composing music for eight films, arranging music or accompanying for four more, producing five, directing two, and editing one.

Rothafel lived with his parents, Gustav, a shoemaker, and Lizzie, at 307 N. Main Street in 1887. His father's shop was two blocks down at 117 S. Main Street. In 1890 they lived at 231 N. Main Street and he worked at 110 S. 2nd Street. They moved back again in 1892 to 307 N. Main Street and in 1894 they lived at 518 W. Oak Street. As a boy Samuel fished and swam in the St. Croix River and he especially remembered sliding down Morris Street in mid-winter. He said, "The most pleasant days of my life were spent in Stillwater." Even by other boys he was considered "adventurous."

In 1895, when Samuel was thirteen, the family moved to New York City. He worked first as a cash boy for $2/week for a Fourteenth Street department store. That job lasted two weeks. He moved through a variety of odd jobs and his parents were beginning to fear he was a dreamer and a loafer until he joined the U.S. Marine Corps. He served for seven years, and for part of that time he was stationed in China, where he witnessed the later stages of the Boxer Rebellion.

Rothafel returned to New York for a while, then went to Forest City, PA, a mining town, to run a store. His first brush with show business came when he opened up a storage room in the back of the store to do a lantern-slide show "nickelodeon" (five-cents a show) for the miners. He returned to the Twin Cities where he became a theater electrician so as to improve his lantern slide show.

While working at the Grand (later the Garrick) in St. Paul, Rothapfel dropped into the office of Theodore Hayes, general manager of the Finkelstein and Ruben movie chain in the Northwest, and suggested the use of a pipe organ to accompany the movies. He thought a full orchestra would be even better. The orchestra idea was dismissed but the organ was tried and was gradually accepted.

Back in New York he talked his way into becoming manager of the Capitol Theater, the largest movie house in New York, and, of course, was the first to use the pipe organ to accompany movies there. His reputation grew with its success and he became a manager of the Regent Theater and the Strand which he upgraded to "de luxe" presentations. He actually composed the music for 1914's *The Avenging Conscience, Thou Shalt Not Kill*, and *The Battle Cry for Peace* (1915). He was one of the first to film an opera, *Carmen* (1915).

In 1918 Rothafel produced his first film, *Devil Dogs*, followed by *Flying with the Marines*, for which he was also director and editor. On its heels came *Fighting along the Piave, Among the Cannibals Isles of the South Pacific,* and, in a dual role, *Under Four Flags,* which he directed as well as produced. The next year he supervised the music for *False Gods*.

During the 1920s Rothafel became a nationally-known radio personality. His moniker was "Roxy" and his show was "Roxy and His Gang." In the midst of radio broadcasting, theater construction, and management, he still found time to revisit his old stomping grounds in Stillwater twice, where he was celebrated as an entertainment hero.

On March 10, 1927, the Roxy Theater opened at Seventh Avenue and Fiftieth Street. It cost $10,000,000 to build, and at the time was the largest theater in the world, with 6,200 seats. The theater opened with the Gloria Swanson film, *The Love of Sunya*, and Miss Swanson herself attended as a guest of honor. A syndicate supported the construction, which began in 1925. A sky-scraper hotel was built above the theater. The *St. Paul Pioneer Press* ran an article on Rothafel on June 21, 1925 with this headline: "Minnesotan, Thought Failure, Builds Largest Movie House." Follow-up articles appeared Aug. 29, 1926, and May 12, 1927.

Rothafel left the Roxy Theater a year later and became operating head of RKO Enterprises at Radio City in New York. In the next few years he wrote the music for eight films. For Minnesotans the most notable was *Mother Machree* starring Minnesota-born Belle Bennett. The Roxy Theater is gone today, but Rothafel's office suite at Radio City Music Hall still boasts his "de luxe" style and is untouched from his last use of it in 1936. Three of his better known songs are "Mother of Three Sons," "Fresh Faust" and "The Negro Burial Ground."

By this time Rothafel was often referred to as "Mr. Impressario," and the name was given added luster when he opened the Radio City Music Hall on December 27, 1932. It was called the "Showplace of the Nation." It also had 6,200 seats in its cavernous orchestra with three mezzanines above. It was an integral part of Rockefeller Center, its address: 1260 6th Avenue between 50th and 51st Streets. It was Art Deco in design, like other Rockefeller Center Buildings—elegance without excess, grandeur without glitz. David Sarnoff of RCA who had dubbed the area "Radio City" joined forces with RKO Studios, Rothafel, and Rockefeller to make the hall a high-quality theater with deluxe entertainment at prices ordinary people could afford.

The entertainment on opening night, lasting five hours, included 96 Roxyettes, four Greek dances and the 110 Tuskegee Choir. It was an extravaganza never to be seen again. Rothafel was thought a genius for combining stage show elements, vaudeville, and orchestra with the movie as the main event. When costs were finally added up a week later, RKO made cuts in expenses right away. As of January 11, 1933, Radio City became a movie house only. The day of the stage show with movie had passed.

Roxy was blamed for the excess in expenses and the dancers were renamed Rockettes to distance them from Rothafel. (It was also easier to say.) In much later days only Radio City could do big format entertainment as it was bigger than all the theaters on Broadway. Due for demolition in the 1970s, it was made a national landmark and refurbished for $70 million.

Rothafel was teased as a child about his name meaning in German "red apple" (Rothapfel). The teasing name was "Little Sammy Rotten Apple." Many years later in a lovingly teasing way it was mentioned again as he returned to his roots in Stillwater and was honored as a local boy who made VERY GOOD in the Big Apple.

Rothafel died of a heart attack at age fifty-three, leaving a widow, a son, Arthur, of San Francisco and a daughter, Bettina (Mrs. George Bijur) of New York.

Roy Shield

LeRoy B. Shield
Born 2 October 1893,
Waseca, MN
Died 9 January 1962,
Fort Lauderdale, FL.

Who'd have thought that the primary composer of music for the Hal Roach Studio comedies of the 1930s was born in Waseca, Minnesota? LeRoy Shield composed a variety of theme, incidental, transition, and background music for Roach from 1929 to 1931. This was plugged into films starring Laurel and Hardy, the Little Rascals, and Charlie Chase. At the time Shield was the West Coast Representative for the Victor Music Company.

Roy was a musically gifted child. At age five he could play piano and organ. At twelve he made his professional debut and at fifteen he became an arranger, composer, and concert pianist. He won a scholarship in piano at Columbia Conservatory in Chicago, followed by music studies at the University of Chicago. He accompanied opera singers like Eva Gauthier on tours in America and he played the works of Ravel, Holst, Baxt, Milhaud, and Casella, often being the first to introduce their works to American audiences.

In 1923, at the age of thirty, Roy joined the Victor Talking Machine Company as a pianist and as "Director of Recording Sessions" and "Manager of Instrumentalists" in New York, and later in Camden, New Jersey. After a move to California in 1926 he was appointed Musical Director in charge of Hollywood Activities. It was there that Roy met Hal Roach and began to compose background music for the Roach comedies.

Shield was a quick study of Roach's needs and came up with tunes like "Good Old Days" which became the theme song for the Our Gang comedies. It was written for the Our Gang 1930 short, *Teacher's Pet*, starring St. Cloud's June Marlowe as the new teacher, Miss Crabtree, who all the Rascals attempt to impress.

Researchers like New York bandleader Vince Giordano, Piet Schreuders of the Beau Hunks Orchestra in Amsterdam, Ronnie Hazzlehurst of the BBC in London, and Guido Nielsen have tracked down Shield's music and recorded it. The Beau Hunks Orchestra has recorded the 121 minutes of dramatic transitions, neutrals, pay-offs and montages onto two CDs, containing seventy-nine "links and bridges" each. Two hours of music may not seem like much, but Roach was adept at recycling the music over and over.

In 1931 Shield was named Director of Music for NBC's Central Division so he moved back to Chicago. He did heaps of arranging and led his orchestra in several NBC musical radio shows, including *Roy Shield and Company* and *Author's Playhouse*. Yet, in 1933, 1935 and 1936, Shield also returned to Hollywood to record more music for the Hal Roach Studios—which never saw fit, by the way, to credit Shield or any other composer for their contributions.

The year 1933 saw the release of *Fra Diavolo* starring Dennis King and Thelma Todd with Laurel and Hardy, and 1936 saw the release *of Our Relations*, another Laurel and Hardy feature. Both films were fully scored by Shield, though he didn't receive a credit. His counterpart at the Roach Studios, Marvin Hatley, did receive credit the next year with his score for the Marx Brothers' *Way Out West* (1937) and he is nominated for an Oscar for Best Musical Score.

Shield never returned to Hollywood after 1936. There is some opinion that he was considered an outsider whereas Hatley was a full-time Roach employee, an "industry man." Shield, feeling a bit used and hurt from the Roach experience, stuck to serious music after that. An interesting sidelight is that Shield earned $500 a week for his score of *Our Relations* while Hatley made only $200 a week for *Way Out West.*

Even on recordings Schield is nearly always uncredited but one can occasionally find a 78-rpm record from the 1930s that credits him and his band, such as "Sing-Song Girl" and "Song of the Big Trail" with LeRoy Shield and the Victor Hollywood Orchestra. He wrote popular tunes such as "You Are the One I Love" and "Illusions;" he composed a symphonic tone poem, "Gloucester," and two suites: "Chicago" and the "Union Pacific Suite."

The peripatetic Shield moved back to New York in 1945 to work closely with NBC's Orchestra leader Arturo Toscanini, and joined him on his nationwide concert tour in 1950. Roy conducted the NBC Concert Orchestra and the NBC Summer Symphony. In 1955 Shield retired at age sixty-two.

Shield married Katharine Williams Dolman who had a son, Mahlon, by a previous marriage. However, Mahlon and Roy were as close as any father and son could be. Roy and Katharine were living in Vero Beach, Florida, in retirement at the time he died. His brother, Walter, survived him.

He was a member of the American Society of Composers, Authors and Publishers. Stanley Adams, President of the fraternity, wrote a memorial statement on Shield for the *New York Times* obituaries on January 10, 1962.

Animators

Ward Kimball

Ward Walrath Kimball
Born 4 March 1914,
Minneapolis, MN
Died 8 July 2002,
Arcadia, CA

Ward Kimball's goal in life was to be an illustrator for the *Saturday Evening Post* and other national magazines but nature took a slightly different course. One of his art school instructors suggested that he apply for a position at the Walt Disney Studios. He did and, a month later, he was hired as an animator. He was hired because he was an artist rather than a cartoonist. That was in 1934 when he was twenty years old.

Ward was born in Minneapolis to a traveling salesman father so he was raised by his grandparents. At eighteen he went to California to enroll in the Santa Barbara School of the Arts, attending for two years. He spent a few months as an apprentice animator at Disney, then did his own animations on the Silly Symphony series of Mickey Mouse shorts. He also worked on the Oscar-winning *The Tortoise and the Hare* (1934).

As the years rolled by, Kimball was invited into Disney's inner circle of advisers known as the "nine old men," a term borrowed from a book of that title about the U. S. Supreme Court and its nine justices, which at the time was obstructing President Franklin D. Roosevelt's New Deal programs.

Kimball was one of several animators assigned to the very first animated feature, *Snow White and the Seven Dwarfs* (1937). Although Disney had won several Oscars for his cartoon shorts, he was advised by all film experts to forget doing a feature (something over sixty minutes in length). Yet, he hired all the artists he could find in the American Southwest and borrowed $750,000 to cover his costs. It turned out that the risk was well worth it as *Snow White* has earned over four hundred times that amount in the years since its original release .

Ward's work on that film was cut out, but he was later assigned to create Jiminy Cricket for *Pinocchio* (1940), also a feature. He based the character on what a real cricket looked like, blending the image into that of a real man with a cane, top hat, and umbrella. Kimball and Cricket shared some traits (see photo), according to Ari L. Goldman of the *New York Times* in that they both seemed like old song-and-dance men of the vaudevillian days. Cricket, like Kimball, was a short, plucky, feisty guy with a big personality, not a guy easily shoved around. Cricket became a co-star of the film along with Pinocchio.

Specifically, Ward's best known works were the five crows in the crow self-confidence sequence in *Dumbo* (1941); Panchito, the finale and title song sequence in *The Three Caballeros* (1945); the Peter and the Wolf sequence in *Make Mine Music* (1946); the two mice and their arch-enemy, Lucifer the Cat, and the stair sequence in *Cinderella* (1950); Tweedledum and Tweedledee, the Cheshire Cat and the Mad Hatter's Tea Party scene in *Alice in Wonderland* (1951); and the Indian Chief in *Peter Pan* (1953).

In the 1950s Ward made the move to television. He worked with German rocket scientist Werner von Braun, both directing and producing *Man in Space* (1955); *Man on the Moon* (1955); and *Mars and Beyond* (1957). He also worked with Von Braun on the Tomorrowland exhibition at Disneyland 1955-56.

Kimball virtually won an Oscar as he did the animated short *Toot, Whistle, Plunk and Boom* (1953) which was awarded the Oscar. It featured an owl who talked about how musical instruments were made and developed. It was the first animated feature done in cinemascope. He later created a thirty-minute featurette for television called *It's Tough to Be a Bird* (1969), which also won an Oscar. Unfortunately, Disney had a strict policy that forbade his artists from receiving specific credit for their work.

Other old Disney "chestnuts" where Ward was a team animator were: *Ferdinand the Bull* (1938); *Fantasia* (1940); *Willie the Operatic Whale* (1946, Nelson Eddy sang for Willie); *Peter and* the Wolf (1946, narrated by Basil Rathbone); *The Adventures of Ichabod and Mr. Toad* (1949); and *Mary Poppins* (1964).

Ward Kimball was a man of many interests. Two special hobbies were jazz and railroads. He played trombone in the Dixieland jazz group, the "Firehouse Five Plus Two," made up of Disney employees, and he had a large-scale railroad and tracks in the backyard of his home. He was a past President of the Train Collectors Association. He even converted Disney himself into being a train enthusiast. He retired from active employment at Disney in 1973 after forty years of service. Among his last contributing works was a sequence to *Bedknobs and Broomsticks* (1971). In 1978 he went on a whistle-stop tour to promote Mickey Mouse's 50th Anniversary. Ward had been responsible for re-designing Mickey when he first arrived at Disney, giving him more expressive eyes and puffier cheeks. He stayed accessible to the studio as a consultant.

About his working days at the Disney Studios, Ward once remarked, "We thought we were always going to be twenty-one years old. We thought we would always be putting goldfish in the bottled drinking water, balancing cups of water on light fixtures, changing labels on cans of sauerkraut juice. We were twenty-one years old, Walt was thirty, leading the pack. Working there was more fun than any job I could ever imagine."

Ward was happily married to Betty Lawyer, whom he met at Disney Studios, for sixty-six years from August 15, 1936, to his death in 2002 at the age of eighty-eight. Besides Betty, he was survived by their son, John, an animator, and two daughters, Kelly Kimball and Chloe Kimball.

Many people felt Disney thought of Kimball as "his right hand man." His was certainly one of the "nine old men" whose opinions Disney respected. His love of trains gained him the job of designing the World of Motion exhibit at the Epcot Center of Disneyworld in Florida. In 1989 Kimball was named a "Disney Legend."

Art Directors

Harry Oliver

Harold Griffith Oliver
Born 4 April 1888,
Hastings, MN
Died 5 July 1973,
Woodland Hills, CA

Harry Oliver began his working life as a "printer's devil" while in school in order to learn to spell better—or so his father hoped. Harry had a pronounced and creative talent for misspelling. In the 1912 St. Paul City Directory he was listed as a carpenter (and scenery painter in St. Paul theaters) but marriage in 1913 and wanderlust took him to Hollywood, California, where Harry became a designer, builder, and painter of movie sets for twenty years, garnering two Oscar nominations for Art Direction along the way. However, as he turned fifty, Oliver gave up his old life to live in the deserts of the Coachella Valley, where he was known as one of California's colorful characters.

Harry was the son of Hastings pioneers, Frederick W. Oliver, born in England in January, 1844, and Mary S. Oliver, born in April, 1856, in Minnesota. Frederick had emigrated from England with his parents in 1850. He was an officer in a Massachusetts regiment in the Union Army in the Civil War. After the war he set up a grocery on 105 East Second Street in Hastings. (The building still stands at 109 East Second Street, the Bathrick Building, as the numbering system has changed slightly over the years.) F. W. was a director on the Hastings Library Association in 1874. They family lived at 500 Second Street.

In 1879 Frederick married Mary Simmons. They had five children of which four survived, all born in Minnesota: Fredrick William (16 June 1883); Amy Silver (3 July 1886); Harold Griffith (4 April 1888); and Frances Mary (16 June 1889).

Harry bragged that he dropped out of school after 4th Grade, but the records suggest that he continued through junior high. The family had moved to St. Paul before the 1910 Census and lived at 57 S. Victoria Street. Harry is listed in the 1912 St. Paul City Directory as a carpenter living at 747 Portland Avenue.

In that same year he married Alice Elizabeth Fernlund. She was a Swedish-American girl raised in a log cabin on the shores of Lake Vermillion where she trapped and hunted. The story goes that after hearing that Alice had captured a large bear cub and trained it as a pet, he hunted her down and married her. The couple soon moved to California to seek a better life. They had two daughters, Amy Fern (Deily) of Placentia, and Mary Alice (Umbach) of Oxenard, both born in California.

By 1919 Harry was working in Hollywood as Technical Director and Art Director though sometimes Associate Art Director or consultant from the Art Department. He spent the transition years, when silent films became talkies, at Fox Studios but also worked for Paramount, RKO, Howard Hughes, and M-G-M Studios, and with Harold Lloyd, Mary Pickford, and Douglas Fairbanks acting as their own producers.

In 1925 Oliver worked on *Ben Hur*, the biggest and most successful extravaganza of its day, with Fred Niblo directing and Cedric Gibbon as Art Director. The chariot race and the sea battle are considered superb even today. Ramon Novarro and Francis X. Bushman starred in this classic. One of the perks of Harry's job was going on location and *Ben Hur* was filmed in Rome. Harry made a stop in Hastings on his way to Italy in 1924.

From that project he went right into *Little Annie Rooney* (1925) starring Mary Pickford, who co-produced the film with United Artists. He was an art consultant on that film. Through Mary Pickford he met Douglas Fairbanks who wanted Harry as associate artist for *The Gaucho* (1927) starring Doug and introducing Minnesota actress Joan Barclay.

Janet Gaynor starred in three of Oliver's films and she won the Oscar for *Seventh Heaven* and for *Street Angel* in 1927-28. Oliver himself was nominated for Oscars for Best Art Direction for both films but didn't win. He began a nice relationship with Fox Studios lasting for ten films through *Sunny Side Up* (1929) with Gaynor; *Song o' My Heart* (1930) starring the great tenor John McCormack, filmed on location in Ireland; and *Lightnin'* (1930) starring the biggest male star of the time, Will Rogers.

William Fox was the only studio owner badly affected by the Wall

Street Stock Exchange Crash and the ensuing Great Depression. His studio was forced to merge with Twentieth Century Films.

Harry free-lanced a few films with Paramount Studios and RKO before moving to M-G-M in 1934. He finished out his career there. He did all the sets for the Howard Hughes production of *Scarface* (1932) one of the earliest and also most violent gangster films. It was directed by Howard Hawks and starred Paul Muni as an Al Capone-like Chicago gangster. Harry was art director on *Movie Crazy* (1932) produced by and starring Harold Lloyd in his last and best comic film sequences, which also offers a nostalgic visit to the Hollywood of the silent era.

Oliver did the art direction for *Tillie and Gus* (1933, Paramount) a marvelous comedy starring W. C. Fields and Alison Skipworth as con-artists and charlatans who return from overseas to help settle an estate. In one classic scene Fields walks into a grand living room and nearly knocks off a Ming Vase with his cane. All eyes are riveted to the rocking vase, which gradually comes to rest again on its pedestal. There is a great steamboat race, too, during the course of which the ship is torn apart in order to feed the boiler for greater steam power.

Viva Villa (1934, M-G-M) was nominated for Best Picture and was a splendid biopic for Wally Beery in the tile role of Pancho Villa. Luise Rainer won the Oscar for Best Actress for *The Good Earth* (1937, M-G-M); Oliver worked as associate art director on both films. Oliver's last major credit was *Of Human Hearts* (1938) with James Stewart, Walter Huston, and Beulah Bondi in a tale about a back-woods preacher and his wayward son.

Harry was noted for his atmospheric settings and controlled environments. It is said that his sets influenced German expressionist art. His specialty was creating really believable exterior sets on the studio's back lot—for example, a New England snow scene for *The Face of the World* (1921, shot in the middle of summer). He did detailed Paris back streets for *Seventh Heaven* and made a complete swamp for *Sparrows* (1926) which convinced the viewing public at the time that the film had been shot in Louisiana. One lasting moment of his set building was the famous "witch's house" in Beverly Hills. It was built to be an administration building for Willat Studio in Culver City in 1921; it was later moved when the studio closed.

As time went by Harry began to grow bored with Hollywood, and in 1941 he decided that he needed a change in life. He had developed a strong attraction to the desert over the years and, as World War II had begun, the time seemed ripe to move there. He bought a parcel of land near Thousand Palms and built with his own hands an adobe home he called Old Fort Oliver. He designed several sketches for other people to build and these were called Storybook Houses of which the witch's house is one. He gave himself the title of Commander while the locals named him the "Desert Rat" after German General Rommel. The philosophic "Rat" wore spectacles and sported a long, gray beard. One favorite saying of his was, "The future is getting here more quickly than it used to." He once announced the startling news that a mosquito has twenty-two teeth.

In 1946 Oliver issued his own newspaper, *The Desert Rat Scrapbook*, a mixture of tall tales, legends, facts, and personal news. It came out four times a year, had a circulation of 30,000 and cost a dime (though the price later increased to two bits.) He had some top-notch writers on his staff, and also borrowed liberally from Mark Twain, Aesop, Benjamin Franklin, George Ade, and Andrew Jackson. Even Lady Bird Johnson read it and corresponded with Oliver. Referring to his spelling problem, he cited former president Andrew Jackson, "It is a poor mind that can think of only one way to spell a word." Oliver also admitted to telling tales but said, "There's a difference between true lies and damn lies, you know. I've forgotten exactly what that means but I tell only true lies."

Oliver coined the word "litterbug," according to Walt Disney, and campaigned fiercely against littering. He even erected billboards on the highway warning against beer-can throwers. In 1969, at eighty-one, beset with heart problems, he moved into the Motion Picture Country Home at 23388 Mulholland Drive, and died, as he predicted, on the Fourth of July, four years later.

An interesting note is that Harry never really liked the sound part of films. Perhaps he thought it took something away from the full appreciation of the visual aspects.

Technical Director

Peter Stolz

Born 23 September 1945, North Hollywood, CA

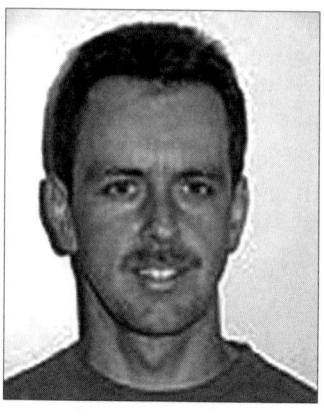

Peter Stolz is the oldest of five boys of Don and Joan Stolz, who ran the Old Log Theatre in Excelsior, Minnesota. He was born in North Hollywood while his dad was in the navy aboard a ship. So perhaps it was natural that one day. like a salmon, Peter would return instinctively to the place of his birth. But instead of following in the footsteps of his theater-director father, he chose his own path to show business success, making special effects for the Indiana Jones films and Star Trek films among others.

The Old Log has operated continuously under one management since 1941, a national record for theaters. It was a summer stock theater during the 1940s and 50s. In 1960 a new, larger, 655-seat theater was opened for year-round use. Peter's brothers, Don, Tom, Tim, and Jon all "cut their show business teeth" and had livelihoods from this theater, which sits on ten acres of woodland near the shore of Excelsior Bay on Lake Minnetonka, a dozen miles west of Minneapolis.

The family lived in Old Edina at 4615 Moorland in the 50s, just a block from movie-house owner and film producer W. R. Frank. Peter attended Benilde School in St. Louis Park, but transferred to St. John's Preparatory School in Collegeville, Minnesota, in his sophomore year. He graduated in 1963.

Peter's professional life began as a set designer at the Old Log. In 1981 he was hired by Ted Moehnke to work on the first of the Indiana Jones trilogy, *Raiders of the Lost Ark* (1981). For six years Peter and Ted worked busily on *E. T. the Extra Terrestrial* (1982), *Star Trek: The Wrath of Kahn* (1982), *Poltergeist* (1982), and *Star Wars: Episode VI – Return of the Jedi* (1983). In each movie Peter was a stage technician working under Ted as the supervisor. However, he was dragon assistant for *Dragonslayer* (1981).

In *Amityville 3-D* (1983) Peter worked on the optical effects crew. He worked with both Bob Finley and Moehnke on *Indiana Jones and the Temple of Doom* (1984) where Peter did miniature pyrotechnics, which he also did on *Starman* (1984) with both Finley and Moehnke. He worked solo on *The Goonies* (1985) as a stage technician and with Moehnke again on *Explorers* (1985); with Finley on *Howard the Duck* (1986) and *The Golden Child* (1986) both as miniature and normal pyro-technicians; and with Ted as pyro-technicians for *Top Gun* (1986). His last visual effects movie was *Batteries Not Included* (1987) starring Jessica Tandy and Hume Cronyn. Then Peter seems to have gone independent. Bob Finley was the tank technician for the great senior film *Cocoon* (1985) also featuring Tandy and Cronyn.

Peter was production designer for *Old Explorers* (1990), written by Dudley Riggs actors Jim Cada and Mark Keller, directed by Bill Pohlad, and filmed at Prince's Paisley Park Studio in Chanhassen.

Leaving visual effects behind, Peter became a special effects man with *Class Action* (1991); a production designer for the made-in-Minnesota film *Embrace of the Vampire* (1994); special effects coordinator for *Murder in the First* (1995); and mechanical effects man for *D3: The Mighty Ducks* (1996), another made-in-Minnesota film about a hockey team of problem kids. He was special effects coordinator again for *A Smile Like Yours* (1997) and, finally, special effects foreman for the TV series, *The Evidence* (2006), his second foray into TV with *Nash Bridges* being the first, 1996.

Peter did special effects for *So I Married an Axe Murderer* (1993); and was special effects pyro-technician for *The Zodiac* (2005).

Minnesota Authors whose Books Have Been Made into Films

(Note: Novelists Houston Branch, Frank Gruber, Jerome Odlum, Max Shulman, and Judith Guest appear in the screenwriter section.)

Charles Baxter

Born 13 May 1947,
Minneapolis, MN

Unlike so many other young American writers … Baxter cares about his people, recognizes the validity and dignity of their lives, grants them humor and individuality," said Jonathan Yardley in the *Washington Post Book World.* Chuck Wachtel of the *Nation* said, "Baxter is a remarkable storyteller…." Theodore Solotaroff, also of the *Nation*, noted that Baxter "has the special gift of capturing the shadow of genuine significance as it fits across the face of the ordinary." A host of critics admire the work of Charles Morley Baxter and the reading populace buys his books. What more could one ask?

To hear Charlie Baxter talk about the philosophic differences of living in Europe versus the U.S., as he eats a healthy new ice cream called Oatscream with a cup of cappucino at The Good Earth Restaurant at the Galleria in Edina, you might guess that the man is an English instructor at the university. You would be close. You might have guessed that he was a full professor except that he looks a dozen years younger than his age with only a sprinkling of gray in his well-trimmed, reddish beard.

In fact, since the autumn of 2003, Baxter has been the Edelstein-Keller Senior Fellow in Creative Writing at the University of Minnesota. His home base was the University of Michigan at Ann Arbor where he was a full professor 1989-1999. Prior to that he was at

Wayne State University for fifteen years. He gained his Ph.D. in 1974 at SUNY (State University of New York at Buffalo) and his B.A. in 1969 at Macalester College in St. Paul, 1969. He graduated from Blake School in Hopkins in 1965.

Charlie's first published works were books of poetry, *Chameleon* (1970) and *The South Dakota Guidebook* (1974). Two volumes of short stories followed, *Harmony of the World* (1984) and *Through the Safety Net* (1985) His first novel was *First Light* (1987). Another book of short stories, *A Relative Stranger*, and another poetry book, *Imaginary Paintings and Other Poems*, both came out in 1990 followed by his second novel, *Shadow Play*, in 1993. *Believers* (short stories and novella) and *Burning Down the House* (essays on fiction) came out in 1997 followed by his editing of *The Business of Memory: The Art of Remembering in an Age of Forgetting* (1999).

Then came *The Feast of Love* (2000), a novel that brought calls from Hollywood. *Feast* was a finalist for the National Book Award. Miramax bought the film rights to Baxter's book and things looked pretty exciting. This was not, however, Baxter's first encounter with film people. One of his early short stories, "Gryphon" (1987-88), was made into a one-hour made-for-TV movie, filmed by Wonderworks and aired by the Disney Channel and PBS with Amanda Plummer starring. The Hallmark Hall of Fame people had also shown interest in *First Light*, but in the end nothing came of it.

Anyway, Mirimax Films bought an option on *The Feast of Love* for the film rights but things became tangled up and delayed, as is often the case. Patricia Rozema was to adapt the novel and direct; her previous film had been an adaptation of Jane Austen's *Mansfield Park*. But after a year, Miramax let their option go, and Lakeshore Entertainment picked up the rights. A screenwriter, Allison Burnett, was assigned to do the adaptation, and the veteran director Robert Benton was assigned to shoot it. The film was shot in Portland, Oregon, in the summer and early fall of 2006 with a large cast, including Morgan Freeman, Greg Kinnear, Jane Alexander, Rahda Mitchell, Selma Blair and Alexa Davalos.

Charlie did not visit the set while the film was in production. "I feel the way most novelists do, which is that the novel is my book, but the movie is their movie, not mine. I didn't want to get in anyone's way. When people ask me whether I'm worried about what would happen to my book, I usually reply, 'They haven't done anything to it. It's still there, the same as it ever was, up there on the bookshelf.'"

The Feast of Love (2007) begins with Charles Baxter, as a character in his own book. He is the first of several narrators as each major character in the book takes his/her turn at narrating his connection with Bradley Smith's life in Ann Arbor, Michigan. We hear from his two wives, his neighbors, and his young employees who house-sit for him.

Charles is the son of John Thomas and Mary Barber (Eaton) Baxter. He has two older brothers, Thomas (deceased) and Lewis. He married Martha Ann Hauser, a teacher, July 12, 1976; they have a son, Daniel John. His most recent novel is *Saul and Patsy*, 2003.

Jon Hassler

*Born 30 March 1933,
Minneapolis, MN*

Minnesota's most Catholic novelist is Jon Hassler. Why think of him as a Catholic writer? He is a Regent's Professor Emeritus at St. John's University in Collegeville, Minnesota; he has been granted an honorary Doctor of Letters degree by Assumption College (Massachusetts), 1994, and the University of Notre Dame, 1996. He has been at St. John's as writer-in-residence since 1980. His books are full of priests, nuns, Catholic schools, Catholic life in Minnesota's small towns, with a few lapsed Catholics thrown in for good measure.

Hassler lived his first ten years in Staples, Minnesota, and his next eight in Plainview, where he graduated from high school in 1951. He has a B.A. from St. John's University and an M.A. from the University of North Dakota. (That institution also awarded him an honorary Ph.D. in 1994.) He taught high school English for ten years before joining the faculty at Bemidji State University. In 1970, while teaching at Brainerd Community College (now Central Lakes College), Jon Hassler began to write.

Jon's first contact with the world of film came in 1981, when Robert Redford bought the movie rights to *The Love Hunter*. That film never got made, but in 1990, Hassler's fourth novel, *A Green Journey* (1985) became a made-for-TV movie under the title *The Love She Sought*, starring Angela Lansbury, Denholm Elliott, and Robert Prosky. Lansbury plays Agatha McGee, an aging school teacher at a Catholic grammar school who has a spiritual crisis and leaves her teaching position to visit a long-term correspondent, James O'Hannon (Elliott) in Ireland.

Agatha McGee appears in four other Hassler novels, including his first, *Staggerford*. Miles Pruitt, Patrick Quinn, and Frank Healy are other recurring characters in these books about characters struggling with transitions in their lives or searching for some central purpose. Hassler also explores the role of the small town as it shapes, and limits, human potential.

His other books include *Simon's Night* (1979) *The Love Hunter* (1981), *Grand Opening* (1987), *Dear James* (1993) *Rookery Blues* (1995), *North of Hope* (1996), *The Dean's List* (1998), *The Staggerford Flood* (2002), *Nancy Clancy's Nephew* (2004), *The Staggerford Murders* (2004), and *The New Woman* (2005). His two children's books are *Four Miles to Pinecone* (1977) and *Jemmy* (1980). He has also published short stories and non-fiction works.

Hassler has won fellowships from the John Simon Guggenheim Foundation and the Minnesota State Arts Board. *Staggerford* was chosen Novel of the Year by the Friends of American Writers and *Grand Opening* was chosen Best Fiction of 1987 by the Society of Midland Authors. The town of Plainview dedicated the Jon Hassler Theatre in his honor.

Jon has married three times; he has three children. He wrote the introductory material for *Stories Teachers Tell*, a collection of anecdotes gathered and edited by his current wife, Getchen Kresl Hassler.

Despite a gradual decrease in his speech function, eyesight, and ability to walk due to progressive supranuclear palsy (a Parkinson's-related disease) Hassler continues to produce books. He is a charming and delightful storyteller with a dry wit and has made the rounds of the lecture tour in the state including The Minnesota Press Club and The Women's Club of Minneapolis, speaking to packed houses as his readers have turned out to honor a celebrated native son.

Thomas Heggen

Born 23 December 1919,
Fort Dodge, Iowa
Died 19 May 1949,
New York City, NY

Thomas Heggen was one of the celebrity columnists of the *Minnesota Daily* student newspaper at the University of Minnesota prior to World War II. He, Max Shulman, and Ted Peterson would duel through articles in the *Daily* and the student body loved it. Heggen's column was called "Saturday's Child;" Peterson's was "Not That It Mattered;" and Shulman's "Sauce for the Gander." They also wrote for *Ski-U-Mah*, a campus humor magazine, and they all studied journalism with professor Mitchell Charnley. Heggen also wrote for the *Literary Review*, the campus literary magazine. Upon graduation each served in the armed forces during World War II with Heggen joining the navy, Shulman the army and Peterson the air force. As a senior Heggen was copy desk editor of the *Daily*.

Professor Charnley said, "Heggen was a writer of the comedy of the pathetic. He could write funny things that could almost make you cry. Peterson was more the kind of guy who wrote the humor of ideas. Shulman wrote the comedy of exaggeration and of contrasting the sensible and the nonsensical." Charnley suspected that Heggen and Shulman might become celebrated writers but was more surprised when Peterson became a renowned communications theorist and expert on twentieth century magazines. He went on to be the Dean of the College of Communications at the University of Illinois. Shulman, (who has his own entry in this book), wrote several popular novels, a couple of Broadway plays, television plays, and a screenplay.

Heggen fell in right away with a smart crowd of wits and writers. Martin Quigley became a public relations consultant in St. Louis; Victor Cohn a staff writer for the *Minneapolis Tribune*; Norman Katkov a fiction and script writer of some prominence following the success of his novel, *Eagel at My Eye*. Bud Nye was a close friend of Shulman's who helped Max write the "Dobie Gillis" scripts. He became an ad executive in New York and his book of fame is *Home Is If You Find It*.

Harry Reasoner, from West High School, was another colleague. He wrote about his experiences at the U in *Tell Me about Women* and later became famous on CBS's *60 Minutes*. Reasoner, slightly geeky at the time and younger than the rest, was a favorite target of Heggen's acerbic wit. Russell Roth, later a copy editor with the *Minneapolis Star*, knew this crowd well from his student days. "Peterson was kind of low-key and didn't hang out much around the paper," Roth said. "Shulman and Heggen were both crazy. Zany, Shulman liked to call it, but they were very different. Heggen was the archetypal stoic Midwestern guy whereas Shulman was a street-smart, hip, urban kid." And then there was *Daily* editor Charles Roberts, who provided Heggen the name he needed for his navy stories. The *Ski-U-Mah* back room in Pillsbury Hall was where their "bull sessions" took place. Peterson got the best marks but Heggen, Shulman, et al. were very competitive as writers.

The Thomas O. Heggen, Sr. family lived at 4621 Beard Avenue South while Tom was at the U for his junior and senior years, 1939 to 1941. He had transferred up here from Oklahoma A & M College where he did his sophomore year, having started at Oklahoma City University. Tom had two sisters. Upon graduation he went to work for the editorial staff of *Reader's Digest* until he joined the navy, serving four years in pure boredom. It was the grueling boredom which triggered the writing of the sketches which became *Mister Roberts*. He was discharged in October of 1945 and returned to his old job at *Reader's Digest*.

Tom Heggen had an unusually talented mentor, his uncle Wallace Stegner. Stegner was a professor of journalism at Stanford University, where he also started the creative writing program. (One of his classes included neophyte authors Robert Stone, Ken Kesey, and Larry McMurtry.) Stegner wrote a number of distinguished novels himself, and was often referred to as the Dean of Western Writers.

In the winter of 1945-46 Tom paid a call on Uncle Wallace and gave him the rough draft of *Mister Roberts*, saying, "Here's a half-assed novel I've written." He was not trying to humorous with this nonchalant remark. How much Uncle Wallace helped or not is not known, but Houghton-Mifflin did pick up the book's publishing rights and released segments of it in the *Atlantic Monthly* magazine in three spring issues.

Meanwhile, Shulman had scored early successes with *Barefoot Boy with Cheek* (1943) followed by *The Feather Merchants* (1944) and *The Zebra Derby* (1946). In 1946 *Mister Roberts* appeared to high acclaim. Theater and film director Joshua Logan and Tom co-wrote the play, *Mister Roberts*, which opened in 1948 and ran for five years. It won all the major theater prizes for the 1948 season. In 1955 the film was made starring Henry Fonda, who also played the first three seasons of the play. It, too, was a smash hit.

A cozy situation occurred with the casting of *Mister Roberts* as there was a strong contingent of Minnesotans in the cast. Minneapolis-born Ralph Meeker was awarded the duty of understudying the title role as well as be a crewman; Duluth-born Charles Nolte was a crewman as was Albert Lea-born Richard Carlson. For Fonda, too, it was "old home week" because he had been close friends with Joshua Logan since their New England summer stock days fifteen years earlier.

Yes, it was great. Even with Tom sitting up in a corner of the balcony with his head most of the time half in a waste basket, it was great. Henry Fonda as Roberts won the Tony for Most Outstanding Portrayal of the season (1948). He also won the Baxter Award and the Academy of Arts and Letters Award.

But Heggen himself found it difficult to come up with a second literary gem to match his navy hit, and in May of 1949, a combination of sleeping pills and excessive alcohol put him to sleep in his tub where he drowned. Whether the death was accidental or intentional has never been established conclusively, and never will be, though many who knew Tom well, including his roommate, Alan Campbell, (former husband of the witty writer Dorothy Parker) rule out the possibility of suicide.

Tom was engaged to Franny when he left for New York. He never wrote her but instead asked his sister, Carmen, to let her know that he was now married to Carol Lynn Gilmer of Oklahoma. They had divorced before he died. His parents and sisters survived him. He left his parents an estate of $557,067 plus a one percent interest in the receipts of the Broadway play *South Pacific*.

Max Shulman claimed to have discovered Heggen "under a large flat stone behind Pattee Hall." Max asked, "What do you think of the Pacific Ocean." Heggen replied, "Oh, about average, I guess." Professor Charnley remembered this, too, about Heggen, "A very sweet, innocent, just angelic-faced girl who worked at the *Daily*, went out of the door of the office to visit the women's room. Heggen ran down the hall and put his hand across the door in front of her and said, 'No one as ethereal and sweet as you could ever have a use for a place like this.'"

Murphy Hall, The journalism building at the University of Minnesota, has had the Heggen Room adjoining its library for some forty years in commemoration of the writer of the blockbuster bestseller, *Mister Roberts*.

(Harry) Sinclair Lewis

Born 7 February 1885,
Sauk Centre, MN
Died 10 January 1951,
Rome, Italy

The first American winner of the Nobel Prize for Literature was Sinclair Lewis. He and F. Scott Fitzgerald both burst into the literary world in 1920 with runaway best sellers. *Main Street* was Lewis's gem and *This Side of Paradise* was Fitzgerald's. While Fitzgerald's book was a middle-weight champion, selling 40,000 copies in its first year, Lewis' book sold 180,000 in its first six months—the heavyweight champion for 1920-21.

Harry Sinclair "Red" Lewis easily has the Minnesota record for books made into movies with nine: *Free Air* (1922); *Mantrap* (1926) starring Clara Bow (the original "It Girl"); *Arrowsmith* (1931) starring Ronald Colman and Helen Hayes; *Ann Vickers* (1933) with Irene Dunne and Walter Huston; *Babbitt* (1934) with Guy Kibbee and Aline MacMahon; *Dodsworth* (1936) with Walter Huston and Mary Astor; *I Married a Doctor* (1936, based on *Main Street*) with Pat O'Brien and Josephine Hutchinson; *Untamed* (1940, based on *Mantrap*) with Ray Milland; *Cass Timberlane* (1947) with Spencer Tracy and Lana Turner; and *Elmer Gantry* (1960) with Burt Lancaster, Jean Simmons, and Shirley Jones, who won the Oscar for Best Supporting Actress.

Sinclair's parents, Dr. Edwin John and Mrs. Emma (Kermott) Lewis had arrived in Sauk Centre in 1883 from Ironton, Wisconsin. Edwin was a man of accomplishments, strict habits, self-discipline, and he wanted his son to be the same. Instead, Sinclair loved art, travel, and adventure. Sinclair's mother died in 1891 when he was six. His father remarried to a kind, caring woman who liked to travel and often took Sinclair with her. As was common in that day Dr. Lewis officed in his home at 811 Third Avenue until 1889 when they moved across the street to 812 Third Ave. where Sinclair lived until he left home. There was a waiting room and a treatment room, and patients came and went all day. Today Third Avenue is now named Sinclair Lewis Avenue.

Young Red Lewis graduated from Sauk Centre High School, spent six months at Oberlin Academy, and entered Yale University in 1903, graduating in 1908. He did not distinguish himself as a student but was a voracious reader. He was also editor of Yale's literary quarterly. In the summers of both 1904 and 1906 he worked his way to London on cattle boats, and in 1907 he took the entire year off to go around the world.

For the next eight years Lewis worked as a journalist in Waterloo, Iowa; New York City; Carmel, California; San Francisco; Washington, D.C.; and back to New York for a longer stay. He was ever restless and stayed that way. He worked as an assistant editor and advertising manager for the publisher George H. Doran Company, 1914-1915, and while there he married Grace Livingston Hegger, who worked for *Vogue* magazine. He had just published his first novel, *Our Mr. Wrenn* (1914), based on his cattle boat voyages, and it enjoyed a degree of critical success, though the royalties were meager.

He published a few stories in the *Saturday Evening Post* which brought him some solid earnings, and his next book, *The Trail of the Hawk* (1915), based on his own courtship and marriage, also did fairly well. He quit Doran to move back to Sauk Centre with Grace to write *The Job* (1917), about social turmoil and injustices in the workplace. Then he fitted out a Model T Ford into a camper and drove with Grace to California and back to New York. *Free Air* (1919), is based on some of these experiences.

With *Main Street* Lewis reached a new pinnacle of success and literary achievement. The title itself became a metaphor for provincial, small-town thinking and values. The book struck a chord with soldiers who had returned from the war in Europe with new ideas about worldliness and provincialism. It helped instigate the "revolt from the village" by those who'd been suppressed in their desire to find their individuality in manner, dress, taste, or thought. In short, the timing for the book was perfect, even if the prose left a little to be desired.

The citizens of Sauk Centre were not unduly thrilled by the unappealing light Lewis had cast on their community. The author himself probably just chuckled about it. The success of the book made him an international celebrity. He began taking frequent trips to Europe, and now he traveled first class. No more cattle boats. He met English writers such as Rebecca West who was charmed by his nonstop, high-powered conversation. Though he always had a complexion problem she overlooked that to comment that he was super-human "as a great natural force, like the aurora borealis." He could charm people off their feet but he had moody fits, too, and could be savagely rude.

Lewis's next novel, *Babbitt*, drew even greater critical praise than *Main Street*. It was focused on a central character, real estate man

George Babbitt, rather than an entire community, and Lewis fully displayed his command of catch-phrases and jargon in his rendering of Babbitt's conversation.

For the next ten years Lewis continued to produce very popular novels at a steady rate, choosing "themes" around which to weave his plots. In *Arrowsmith* (1925) the title character finds salvation in his reverence for science. With *Elmer Gantry* (1927) Lewis satirized evangelical religion. The book was censured in Boston and denounced by clerics of all faiths, though Lewis's attack was focused on a form of religious hucksterism that is still alive and well today.

In time Lewis became, along with Hemingway, Dos Passos, and other young writers, a part of the rough new generation that chronicled an entirely different world than the one made familiar by patrician novelists such as Edith Wharton, Henry James, or William Dean Howells. His voice of satire was fresh and vital—some say that it is unmatched in American literature until the arrival of Philip Roth's *Portnoy's Complaint*.

Lewis's last book of the decade was *Dodsworth* (1929). It depicts the daily life of an ill-matched couple traveling in Europe. Following a crisis Dodsworth finds a new woman companion who helps him to understand how practical work and art can be combined to form a worthwhile career.

Sinclair himself divorced his wife Grace in 1928 and married journalist Dorothy Thompson later that year after a whirlwood courtship. They had met in Europe. They produced a son, Michael, born in 1930. For many years it was a satisfying, intellectual marriage though it dissolved eventually. Lewis moved to new living quarters every year or two including Duluth, Lowry Hill in Minneapolis, and Excelsior.

An amusing note is that Sinclair Lewis settled in Excelsior in 1950 with hopes of staging a play he'd written at the Old Log Theatre, but manager-director Don Stolz, to his perpetual chagrin over fifty years later, told him it was not stageworthy. He has laughed in a self-chiding way, saying, "How do you tell a Nobel Prize winner that his script isn't good enough to be staged?" Don was young enough then to be brash and foolish. An older Don Stolz would have worked elbow to elbow with Lewis to make it stage worthy. The next year Lewis was dead.

Lewis did have a few of his plays staged in New York or elsewhere earlier in his career: *Hobohemia* (1919); *Dodsworth* (1934, adapted from his book by Sidney Howard); *Jayhawker: A Play in Three Acts* (1935); *It Can't Happen Here* (1938, from his novel); and *Angela Is Twenty-Two* with Fay Wray (1938, in Columbus, Ohio).

Even before Lewis hit it big with *Main Street* his early stories and novels were attracting attention in Hollywood. His debut film, *Nature Incorporated* (1916), came from a short story, as did *The Unpainted Woman* (1919). His first filmed novel, *Free Air* (1922), came also from this "apprentice" period of writing.

Silent film stars Monte Blue and Florence Vidor played Dr. Will and Carol Kennicott in *Main Street* (1923), by which time the novel had sold half a million copies. Also in 1923 appeared another filmed short story, *The Ghost Patrol. Babbitt* (1924) followed, with Willard Louis and Mary Alden.

During the thirties the film studios found better ways to present Lewis's often ascerbic vision of American life. The sonorous-voiced Ronald Colman starred in *Arrowsmith* (1931), the portrait of a man committed to the sacred exactness of science in an age ruled by gossip and opinions based on hot air. A number of his later novels, though not so well regarded as those of the twenties, were also made into popular films, including *Ann Vickers* (1933); *It Can't Happen Here* (1935) and *Kingsblood Royal* (1947). *Cass Timberlane: A Novel of Husbands and Wives* (1945) became a popular movie. Lewis remained in the public eye throughout his adult life.

Red drank more heavily with the passage of time, however, and never seemed to find a place where he could settle and be happy. He was always on the move and drinking lots of booze when he got there, only to realize soon enough that he needed to go somewhere else. He remained dissatisfied with many things including himself, and he could find no peace or soulful sofa where he could kick off his shoes and rest; and that spirit haunts the characters in his books, too.

When Lewis became the first American to win the Nobel prize, part of the citation read, "Sinclair Lewis…for his vigorous and graphic art of description and his ability to create, with wit and humor, new types of characters." To many Europeans, Lewis was America, brash, bright, and highly energetic, especially in his condemnations but also in his praise of this or that. He was America's first international icon and cultural ambassador-at-large to Europe. He was a free-spirited American who said what was on his mind; he was listened to and praised for it.

Tim O'Brien

Born 1 October 1946,
Austin, MN

Most critics agree that Timothy O'Brien is the best literary spokesman of the Vietnam War
experience. But for O'Brien that
war-time experience "was the dark,
jarring experience that made [me] a
writer." He described the war as the "Lone Ranger watershed event
of my life." Upon graduating from Macalester College in St. Paul, he
could not decide whether to flee to Canada to escape the military
draft or to submit to it and serve his country in the armed forces. He
chose to serve.

O'Brien served in Vietnam from January, 1969 to March, 1970,
in the Fifth Battalion, Forty-Sixth Infantry of the U. S. Army's Ameri-
cal Division, which patrolled the deadly Batangan Peninsula and the
villages of My Lai after the massacre in the area in March, 1968. A
wound ended his tour of duty, but he returned to America sound in
mind, body, and spirit—unlike many of his peers. As this "watershed
event" percolated in his brain, he jotted everything down as a personal memoir, including clippings out of newspapers and magazine
articles about the war, and then found a publisher. *If I Die in a Combat
Zone, Box Me Up and Ship Me Home* was issued in 1973.

In O'Brien's first novel, *Northern Lights* (1975), the war serves as
a backdrop for a story involving two brothers who survive a disastrous skiing trip in the wilds of Northern Minnesota. For his second,
Going after Cacciato (1978), he faces the war experience head-on. The
men in a platoon pursue a deserter but the chase seems more men-
tal than physical. The soldiers develop greater skills in imagination
and can visualize better both the terrible reality of Vietnam and their
own ability to endure it. As they pursue the deserter, many scenarios
are played out in the soldiers' minds, and the horrors of their daily
existence create the fabric upon which the tale unfolds. Thoughts of
sentry duty, ambush, patrol, and death weave their way in and out of
Cacciato's escape.

Going after Cacciato (1978), won the National Book Award, and
it was natural that Hollywood would begin to sift through O'Brien's
novels and short stories for material. His novel *In the Lake of the
Woods* (1994) was filmed for TV in 1996, with Peter Strauss, Kathleen

Quinlan, and Peter Boyle; Strauss plays John Waylan who loses a bid for the U. S. Senate as a result of allegations relating to his experience as an officer in Vietnam. He and his wife, Kathy, retreat to the Minnesota north woods to examine his life and also their marriage. Then Kathy disappears. O'Brien has said that in this "postmodern" detective novel he explored what "deceit can do to the human heart," that there so often are secrets husbands and wives hide from each other, secrets that torment later, and that men and women never really truly know one another regardless of how long they've been together.

Two years later one of O'Brien's short stories, "Sweetheart of the Song Tra Bong" was filmed as *A Soldier's Sweetheart* (1998) with Kiefer Sutherland and Georgina Cates. Sutherland is a medic in Vietnam who moves his girlfriend to his outpost. When she disappears he must go out and search for her.

O'Brien has contributed stories for *Esquire*, *Redbook*, *Harper's*, *Gentlemen's Quarterly*, *McCall's* and Prize Stories of 1976, 1978 and 1982 besides penning five novels and a book of short stories, *The Things They Carried* (1990). *The Nuclear Age* (1981) and *Tomcat in Love* (1998) are his other novels. He graduated summa cum laude in political science from Macalester in 1968. He won a Purple Heart in Vietnam. He was a reporter for the *Washington Post* (1971-1974). Besides winning the National Book Award (1978), he won the Bread Loaf Writers Conference award; and a National Endowment for the Arts award. He also did graduate school studies at Harvard University. In 1973 he married Ann Elizabeth Weller; they divorced in 1995.

While O'Brien is labeled a "war writer," he argues that "war stories aren't about war—they are about the human heart at war." His fictional portrayals of the Vietnam War vividly brought the fears, horrors and torment of wartime experience to the wilderness of Minnesota and beyond.

O'Brien grew up in Worthington. When he was nine years old, he wrote "Timmy of the Little League." His life is simple and disciplined, working from early morning to dinner time including weekends. He is the son of William T. (an insurance salesman) and Ava E. (a teacher) (Schultz) O'Brien.

Larry McCaffery of the Chicago Review asked O'Brien what could he teach people about war, after having witnessed a good deal of violence and death. He replied that you must try to instill some insight and wisdom but experience doesn't make someone a teacher. Instead of teaching "I wanted to use stories to alert readers to the complexity and ambiguity of a set of moral issues—but without preaching a moral lesson."

Martha Ostenso

Born 17 September 1900,
Bergen, Norway
Died 24 November 1963,
Seattle (or Tacoma), WA

Martha Ostenso's award-winning book, *Wild Geese*, (1925) was filmed three times, in 1927, 1961 and 2001, truly a testament to the timeless quality of the novel. What was the award she won? Dodd, Mead, and Company chose her novel as the best that year among 1,700 entries, and she received a cash prize of $13,500. That amount would perhaps be $75,000 today. Ostenso wrote seventeen other books but only one was filmed, *And They Shall Walk: The Life Story of Sister Elizabeth Kenny.* The title of the film was simply **Sister Kenny** (1946) starring Rosalind Russell as the great polio fighter-nurse from the Australian bush.

Martha's family immigrated to the United States in 1902 and moved north to Canada in 1915, settling on a large farm in the rural Manitoba area. Her parents were Sigurd Brigt and Lena (Tungeland) Ostenso. In 1918 she went to the University in Manitoba to become a teacher, and she eventually took a job in Hayland, in the interlake area. She later worked as a reporter for the *Manitoba Free Press*, and in 1922 she moved to New York City to study fiction writing at Columbia University. She went with Douglas Leader Durkin, who had been one of her English professors at the University of Manitoba. Durkin supplied her with plots and edited her finished manuscripts. Their relationship remained fruitful and they eventually married on December 16, 1944. While living in New York she also worked as a social worker in Brooklyn.

Ostenso's work deals with life in the Canadian West and American Midwest, a genre sometimes referred to as Prairie Realism. Both she and Douglas had lived in many small towns in Minnesota, Manitoba, Wisconsin, and the Dakotas, and these experiences provided the fodder for her books Her themes are the will to power, rebellion, self-searching, marital strife, and the relationships of people to the land.

When Martha's first book, *A Far Land*, appeared in 1924, a reviewer from the Boston Transcript described the poems as "clear and vivid," and James Roty of the Nation said, "Miss Ostenso's product is genuine and personal. She has her own way of listening to the world and of responding to it with a delicate falling music."

Those talents were clearly in evidence in *Wild Geese*, which depicts the struggles of a farm girl to escape her father's punishing work routine and repressive parental oversight of her personal life. With the help of a more sophisticated girlfriend, the heroine finally escapes to the city.

Minnesota's Belle Bennett starred in the 1927 film as our heroine's mother—a roll she had already done so well in **Stella Dallas** (1925) and a half dozen other films. Russell Simpson played the domineering father. (Russell also played Henry Fonda's Okie father in **The Grapes of Wrath**). The silent, black-and-white film was seventy minutes long.

Ostenso churned out a long succession of popular novels followed the success of *Wild Geese*, including *The Dark Dawn* (1926), *The Young May Moon* (1929) and *The Mandrake Root* (1938) in which we see a professor drawn to the wiles of the sexually aggressive wife of a pious farmer. *O River Remember!* (1943) follows the tribulations of a farm family in the Red River Valley.

During the 1930s, due to the success of these and other novels, Martha and Douglas typically earned between $30,000-40,000 per year on book royalties alone. Perhaps due to their hardscrabble early years, the couple went in for the luxurious life in a big way, owning stylish cars, boats, and homes in Beverly Hills. In 1931 they built a lavish lodge home on Wilson Bay of Gull Lake near Brainerd, where they entertained Henry Fonda, John Barrymore, Douglas Fairbanks ,and Mary Pickford.

Wild Geese was largely ignored in Canada until the mid-1940s when Clara Thomas did an anthology on Canadian writers and Ostenso's book was praised as a classic depiction of the hard life in the Canadian West. However, because of her early success with writing in America, where she was assured of a literary career, Ostenso never moved back to Canada.

Ostenso worked with Sister Kenney herself on her second filmed book, *And They Shall Walk: The Life Story of Sister Elizabeth Kenny*. Alexander Knox wrote the screenplay, and the film's producer and director, Dudley Nichols, assisted in the adaptation. The story of Sister Kenny's struggles to gain acceptance for her novel methods of treating polio in the face of the conservative medical establishment was one that paralleled Ostenso's own early struggles. Perhaps the story also appealed to Ostenso because of it's Midwest connections. It was in Minnesota that Sister Kenny finally found support and encouragement for her techniques. In 1943, with the encouragement of local hospitals and University of Minnesota staff, she founded the Elizabeth Kenny Institute in Minneapolis. That institution later merged with Northwestern Hospital in South Minneapolis and continues to be a viable treatment center for polio and other musculo-skeletal degenerative diseases.

Some of you may have wondered why two people, so much in love as Martha and Douglas were, waited to marry until 1944. The answer is simple. Douglas had been married but estranged from his wife the whole time he knew Martha. When he became free in 1944, they promptly married, and were together until her death. The last years were rough sailing. Martha eventually declined into alcoholism, and she died of cirrhosis of the liver in 1963.

Two years before her death, Germany and Austria joined together to make *Ruf der Wildgänse* which was *The Cry of the Wild Geese* in the U.S. TV title. Coming full circle, the Canadians made an adaptation called *After the Harvest* for TV in 2001. This production starred Sam Shepard as Caleb Gare.

Anne Tyler

*Born 25 October 1941,
Minneapolis, MN*

A nne lived at 64 Bedford in Apt. 6 in Minneapolis until the age of six when her Quaker family moved to Raleigh, North Carolina. Her father, Lloyd Parry Tyler, was an industrial chemist with the Minnesota Highway Department-Lab and her mother, Phyllis Mahon Tyler, was a social worker. Anne began writing short stories at age seven. Her favorite childhood book was *The Little House* by Virginia Lee Burton. She credits this book with showing her "how the world worked, how the years flowed by and people altered and nothing could ever stay the same." Eudora Welty, a noted Southern short story writer, was the other main influence on her. Her favorite books are *Anna Karenina, Pride and Prejudice,* and *The Great Gatsby.*

Tyler attended Duke University in Durham, North Carolina, graduating Phi Beta Kappa at nineteen in 1961. At Duke she twice won the Anne Flexner Award for Creative Writing and the school's literary magazine, the *Archive*, published her first story, "Laura." She did graduate work in Russian studies at Columbia University and worked a year as a bibliographer of Russian materials at Duke, ordering books from the Soviet Union. In 1963 she married Taghi Modaressi, an Iranian-born psychiatrist ten years her senior. The marriage ended with his death in 1997. Anne has two grown daughters she still lives in Baltimore, Maryland, the setting of many of her novels.

The *New Yorker*, the *Saturday Evening Post*, *Redbook*, *McCall's*, and *Harper's* have published Ms. Tyler's short stories. Her first published novel was *If Morning Ever Comes* (1964). In 1967 she became a full-time writer. A few of her novels are *Earthly Possessions* (1977, which won an American Academy Award); *Morgan's Passing* (1980); *Dinner at the Homesick Restaurant* (1982); *Ladder of Years* (1996); *A Patchwork Planet* (1998); and *The Amateur Marriage* (2003). Her nineteenth and most recent book is *Digging to America* (2006).

Tyler's tenth novel, *The Accidental Tourist* (1985), opened Hollywood's doors to her and since then six of her books have been made into films. It was filmed in 1988 with William Hurt, Kathleen Turner, Geena Davis, directed by Lawrence Kasdan. Hurt (Macon Leary) writes travel guides for businessmen who hate to travel. He is devastated by his son's death in a fast food diner and tunes out of life. His wife leaves him. He finds a new love interest (Davis) and lives with her and her son, then learns that his wife wants him back. The film was nominated for a Best Picture Oscar, Best Musical Score and Best Screenplay. Geena Davis won the Best Actress Oscar.

In 1989 Tyler won the Pulitzer Prize for Fiction for *Breathing Lessons,* the story of a long-married couple who finally come to grips with their problems during a 90-mile trip to a friend's funeral. It was filmed for TV in 1994. Her other books-into-film for TV are *Saint Maybe* (1998), *A Slipping-Down Life* (1999), *Earthly Possessions* (1999), and *Back When We Were Grownups* (2004).

Guy Pearce plays North Carolina rock singer Drumsticks Casey in *A Slipping-Down Life* while Lili Taylor plays a shy, young Evie Decker, who is infatuated with him. The power of this attraction makes her come out of her shell.

Charlotte Emory (Susan Sarandon) in *Earthly Possessions* (1999), is a bored housewife who runs away from her minister-husband but is captured as a hostage by a bank robber (Stephen Dorff), becoming an accomplice to his escape. She learns that he needs money to rescue his pregnant girlfriend from a home for unwed mothers.

In *When We Were Grownups* (2001) Rebecca Davitch is the mother of a big family. She discovers that "she has turned into the wrong person." She is a grandmother who is "wide and soft and dimpled, with two short wings of dry, fair hair flaring almost horizontally from a center part." However, she believes it is not too late to make changes and tries to find her true self from her past.

How does Anne rate with other writers? Eudora Welty said, "If I could have written the last sentence of *Dinner at the Homesick Restaurant* I'd have been happy for the rest of my life." After reviewing five of her early novels for the *New Yorker*, John Updike remarked, "She's not merely good, she's wickedly good." She was the only woman on *Time* magazine's 1990 list of the ten best books of the 1980s.

The oldest of four children, Anne Tyler is reclusive and has no "guilty secrets or secret hobbies." She gets ideas while vacuuming and daydreaming. Lisa Allardice of the *Observer* wrote of her interview with Tyler on Sunday, January 4, 2002, "The morning after Anne Tyler won the Pulitzer Prize in 1989, she politely dismissed an inquisitive reporter with the explanation that she was too busy writing to talk; they had interrupted her in the middle of a sentence. She was 'allergic' to interviews. Tyler is a writer not a celebrity."

Will Weaver

Born 19 January 1950,
Park Rapids, MN

Will Weaver freely admits that he lives in the past and has lived there quite a bit of his adult life. That is not to say that he ignores the present or that he never thinks about the future, but memories of his growing-up years are as vivid as when he lived them. Compressed into a few short years, a teenager experiences the extreme of highs and lows, utterly sad days offset by completely joyous days. With this awareness always in mind Weaver has devoted much of his writing life to books for young adults with three novels and two books of short stories.

However, two works that he wrote for adults have caught the attention of film makers. His novel, *Red Earth, White Earth* (1986), was adapted for TV and aired on CBS in 1989. More recently, the title story from his collection, *A Gravestone Made of Wheat* (1989), was filmed in 2005 as *Sweet Land*. It was premiered October 22-23, 2005, at Hamptons International Film Festival where the film received the Audience Acclaim Award and Elizabeth Reaser won the prize for Best Newcomer. *Sweet Land* opened October 24, 2005, at the Riverview Theater in South Minneapolis for its Twin Cities' premiere.

The film details the life of a Norwegian-immigrant farmer in the years following World war I who discovers that his mail-order bride is not Norwegian but German. She arrives with great hopes for love, only to face quite a few obstacles put up by the tight-knit Norwegian community. The film also brushes across more recent farm generations, though its most appealing sections draw their strength from the rural immigrant experience.

Sweet Land was directed by Minnesota-trained Ali Selim, who had bought the film rights to the book ten years earlier. This independent feature was made with a budget of just over $1 million. Weaver himself appears in the film as a farmer, but he has no lines of dialogue. The production schedule was six days a week and twelve hours a day.

Chippewa County sites used during filming include the Pioneer Village, the Milwaukee Road Depot, the Swensson Farm Museum, and Heritage Hill, which has a fine collection of antique farm machinery. The majestic farmland and countryside around Montevideo also figures prominently in the film.

Will began teaching at Bemidji State University in 1979, and joined the staff full-time in 1981. Politically, he is a "progessive." He received his B.A. from the University of Minnesota, 1972, his M.A. from Stanford University, 1979. While studying at Stanford, he found his writing voice. To develop that voice he found it necessary to return to his roots and he has stayed in the Bemidji area ever since.

His avocations are mountain hiking, hunting, fishing, studying the short story form, and rock 'n' roll. He is the son of Harold Howard (a farmer) and Arlys A. (Swenson) Weaver. Will married Rosalie Mary Nonnemacher (a teacher), March 2, 1975. They have a boy and a girl, Caitlin Rose and Owen Harte Weaver. Weaver has been the recipient of numerous regional and national awards for both his adult and juvenile fiction. He feels that his mission is to educate people through his writing about disappearing life styles.

Laura Ingalls Wilder

Born 7 February 1867,
Pepin, WI
Died 10 Febray 1957,
Mansfield, MO

L aura Ingalls Wilder has only a fleeting connection with the world of film, but her books for children are prairie classics, and her story is well worth telling.

Her family moved often, living in Wisconsin (twice), Iowa, Minnesota (twice), South Dakota, Missouri, and Kansas by the time Laura Elizabeth was fourteen years old. Their stay in Walnut Grove was a bit longer than the rest of their stops, which is probably why it's featured in the popular television series based on her books, *Little House on the Prairie*, which ran for nine seasons between 1975 and 1984 (check).

During her infant years the family was forced to leave Kansas when they discovered their farm was located on Osage Indian land. In 1870 the entire family came down with malaria and nearly died so they returned to Pepin, Wisconsin, where Laura first attended school.

In 1874 her father, Charles Ingalls, sold the log cabin he had built from logs he felled himself and the family moved to Walnut Grove, where they lived in a cramped dugout house with a sunken floor and sod walls. The interior walls were eventually whitewashed.

Charles eventually built a wood-framed house, but he had to buy the lumber. There weren't enough trees in the vicinity to make a proper log cabin. The Ingalls settled on the banks of Plum Creek, a mile from the town of Walnut Grove where they were active in church activities, and Laura and Mary attended school. Grasshoppers, locusts, and the death of siblings, are a few of the hardships and disasters that plagued Laura's early years. Laura's sister Mary contracted a fever and became blind for life. Charles often left town in search of work, and at various times was a hotel keeper, a butcher, a carpenter, and even a Justice of the Peace. The occupations which most endeared him to his family were his fiddle playing and his storytelling.

Charles finally landed a well-paying job when his brother-in-law, who worked for the Chicago-Northwestern Railroad, offered him a position as a company storekeeper, bookkeeper, and timekeeper in De Smet, in Dakota Territory. Charles made a claim of 160 acres three miles from De Smet near Silver Lake. The Homestead Act allowed persons to own acreage outright if they cultivated it and built some kind of home in which the family lives for at least part of each of five years. Here Charles made a promise to his patient Caroline that he would move no more.

They barely survived the harsh winter of 1880-1881 as snow piled up to forty feet high on the tracks. When the spring thaws came in May, Laura took a job in town to earn money to send Mary to Iowa to a school for the blind. Laura was shy and found socializing diffi-cult, and she would often retreat to her books. She was a good student especially in English but she never graduated. Why?

At fifteen Laura was offered a teaching position at a small school fifteen miles from De Smet. She took a room at the Bouchie family. Shortly after she met Almanzo, ten years her senior. He took her to and from De Smet on weekends in his buckboard carriage. They became engaged in the summer of 1884 and were married a year later.

Laura was twenty-eight at the time. The couple moved to Man-sfield, Missouri, in the Ozark Mountains, where they settled and stayed. The couple had a daughter, Rose, born in 1886.

During the 1930s Laura decided to write down her family memo-ries, encouraged by many of the people who had heard her stories. Eight "Little House" books were published between 1932 and 1943. Her earliest memories, which appear in *Little House in the Big Woods* (1932) were of the years in Pepin, Wisconsin, but the others are devoted largely to prairie living. The second book, about their life in Independence, Kansas, was *Little House on the Prairie* (1935) followed by *On the Banks of Plum Creek* (1937), which details their life in Wal-nut Grove. The next book, about their life in De Smet, South Dakota, was *Little Town on the Prairie* (1941).

The other Little House books are *Farmer Boy* (1933), Laura's meeting Almanzo; *By the Shores of Silver Lake* (1939); *The Long Win-ter* (1940); and *These Happy Golden Years* (1943). When Laura wrote the series had no idea of the fame she would attract, though her books have by now been translated into more than forty languages

Since Laura lived just past her ninetieth birthday, we really reach into pioneer history in discussing her and her family. Her father was born in 1836 and her mother on December 12, 1839. They were married February 1, 1860, so her parents were married more than 150 years ago. Though Laura went on an occasional book tour, her life remained relatively unchanged as a farm wife, though her fan mail grew steadily from year to year.

Bits of trivia: Laura was the first woman to fly across the United States. She made a nine-stop trip from Roosevelt Field in New York to Glendale, California. Charles Ingalls was related to Mary Ingles, a Mayflower passenger whose story is told in the book and film, *Follow the River*. Laura outlived all her siblings. Mary died in 1928; Carrie in 1946; and Grace in 1941. Almanzo, her darling Manly, died October 23, 1949, after sixty-four years of marriage Sadly, he outlived three of his four daughters. Their only son lived only a few days after birth and died August 10, 1889.

L aura's pioneer tales got a new lease on life when they came to the attention of actor Michael Landon. He felt they had a good deal of promise, and he convinced NBC to give him almost total control of the TV series that became *Little House on the Prairie*. He not only starred as Laura's father, but was also executive producer and a frequent writer of the shows, which ran for nine seasons from 1974 to 1983. Although the story-lines bear little resemblance to those in Wilder's work, this is the version most widely known to people today.

After such popularity on TV it was natural that a movie should come from it. Finally, in 2000 one was made for TV: ***Beyond the Prairie: The True Story of Laura Ingalls Wilder*** with Richard Thomas, Lindsay Crouse, Barbara Jane Reams, and Tess Harper.

There is a cozy, log cabin-styled Laura Ingalls Wilder Center in Pepin, Wisconsin, her place of birth, and it is full of bric-a-brac related to her history. Wilder was inducted into the Hall of Famous Missourians in 1993 and there is a Laura Ingalls Wilder Library in Mansfield, Missouri. Walnut Grove also has its own cozy tourist center, complete with a facsimile of the original sod hut the family lived in there.

August Wilson

*Frederick August Kittel
Born 27 April 1945,
Pittsburgh, PA
Died 2 October 2005,
Seattle, WA*

The best playwright of the Baby Boomer generation was August Wilson, who lived some twenty years in St. Paul. He became the voice for the African-American experience in the late twentieth Century. Wilson won two Pulitzer Prizes, for *Fences* and *The Piano Lesson*; six New York Drama Critics Circle Awards; a Drama Desk Award; a Whiting Writers Award; and a Tony. He also received Rockefeller and Guggenheim Fellowships in Playwriting. Shows what you can do with a ninth-grade education!

August grew up with five siblings in the Hill District of Pittsburgh. His black mother, Daisy Wilson of North Carolina, was resilient and principled, and his white, German-immigrant father was abusive, though seldom at home.. He was bright in school but he dropped out in the ninth grade after being falsely accused of plagiarism by a bigoted teacher. By then he knew that he wanted to be a poet, and he continued his education reading voraciously at the public library.

Wilson began his creative life as a poet. With $20 earned from writing his sister's term paper, he bought a Royal typewriter which he carried everywhere. He was inspired by the Black Arts Movement and the Civil Rights Movement in the 1960s, and labeled himself a Black Nationalist. In 1968 he co-founded the Black Horizons Theater on the Hill and wrote and directed there over the next ten years.

Theater director/actor Claude Purdy invited Wilson to move to St. Paul, which he did in 1978. He just fell in love with St. Paul with its civilities like Summit Avenue and heated bus shelters. The next year he landed a job writing historical skits for the Science Museum of Minnesota. He and Judy Oliver, his second wife, lived in an apartment on Selby Avenue until 1990. In 1977 a good friend of Purdy's, Lou Bellamy, founded and became artistic director of the Penumbra Theatre in St. Paul. He staged Wilson's debut play, *Black Bart and the Sacred Hills*, in 1981. This satirical Western was adapted from

162

his earlier poems. Bellamy knew a good thing when he saw it, and continued to support Wilson's talent by staging his plays.

In 1982 Wilson was writing the first draft of *Ma Rainey's Black Bottom* and working as a cook for Little Brothers of the Poor on Lake Street in Minneapolis. He was also a cook at Nora's on Lake St. across from Lake Calhoun. Cooking was his main source of income during his twenty years in Saint Paul, and he was good at it. That same year he wrote *Jitney* in ten days—in bars on St. Paul's Cathedral Hill. The Minneapolis Playwrights Center (Lab) submitted the play to the Jerome Foundation which awarded Wilson $2,400 on a Jerome Fellowship to have his play, about a 1970s Gypsy cab station in Pittsburg, read professionally.

Though he had sent plays to the National Playwrights Conference of the O'Neill Theatre Center in New Haven, Connecticut, and been rejected each time, *Ma Rainey's Black Bottom* was accepted for a workshop in 1982. This began a long association with Lloyd Richards, head of the Playwrights Conference and Dean of the Yale School of Drama. By 1983 the play was fully developed and staged at the Yale Repertory Theatre. It made its debut on Broadway in 1984 running for 275 performances and winning the New York Drama Critics Circle Award. Ma Rainey was Wilson's first commercial success.

The play is set in a Chicago recording studio in 1927. The drama turns on a power struggle between Ma, a black singing star, her lead musician, and the white recording studio boss. A fiery trumpeter adds to the mix of the play's tensions. Penumbra staged it in 1987. It became the first of ten plays designed to tell the story of the African-American experience in each decade of the century.

Whoopi Goldberg starred as Ma Rainey in a re-staging on Broadway in 1997. Imagine her saying these words, "White folks don't understand about the blues. They hear it come out, but they don't know how it got there. They don't understand that's life's way of talking. You don't sing to feel better. You sing 'cause that's a way of understanding life."

Fences was staged on Broadway in 1987. It focuses on a character named Troy Maxson who learned to play baseball in prison but was barred from playing in the major leagues because of his color. Though a talented athlete, he is forced to earn his living as a sanitation worker. Adding further dimension to the story is the fact that Troy's son wants an athletic scholarship, something unthinkable in Troy's day.

Fences won the 1987 Pulitzer Prize. James Earl Jones originated the role of Troy Maxson.

Joe Turner's Come and Gone won the New York Drama Critics Circle Award. It opened at the Yale Repertory Theatre in 1986 and on Broadway in 1988.

The Piano Lesson was a finalist for the Pulitzer in 1989, and won it in 1990, along with the New York Drama Critics Circle Award. It's about a brother who comes home to collect his half from the sale of the family piano, only to fins that his sister, slated to receive the other half, doesn't want to part with it.

Two Trains Running enjoyed critical success and won the New York Drama Critics Circle Award. It's main character is a waitress who scars her legs to ward off skirt-chasing men. Lawrence Fishburne and Cynthia Martells starred in the original staging.

Wilson's plays are full of traditionalism, African-American art and ritual, but they also have linear narrative and serious dramatic tension. Most theater-goers are white, however, and Wilson urged black communities to build and develop theaters for their neighborhoods to get the black people involved, to expand the theater's voice, and make fuller connections with the black community generally.

Lou Bellamy credits Wilson as being one of the Penumbra Theater's longest and most loyal supporters, "Everybody knows that Claude brought him here and one half hour after he got off the plane from Pittsburgh, August was sitting in here. But what they don't know is that the play wasn't pulling very well, and August used to come every night with his wife just to sit in the audience and help us. It was just to fill up a seat but he wanted to help.

"He has always been very generous to us. His name does so much. Most of our national recognition comes from our relationship with him. We are mentioned in his biography in theater programs." Yes, a Wilson play helps pay the bills in any theater. Penumbra Theatre is now a nationally renowned.

An exciting partnership occurred between the Guthrie Theatre and Penumbrain 1997, as Joe Dowling, Guthrie's Artisitic Director, opened its doors to let Penumbra stage *Fences*. Penumbra had total artistic control and the Guthrie provided the marketing and promotion. The play was a success on every level.

On the other hand, Wilson's associations with Hollywood have been shaky at best. *The Piano Lesson* (1990) was a made-for-TV movie. August wrote the teleplay and produced. It was aired on Hallmark Hall of Fame, CBS, February 5, 1995. Charles S. Dutton starred as Boy Willie; Alfre Woodard played his sister, Berniece Charles. Carl Gordon played the role of Doaker.

Film rights for *Fences* were optioned by Eddie Murphy in 1988 but the project never got going. Wilson wrote a screenplay for Murphy but in 1998, after ten years, the film option expired. Paramount Studio picked up the movie rights to *Fences* but nothing has come of that either. There was a snag in that Wilson insisted that a black director do the film, suggesting Lloyd Richards, who had been involved in shaping Wilson's plays for Broadway time and again.

Some very important people wanted to film *Joe Turner's Come and Gone* and do you know who they were? Harry Belafonte bought the film rights. In the cast would be himself, Sidney Poitier, Morgan Freeman, Denzel Washington and Danny Glover. "There shouldn't be any problem getting money to put those five guys in a film," Wilson said. Yet, it was never filmed.

August's first wife was Brenda Burton, a Muslim nurse. They were married in 1969, and divorced three years later. They have a daughter, Sakina Ansari. Wilson had no children with his second wife, Judy Oliver, a social worker (1981-1990). His third wife was costume designer Constanza Romero (1994-his death); they had a daughter, Azula Carmen.

August Wilson was the subject of a British-made documentary in 1990 after winning his second Pulitzer (for *The Piano Lesson*). Constantly in search of the "black experience in America," Wilson said, "We are Africans in America. We are blacks in America, and we should be allowed to be that. And it's rather ridiculous, really, if you've ever seen anything like this, where you have an African on stage and you're asking him to deny that he's African." From this statement it's obvious he is opposed to colorblind casting—putting black actors into non-black roles. Lou Bellamy has also opposed the practice.

When he was poor and unknown, Wilson always had plenty of time to write or stroll down Selby Avenue. After his second Pulitzer, he had no time for himself at all. It was stressful to give up writing time to accept the many invitations he received to speak or appear around the country but when a teacher at the Paul Robeson School in New York, for example, invited him to address the class, how could he say no? Often he was saddened after such an appearance because it reminded him that blacks often don't even know their own history.

No playwright of his generation has been more successful than Wilson. His first eight plays were staged in New York, seven of the them on Broadway, and he has received innumerable awards. Let us hope that with time a few more of these gems of vernacular poetry and social insight make their way to the big screen.

Wilson succumbed to liver cancer in October of 2005.

Kathleen Winsor

Born 13 October 1915,
Olivia, MN
Died 26 May 2003,
New York City, NY

Forever Amber (1944) was the best-selling book of the 1940s selling over three million copies in sixteen languages, bringing fame and fortune to Kathleen Winsor.

Kathleen was born in Olivia, Minnesota, where her father, Harold, sold real estate. Her mother, Myrtle, was a homemaker. The family lived at 147 Sixth Street. Her younger brother, Edward, was born in 1918. By the 1920s everyone had heard about the West Coast and what opportunities could be had there for those with adventurous hearts, so in late 1921 the family picked up and moved west to Berkeley where Kathleen did all her schooling.

After high school Kathleen attended the university in her home town. At twenty she married campus football star Robert Herwig. He had just finished his senior honors thesis on King Charles II of England, a topic that so captivated Winsor that she proceeded to read 356 books on the topic herself. With this background she wrote her thousand-page classic.

Success changed Winsor completely. As she became a celebrity, she grew tired of Herwig and divorced him in 1946. Later that year she became the sixth wife of band leader and clarinetist Artie Shaw, who sandwiched her in between Lana Turner and Ava Gardner.

Otto Preminger directed the film version of *Forever Amber* (1947) with Linda Darnell in the role of Amber St Clair. Cornell Wilde, George Sanders, Jessica Tandy, and Richard Greene round out the cast. Amber is a sixteen-year old, ambitious country girl determined to raise her humble status to one of comfort, wealth, and respect. The plot is long and convoluted, with numerous trysts, marriages, and deaths, to which added spice is provided by the trappings of court ceremony and the great London fire and plague of 1666.

The Catholic Legion of Decency condemned the film with a Class "C" rating (the worst) and strongly objected to the character of Amber, who seemed to be suffering from nymphomania. "I don't write dirty scenes," Kathleen protested. "I wrote only two sexy passages, and my publishers took both of them out."

By equating the film with pornography the Legion of Decency provided loads of free publicity, and the public was knocking down the doors to see the film.

The book had already stirred up a grand controversy because it seemed to glorify the life of a courtesan, though some readers, including the *Catholic World*, held that it was accurate in many details of the period and showed thorough research. And why not? It had taken her five years of research and writing to finish the book.

There was more than a little speculation that Winsor would star herself in the film, as she was as pretty as any actress could be for the part. Taylor Caldwell, a peer in the field of historical fiction, commented that Winsor's beauty worked to her disadvantage, "Her pretty face has always gotten in the way of the fact that she is one of America's most magnificent novelists." And she did use herself as the model for the character in her follow-up book, *Star Money* (1950) which dealt with a novelist's success and fame.

Winsor's career began as a receptionist and reporter for the *Oakland Tribune*. After writing her first five books, she took a pause to be a story consultant for the TV series, *Dreams in the Dust* in 1971. In all she wrote eight books, and some critics discerned improvements in her prose, though none of her later works approached the popularity of *Forever Amber*.

Kathleen was childless, but had four husbands: Robert J. Herwig, 1936-1946; Artie Shaw, 1946-1949, Robert Krakower, attorney, 1949-1953; and Paul A. Porter, attorney, 1956-1975. She died at eighty-seven.

Movies Made
in Minnesota

Activity code: producer = p; director = d, writer = w, editor = ed; composer = m, cinematographer = ph, art director = ad, production designer = pd, costumer = c. Data provided by IMdb and *Halliwell's Film Guide*.

1. ***Evangeline*** (1929), 87m; p/d: Edwin Carewe (Edwin Carewe Productions); starring Dolores del Rio (Evangeline), Roland Drew (Gabriel), Alec B. Francis (Father Pelican), Donald Reed (Baptiste) and Paul McAllister (Benedict Bellefontaine); from the poem by Henry Wadsworth Longfellow. Shooting sites included Minnehaha Falls in Minneapolis. This is not a full "talkie" but had some "talk sequences."

In Acadia, (now part of the Canadian province of Nova Scotia), young Evangeline is bethrothed to Gabriel. But before their wedding can take place, the British imprison the men and send them into exile with their lands forfeit to the Crown. Evangeline follows the exiled men to Louisiana in hopes of finding her beloved.

2. ***Smith of Minnesota*** (1942), 66m, Columbia Pictures; d: Lew Landers; w: Robert Hardy Andrews; biopic starring Minnesota Gopher Football's All-American (1941) halfback Bruce Smith as himself; Minnesota actress Arline Judge (as Smith's love interest), Don Beddoe and Rosemary DeCamp as his parents, Mr. & Mrs. Lew Smith, and a cast of thousands.

Real game footage (from 1941 Minnesota Gophers movie reels as National Champs) showcases Smith during the golden days of Gopher football under the great coach Bernie Bierman. The University of Minnesota's Memorial Stadium is the site of much of the real game footage. Staged game footage was done in Hollywood.

3. ***An American Romance*** (1944), 151m, MGM, d: King Vidor; w: Herbert Dalmas, William Ludwig; ph: Harold Rosson; m: Louis Gruenberg; featuring Brian Donlevy, Ann Richards, John Qualen, St. Paulite Walter Abel, and Stephen McNally. Film sites include the docks of Duluth; a iron mine in Hibbing; and the Mesabi Range.

The story of a European immigrant who becomes a master of industry; a patriotic rendering of the "American Dream."

4. **Swedes in Minnesota** (1945) 16m, U.S. Office of War Information, Overseas Branch. This film examines why Swedish immigrants have come to the United States and why they feel at home here. Ingrid Bergman visits the Swedish consulate in New York, the American Swedish Museum in Philadelphia and various sites in Minnesota, including Lindstrom and Scandia in Chisago County.

5. **A Boy, a Girl and a Dog** (1946), 77m, Film Classics, Inc.(p: W.R. Frank); d: Herbert Kline, who adapted it from a Leopold Atlas story; co-w: Irving Fineman, Maurice Clark; m: Willy Stahl; ed: Marguerite Francisco; ph: Edward A. Kull; featuring Sharyn Moffett, Jerry Hunter, Harry Davenport, Lionel Stander, W. R. "Bill" Frank, Jr. It is Frank's fifth film production, considered a "down-to-earth, close-to-your-heart, full-of-fun movie; A kid's movie, Ms. Moffett is "the darling little heart stealer" from **My Pal Wolf** and one critic called Jerry Hunter "Hollywood's greatest boy discovery since Jackie Coogan in **The Kid**." Frank appeared in this film.

6. **The Great Dan Patch** (1949), 92m, United Artists (exec.p: W.R. Frank): p/w: John Tainter Foote; d: Joseph Newman; m: Rudy Schrager; ph: Gilbert Warrenton; ad: Jerome Pycha, Jr. Jacque Mapes; featuring Gail Russell, Dennis O'Keefe, Ruth Warwick, Charlotte Greenwood, Henry Hull, Arthur Hunnicutt and John Hoyt.

The somewhat bowdlerized story of the famous pacer and his owner M. W. Savage. It premièred at the Boulevard Twins Theater on Lyndale Avenue at 53rd St. in South Minneapolis. Airport searchlights helped movie-goers feel more festive. Frank had to join SAG (Screen Actors Guild) with this third film appearance. Sites used were a horse ranch and pasture land between Savage and Shakopee, Minneosta.

7. **Airport** (1970), 136m, Universal/Ross Hunter (Jacque Mapes); wd: George Seaton from a novel by Arthur Hailey; ph: Ernest Laszlo; m: Alfred Newman; ed: Stuart Gilmore; ad: E. Preston Ames, Alexander Golitzen; c: Edith head. Starring Dean Martin, Burt Lancaster, Jean Seberg, Helen Hayes, Van Heflin, Jacqueline Bisset, George Kennedy, Maureen Stapleton, Dana Wynter, Lloyd Nolan, Barbara Hale, Gary Collins, Jesse Royce Landis and Minnesota actors Larry Gates, Marion Ross and Nancy Nelson. Partly filmed at Minneapolis-St.Paul International Airport and Lindbergh Terminal. Veteran director Henry Hathaway directed blizzard scenes on the airport's tarmac. When snow lightened up too much, filming was done in Detroit's International Airport.

An old-fashioned all-star version of Alex Hailey's best-seller about impending catastrophe at the Twin Cities Airport. Judith Christ called it "The best film of 1944." Helen Hayes won an Oscar for Best Supporting Actress. The film received eight Oscar nominations. Critics called this one of best examples of pure Hollywood dazzle.

8. *The Emigrants* (1970), 191m, Svensk filmindustri (Bengt Forslund), w/d/ed/ph Jan Troell, m: Erik Nordgren; starring Max von Sydow, Liv Ullmann, Eddie Axberg and Svenolof Bern. This Swedish production (entitled Untvadarna), based on the Moberg novels, received Academy award nominations for Best Picture, Best Script-Best Direction for Jan Troell and Best Actress (Liv Ullmann) and Best foreign Film. Film sites include Marine on St. Croix, where the characters depicted in the novels actually settled.

9. *The New Land* (1972), 102m (204m in Sweden), a sequel by Jan Troell, once again with Max von Sydow and Liv Ullmann.

10. *Slaughterhouse Five* (1972), 104", Universal/Vanadas (Paul Monash); d: George Roy Hill; w: Stephen Geller from a Kurt Vonnegut, Jr. novel of the same title; m: by J.S. Bach played by Glenn Gould; ph: Miroslav Ondricek; pd: Henry Bumstead; featuring Michael Saks, Valerie Perrine, John Dehner, Ron Leibman, Sharon Gans, Eugène Roche, Sorrell Booke and Minnesota actor Warren Frost. Some film sites were old Hwy 12 near Parade Stadium, large lakefront home on Lake Minnetonka, Elks Club off Hwy 12 (I-394).

Kurt Vonnegut's anti-war, space/time fantasy film with local boy George Roy Hill in the director's chair. Hill appeared at the Cooper Theater in St. Louis Park for the premiere; his favorite film. He gave an introductory talk and shook hundreds of hands.

11. *The Heartbreak Kid* (1972), 106m, (TCF) Palomar (Edgar J. Sherick); d: Elaine May; w: Neil Simon from a story by Bruce Jay Friedman; m: Garry Sherman; ph: Owen Roizman. Featuring Cybill Shepherd, Charles Grodin, Minneapolis actor Eddie Albert (Oscar nominee for Best Supporting Actor), Jeannie Berlin (Oscar nominee for Best Supporting Actress); Audra Lindley, Art Metrano and William Prince. Filming sites included the Mall near Vincent Hall at the University of Minnesota Campus and the chapel of St. Martin's-by-the-Lake Episcopal Church near Navarre on Lake Minnetonka. University of Minnesota student Jim Westcott began his film career with this movie.

12. *You'll Like My Mother* (1972), 92m, Universal/Bing Crosby Productions (Mort Briskin); d: Lamont Johnson; w: Jo Heims based on a novel by Naomi Hintze; ph: Jack Marta; m: Gil Melle. Featuring Rosemary Murphy, Patty Duke, Richard Thomas and Sian Barbara Allen. Filmed at the Congdon Mansion "Glensheen," 3300 London Road in Duluth overlooking Lake Superior.

13. *The Wrestler* (1974 aka **The Maim Event**), 95m, Entertainment Ventures Inc; p: W.R. Frank, Jr., exec. p: Verne Gagne; d: Jim A. Westman; w: Eugene Gump; ph: Gil Hubbs; m: William A. Castleman, William Loose; ed: Neal Chastain. Featuring Ed Asner (as Frank Bass), Verne Gagne (Mike Bullard), Billy Robinson (English champion), Minneapolis *Star Tribune* columnist, Jim Klobuchar, Bob McNamara (great 1950s Gopher Halfback), The Crusher, Dusty Rhodes, Larry Hennig, Greg Gagne, Rick Flair, Nick Bockwinkel, Hardboiled Haggerty, Lord James Blears, Dick Murdoch, Superstar Billy Graham, Sam Menacher (mob boss), Elaine Giftos (Bass's secretary), Sarah Miller (Betty Bullard), Jim Brunzell, Pedro Morales, Vince MacMahon Sr., Jack "Wildman" Armstrong, the Bruiser, and Harold "Odd Job" Sakata.

Gamblers, mobsters, unscrupulous wrestlers, money-grubbing promoters, and fixers corrupt the wrestling industry. Frank Bass attempts to bring honesty and fairness back by persuading an over-the-hill champion to win a final match. Verne uses drop kicks and his trademark sleeper hold to win the crucial match. Film sites include: Verne Gagne's home near the Narrows Bridge in Lake Minnetonka; buildings in St. Paul; Mayslack's Restaurant-Bar near 14th & University Ave. N. E. Mpls (partly in honor of Stan Mayslack's former wrestling days); and an empty warehouse in Chicago. Entertainment Ventures (EVI) presented this Gagne-Frank Production. Each producer put up a quarter of a million dollars and it was screened nationally.

14. *Ice Castles* (1978), 109m, Columbia/International Cinemedia Center (John Kemeny); d: Donald Wrye; co-w: Donald Wrye and Gary L. Baim; m: Marvin Hamlisch; ph: Bill Butler; pd: Joel

Schiller; featuring Robby Benson, Lynn-Holly Johnson, Colleen Dewhurst, Tom Skerritt, Jennifer Warren, David Huffman and Minnesota's James Cada.

Hennepin Avenue between 7th and 8th Sts. was flooded to film some of the skating scenes in this ice-skating romance. Other sites include Mariucci Arena at the U of M; The Met Center, 7901 Cedar Avenue, Bloomington; and general shots around South St. Paul.

15. *Foolin' Around* (1979), 101m, Columbia/Arnold Kopelson; d: Richard T. Heffron; w: Mike Kane, David Swift; m: Charles Berstein; ph: Philip Lathrop; featuring Gary Busey, Annette O'Toole, Cloris Leachman, Tony Randall, John Calvin and Minnesota actors Eddie Albert and Wayne A. Evenson. Film sites include: St. Paul Cathedral, 239 Selby Avenue; Central Lutheran Church, 333 S. 12th St., Minneapolis; Lake Minnetonka; and the University of Minnesota.

16. *Take This Job and Shove It* (1980), 106m, Avco Embassy/Cinema Group (Greg Blackwell); d: Gus Trikonis; w: Barry Schneider from a story by Schneider and Jeffrey Bernini from a song by David Allan Coe; m: Billy Sherill; ph: James Davis; ad: Jim Dultz; ed: Richard Belding. Featuring: Robert Hays, Barbara Hershey, David Keith, Art Carney, Eddie Albert, Tim Tomerson, Penelope Milford, Charlie Rich and Martin Mull. Filming took place in Minneapolis.

17. *Off the Minnesota Strip* (1980, Universal-TV/Cherokee Productions); 104m; d: Lamont Johnson; p/w: David Chase who won an Emmy for his script; c: Donald M. Morgan; ed: Diane Adler, George R. Rohrs; pd: Vincent M. Creciman; featuring Hal Holbrook and Michael Learned (as Mr. & Mrs. Johanson), Mare Winningham (as runaway Micki Johanson), and Heather McAdam.

18. *The Willmar 8* (1981), 50m, GTY; d: actress Lee Grant's directing debut; documentary shot in Willmar portraying eight ordinary women who risk their jobs, friends, family, and position in the community to begin the longest bank strike in American history.

19. *The Personals* (1982), 90m, New World Pictures (Patrick Wells, Peter Markle); w/d: Markle, ed: Stephen E. Rivkin (Assoc p); m: Will Sumner; co-ph: Markle, Gregory M. Cummins; sound: Matthew Quast; featuring Bill Shoppert (assoc. p), Chris Forth, Karen Landry, Michael Laskin, James Cada, Paul Eiding, Victoria Dakil, Patrick Thomas O'Brien, all Minnesota actors.

Film sites include: Lakes Calhoun and Harriet, Lake of the Isles; Peter Markle's house at 2217 Humboldt Avenue S., Shoppert's apartment, Well's house, and the Minneapolis Institute of Arts.

20. *Purple Haze* (1983), 97m, Triumph Films (Thomas A. Fucci); d: David Burton Morris; exec.p: Victoria Wozniak; w: Tom Kelsey, Morris, Wozniak; ph: Richard Gibb; ed: Dusty Dennison; Choreographer: Peter Thoemke; featuring Peter Nelson, Chuck McQuary, Bernhard Baldan, Susanna Lack, Bob Breuler, Johanna Bauman, Katy Horsch, Heidi Helmer, Tommy O'Brien, Dan Jones, Don Bakke, James Craven, Jean Ashley, Sara Hennessey, John Speckhardt, Michael Bailey, Steve Gjerde, Peter Thoemke.

A young man with problems drops out of college in the late 1960s and returns home to await his draft notice. This film won the Grand Prize for Best Feature Film at the Sundance Film Festival. Film sites include under the Ford Parkway Bridge in St. Paul. (See Morris's bio for details.)

21. *Wildrose* (1984), 95m, New Front Films/Ely Lakes Films; d: John Hanson; p: Sandra Schulberg; w: Eugene Corr, Hansen, Schulberg; ed: Arthur Coburn; m: Bernard Krause, Gary Malkin, Chris Williamson; ph: Peter Stein; ad: Shirley Morton, Cate Wittemore; featuring Tom Bower, Cinda Jackson, Lisa Eichhorn, Lydia Olsen, Vienna Maki and Minnesota actors James Cada, Bill Shoppert, James Stowell, and Steve Yoakam.

One woman's struggle for the right to work unharrassed in the mines. This film had a special showing at MOMA in New York City. Film sites include the Iron Range, an abandoned mine near Eveleth, and Bayfield, WI. See Hanson's bio for details.

22. *Purple Rain* (1984), 111m, Warner Bros. Pictures/Purple Films (Robert Cavallo, Steven Fargnoli, Joseph Ruffalo); m/star singer: Prince (The Kid); d: Albert Magnoli; co-w: Magnoli and William Blinn; featuring Jerome Benton, singer Morris Day and the Time ("Jimmy Jam" Harris and Terry Lewis), Apollonia Kotero, Olga Karlatos (as the mother), Clarence Williams III (as the father), Billy Sparks, Jill Jones, Dez Dickerson, Brenda Bennett, Susan Moonsie, Kim Upsher, Sandra Claire Gershman, Alan Leeds, Charles Huntsberry. Film sites include: First Avenue Club, 29 North 7th Street in Minneapolis; and Eagan. Prince won an Oscar for Best Original Song Score and singing "When Doves Cry." *Purple Rain* soundtrack won three Grammy Awards.

23. *Friday the 13th: The Final Chapter* (1984), 91m, Paramount (Frank Mancuso, Jr.; aka *Friday the 13th: Part IV*); d: Joseph Zito; w: Barney Cohen; ad: Joao Fernandes; m: Harry Manfredini; pd: Shelton H. Bishop III; ed: Joel Goodman; featuring E. Erich Anderson, Judie Aronson, Peter Barton, Kimberly Beck, Crispin Glover, Camilla More. Film sites include Lake Minnewashta, Chanhassen, MN.

24. *That Was Then... This Is Now* (1985), 102m, Paramount/ Media Ventures (Gary R. Lindberg and John M. Ondov); w: Emilio Estevez from an S.E. Hinton novel; d: Christopher Cain; m: Keith Olsen; ed: Ken Johnson; ad: Chester Kaczenski, ph: Juan Ruiz-Estevez. Starring Emilio Estevez, Morgan Freeman, Craig Sheffer, Kim Delaney, Jill Schoelen and Barbara Babcock.

Film sites in this version of the S. E. Hinton young-adult novel include St. Paul's Jackson Street, Geranium Street, Mario Street, East Seventh Street, Smith Avenue (Terry's house), Capitol Hill area (for the final race scene), and Midway Hospital, 1700 University Avenue West; Nicollet Island, Uptown area in Minneapolis; and Fort Snelling National Cemetery, 7601 34th Avenue, Richfield.

25. *Blood Hook* (1985), 85m, Trauma Films/Prism Pictures/ Golden Chargers/ Spider Lake Films, Ltd (David Herbert); d: Jim Mallon; w: Larry Edgerton, John Gallagher; m: Kevin Murphy, Thomas A. Naumas; ph/ed: Marsha Kahm; ass't ed: Ali Selim; featuring Mark Jacobs, Lisa Todd, Patrick Danz, Sara Hauser, Don Winters, Bill Lowrie, Paul Drake, Christopher Whiting, Bonnie Lee, Paul Herman and noted Minnesota actors Don Cosgrove and Dale Dunham.

"During a local 'Muskie Madness' fishing contest people are mysteriously dragged into the lake and killed by a giant hook.

26. *One More Saturday Night* (1986), 95m; Columbia Pictures/AAR Films/ Delphi V Productions/Rastar Films; d: Dennis Klein; w: Al Franken, Tom Davis, featuring Franken (Paul Flum) and Davis (Larry Hays); Film sites include St. Cloud, Minnesota.

Teenagers and adults alike try to drum up dates for the weekend in a small Minnesota town. The writers, Al Franken and Tom Davis, are the real stars. A very funny movie.

27. *God's Country* (1986), 90m; PBS-TV; p: Vincent Malle; d/ narrator: Louis Malle; ph: Charlie Clifton, Louis Malle; ed: James Bruce; documentary of prosperous farming community of Glencoe, MN., about 60 miles west of the Twin Cities.

In 1979 Malle interviewed several farm families around Glencoe before being called away to work on other projects. He returned in 1985 and discovered that farm foreclosures and a crumbling economy had soured the attitudes of many farmers.

28. *Rachel River* (1987), 90m, p: American Playhouse/Marx/ Smolan (Timothy Marx); d: Sandy Smolan; w: Judith Guest from stories by Carol Bly; ph: Paul Elliott; m: Avro Part; pd: David Wasco; ed: Susan Crutcher. Featuring: Pamela Reed, Viveca Lindfors, James Olson, Craig T. Nelson, Alan North, Jo Henderson, Jon DeVries and Zeljko Ivanek and Minnesota's Ollie Osterberg. A small-town drama filmed in Minnesota's Arrowhead country.

29. *Patti Rocks* (1987), 87m, Premier/Film Dallas (Gwen Field and Gregory M. Cummins); d: David Burton Morris; co-w: Morris, Chris Mulkey, Karen Landry, John Jenkins; ph: Greg M. Cummins, m: Doug Maynard. Featuring Chris Mulkey, Karen Landry, John Jenkins, David L. Turk, Stephen Yoakam, Joe Minjares, and Buffy Sedlacheck all from Minnesota. A married man takes an old buddy on a ride to see his pregnant girlfriend. Film sites used were Midway Chevrolet, The Ace Box Tavern, and Dayton's Bluff, all in St. Paul; and some scenes in Minneapolis.

30. *Hometown Boy Makes Good* (1988), 88m, Warner Home Video/ HBO; d: David Burton Morris; w: Allen Rucker; ph: Sharon Seymour; featuring Cynthia Bain, Phil Brock, Anthony Edwards, Jeff Gadbois, Chris Mulkey, Terry Hardin, Harry Shearer, Tony Sporadakis, Melvin Kirkpatrick, Grace Zabriske.

"A small town boy moves to the big city to attend medical school. He drops out but never tells his mother who has already boasted near and far about his great psychiatric practice. Feeling guilty, he goes home to confess the truth but the mayor intercepts him to invite him to start a practice in his boyhood town." IMDb

31. *Far North* (1988), 89m, Rank/Alive Films/Nelson/Circle JS (Malcolm R. Harding, Carolyn Pfeiffer); wd: Sam Shepard, m: The Red Clay Ramblers, J.A. Deane; pd: Peter Jamison; ph: Robbie Greenberg; ed: Bill Yahraus. Starring Jessica Lange, Tess Harper, Charles Durning, Donald Moffat, Ann Wedgeworth, Patricia Arquette.

Sam Shepard's debut in directing - about a family squabbling around the bed of their sick father. Filmed around Jessica Lange and Sam Shepard's cabin home south of Duluth.

32. *Catch Me If You Can* (1989), 105m, Medusa Management Company Entertainment Group/Sterling Entertainment (Jonathan D Krane); wd: Stephen Sommers; ph: Ronn Schmidt; m: Tangerine Dream; ad: Stuart Blatt; ed: Bob Ducsay. Featuring Matt Lattanzi, Loryn Locklin, Grant Heslov, Billy Morrissette, M. Emmet Walsh.

To raise money for a school a high school senior becomes a champion drag-racer and wins the heart of the girl who is class president. Filmed in St. Cloud. (See the entry on Sommers for details.)

33. *The Comeback* (1989), 94m, CBS-TV (Ron Roth); d: Jerrold Friedman; w: Percy Granger from a Seymour Epstein story; ph: Bojan Bazelli, William F. Carlson; ed: Anthony Redman; pd: Michael Molly; m: Craig Safan; featuring Robert Urich, Mitchell Anderson, Kofi Brewer, Ronny Cox, Aaron Fletcher, Harvey Martin, Brynn Thayer, Pete Turner, Paul Meshejian, Chynna Phillips and Minnesota actors Allen Hamilton, Mark Bradley, Terry O'Sullivan and Peter Syvertsen. Film sites include a Lake Minnetonka home and the Lumber Exchange Bldg, 425 Hennepin Avenue in downtown Minneapolis.

A former NFL football star returns to Minnesota to visit his ex-wife and son, with disastrous results.

34. *Old Explorers* (1989), 100m, Taurus Entertainment Company/River Road Productions (Robert Schwartz); d: William Pohlad; w: James Cada, Mark Keller, Pohlad; ed: Miroslav Janek; ph: William F. Carlson; pd: Peter Stolz; featuring James Whitmore, José Ferrer, William Warfield, Jeff Gadbois, Jonathan Coder, Caroline Kaiser. (For details see Bill Pohlad entry.)

35. *Graffiti Bridge* (1990), 95m, Warner Bros. Pictures/Paisley Park (Arnold Stiefel, Randy Phillips); wdm: Prince; ph: Bill Butler; pd: Vance Lorenzini; ed: Rebecca Ross. Players: Prince (as The Kid), Morris Day, Ingrid Chavez, Jerome Benton, Mavis Staples, Tevin Campbell, Robin Power, T. C. Ellis, Jill Jones, members of The Kid's band, members of Grand Slam Dancers, George Clinton and his Funkestra band, members of The Time especially Terry Lewis and "Jimmy Jam" Harris, and D.Williams, Jevetta Steele, Jeralyn Steele and Fred of The Melody Cool Choir..

Two club owners disagree over the kind of music to feature. Prince reprises his "Diamonds and Pearls." Tagline is: "Music is the Power; Love is the message; and Truth is the answer." Prince had total control ala Chaplin. Film sites include Eden Prairie and Paisley Park Studio in Chanhassen.

36. ***Drop Dead Fred*** (1990), 99m, Rank/Working Title/Polygram (Paul Webster); d: Ate de Jong; w: Carlos Davis, Anthony Fingleton, story: Elizabeth Livington; ph: Peter Deming; m: Randy Edelman; pd: Joseph T. Garrity; ed: Marshall Harvey. Featuring: Phoebe Cates, Rik Mayall, Marsha Mason, Tim Matheson, Bridget Fonda, Carrie Fisher, Keith Charles, Ashley Peldon, Daniel Gerroll.

An imaginary childhood friend comes back to visit a woman already beseiged with problems. Film sites include: Harriet Island, Lowry Hill, the Walker Art Center, Gaviidae Commons, the Wells Fargo Tower and Prince's Paisley Park Studio in Chanhassen.

37. ***Voices Within: The Lives of Trudi Chase*** (1990), 120m, ABC-TV/ New World Television (Lamont Johnson, Martin Mickelson, Harry Sherman); d: Lamont Johnson; w: E. Jack Neuman from the Trudi Chase book, *The Troops for Trudi Chase*; m: Charles Fox; ph: William Wages; ed: Susan B. Browdy; pd: Paul Peters; featuring Shelley Long, Tom Conti, Val Bettin, Frank Converse, Jon Beshara, Melinda Kordich, Jamie Rose, Bruce Westphal, Marion Collier, Steve Porter, Carl Ciarfalio, and Minnesota actors Dale Dunham, Nancy Gormley, Joe Minjares, David Fox-Brenton, and Susan Eisenberg.

The true story of a woman in therapy for a multiple-personality disorder. She reveals twenty-two at first but later reveals another seventy wanting be break free.

38. ***Stranger Within*** (1990), 60m, ABC-TV (Barry Rosen, Paulette Breen); d: Tom Holland; w: John Pielmeier; ph: James Hayman; m: Vladimir Horunzhy; ed: Scott Conrad; pd: Ray Storey; featuring Kate Jackson, Rick Schroder, Kelsey Rose, Clark Sandford, Chris Sarandon, Pamela Danser, Rose Swanson, Zachary Hunke, and Minnesota actors Oliver Osterberg, Dale Dunham and James Harris.

Mare Blackburn is excited to see a young man return to this small Minnesota town after a sixteen year absence, supposedly from abduction, but she soon realizes that he is a dangerous psychopath. Rick Schroeder, the young man, was nominated for a Golden Globe for Best Actor in a mini-series or a movie-made-for-TV, 1991.

39. ***American Dream*** (1990), 98m, p: Athur Cohn, Barbara Kopple; d: Kopple, Cathy Caplan, Lawrence Silk, Thomas Haneke; m: Michael Small; ed: Caplan, Haneka, Silk; ph: Tom Hurwitz, Mathieu Roberts, Nesya Shapiro; featuring Jesse Jackson and Ray Rogers as themselves. Cohn and Kopple won an Oscar for the Best Documentary Feature. Film site was Austin, MN.

"'American Dream' is a sobering and fascinating documentary depicting the social, economic and emotional ramifications of a labor strike initiated by employees at the Hormel meatpacking plant in Austin, Minnesota. Although the film depicts events that took place in 1986, the content is every bit as relevant today.

"Like 'Roger & Me,' the acclaimed documentary by Michael Moore that savaged General Motors and the 80s corporate ethos of 'profits above everything else,' 'American Dream' is a priceless portrait of blue-collar work and life in small-town America.

40. *The Keys* (1990), 94m, Universal TV/Desparado Pictures (Stanford Blum)/ CIC-TV-Brazil; d: Richard Compton; w: Maurice Hurley, Eduardo de Gregorio, Marilu Parolini; m: Dale Menten; ph Geoffrey Erb; ed: Boyd Steer; featuring Geoffrey Blake, Brian Bloom, Scott Bloom, Dennis Boutsikaris, Paul Calderon, Barry Corbin, Alicia Coppola, Roberto Escobar, Ben Masters, Iris Peynado.

41. *Equinox* (1991), 110m, Metro Tartan/SC Entertainment (David Blocker); wd: Alan Rudolph; m: Rachmaninov, etal; ph: Elliot Davis; pd: Steven Legler; ed: Michael Ruscio; featuring Matthew Modine, Lara Flynn Boyle, Marisa Tomei, M. Emmet Walsh, Kevin J. O'Connor, Minnesota actors Shirley Venard, Jack Walsh, Isabell Monk O'Connor, and Wayne A. Evenson.

A morgue attendant discovers that a dead woman has left a trust fund for a pair of twin boys. She tracks them down, finding a shy garage mechanic and a wild killer. A bit related to ***Pulp Fiction***. The film was shot in Russell's Bar (formerly Richard's) 4th St. next to the Grain Exchange in Minneapolis and St. Paul sites.

42. *Highway 61* (1991), 102m, Shadow Shows/ Telefilm Canadian/ Film Four International(Colin Brunton, Bruce McDonald); d: Bruce McDonald; w: Don McKellar; ph: Miroslaw Baszak; m: Nash the Slash; ad: Ian Brock; ed: MichaelPacek; Film sites include Duluth, MN. A naïve, small-town barber and jazz trumpeter travel to New Orleans with a delinquent roadie tagging along. She has stolen some drugs and stashed it in a corpse.

43. *Lucky Day* (1992), m, ABC-TV (John Lugar); d: Donald Wrye; co-w: John Axness, Jennifer Miller; m: David Bell; ph: Jon Kranhouse; ed: Craig Bassett; pd: Cate Bangs; featuring Amy Madigan, Olympia Dukakis, Chloe Webb, Terence Knox, John Beasley, Ann Bainbridge and Minnesota actors Allen Hamilton, James Cada, Peter Syvertsen,

David Anthony Brinkley; it was nominated for an Emmy.

Strong performances by Madigan, Dukakis, and Webb really make this a woman's film. Amy as Kari takes over the care of her younger sister Allison (Chloe Webb) from her snooty mother (Dukakis) who attempts to re-assert her authority when Amy wins the lottery. Filmed in St. Paul and in Minneapolis especially on E. Lake Street.

44. *Crossing the Bridge* (1992), 103m, p: Outlaw Productions (Jeffrey Silver, Robert Newmyer); d/w: Mike Binder; m: Lisa Haley, Peter Himmelman; ph: Newton Thomas Sigel; ed: Adam Weiss; ad: Jack Balance; featuring Josh Charles, Jason Godrick, Stephen Baldwin, Cheryl Pollak, Rita Taggart, and Minnesota actors James Cada, Isabell Monk O'Connor, Chris Forth, Bill Shoppert, and David Anthony Brinkley. Three teenage buddies from Detroit learn about friendship and loyalty. Film sites include the Hennepin Avenue Bridge in downtown Minneapolis and the University of St. Thomas.

45. *Laurel Avenue* (1992), 155m (2 parts), HBO-TV (Jesse Beaton, Tony To); d: Carl Franklin; w: Michael Henry Brown from a story by Paul Aaron; m: Harold Wheeler; ph: James Glennon; ed: Carole Kravetz; pd: Maxine Shepard; featuring Robin Stubbins White, Mary Alice, John Beasley, Tony Brubaker, Juanita Jennings, Marvette Knight, T.C. Ellis, Robin Hickman, Gary Groomes, Chrys Carol, Randy Carter, Scott Lawrence, Lotis Key, Dan Martin, Darvone Manikong, Shawn Skie, Khnadi Simone, Jay Brooks, Monte Russell and Minnesota actors Michael Tezla and Buffy Sedlachek.

A weekend in the life of the Arnett family involving contacts with a preacher, a drug dealer, and an innocent young school girl. Shot at the corner of Laurel and Chatsworth in St. Paul.

46. *Twenty Bucks* (1992), 91m, Triton Pictures (Karen Murphy); d: Keva Rosenfeld; co-w: Leslie and Endre Bohem; m: David Robbins; ph: Emmanuel Lubezki; ed: Michael Ruscio; pd: Joseph Garrity; featuring Linda Hunt, David Rasch, George Morfogen, Bubba Baker, Brendan Fraser, Elizabeth Shue, Steve Buscemi, Spalding Gray, Rosemary Murphy, William H. Macy, Christopher Lloyd, Minnesota actors John Paul Gamoke, Jim Westcott and Nancy Gormley. Film sites include the Minneapolis-St. Paul International Airport.

The film follows the life of a $20 bill as enters and leaves the hands of a street person, an aspiring writer, a stripper, two thieves and several other colorful characters.

47. *The Mighty Ducks* (1992), 101m, Buena Vista/Walt Disney

(Jordan Kerner, Jon Avnet); d: Stephen Herek; w: Steven Brill; ph: Thomas Del Ruth; m: David Newman; pd: Randy Ser; ed: Larry Bock, John F. Link. Featuring: Emilio Estevez, Joss Ackland, Lane Smith, Heidi King, Josef Sommer, Joshua Jackson, Aaron Schwartz, Elden Henson, Marguerite Moreau, Garette Ratliff Henson, J.D. Daniels, Shaun Weiss, Brandon Quintin Adams, M.C. Gainey, and Minnesota actors Peter Syvertsen and Dale Dunham.

Film sites include: Courtroom scenes in St. Cloud; Elliot Park, Gaviidae Commons on the Nicollet Mall at 555 Nicollet Avenue, and the Theodore Wirth Park (for Han's shop) at 1339 Theodore Wirth Parkway in Minneapolis; Rice Park and Mickey's Diner at 36 W. 9th St. in St. Paul; Cook Memorial Arena (where District 5 becomes the Ducks and they get their jerseys) at 11091 Mississippi Blvd in Coon Rapids; New Hope; and the Met Center in Bloomington.

A film about a lawyer who turns a group of drop-outs into a winning hockey team. Many of the young hockey players are local kids.

48. *Bound and Gagged: A Love Story* (1992), 94m, Metro

Tartan/ Cinescope (Dennis J. Mahoney); wd: Daniel B. Appleby; ph: Dean Lent; m: William Murphy; pd: Dane Pizzuti Krogman; ed: Kaye Davis. Featuring Ginger Lynn Allen, Karen Black, Chris Denton, Elizabeth Saltarrelli, Mary Ella Ross, and Minnesota actors Chris Mulkey, Randy Adamsick, Garth Schumacher, Bill Shoppert, Joe Minjares, and Phyllis Wright. Filmed entirely in Minnesota.

A movie about abuse, and unstable marriages, and abduction.

49. *Untamed Heart* (1993), 102m, M-G-M (Tony Bill, Helen

Buck Bartlett); d: Tony Bill; w: Tom Sierchio; ph: Jost Vacano; m: Cliff Eidelmann; ed: Mia Goldman; pd: Steve Jordan. Featuring Christian Slater, Marisa Tomei, Rosie Perez, and Minnesota actors Allen Hamilton, James Cada, Claudia Wilkens, Sally Wingert, Nancy Marvy, Joe Minjares, Vincent Kartheiser, Sarquetta Senters, Isabell Monk O'Connor, John Paul Gamoke, and Buffy Sedlachek.

Film sites include: Jimmy (the Greek)'s Coffee Shop at 4th St. N.E. and Central Avenue in Mpls, the Met Center, 7901 Cedar Ave S. Bloomington, Nicollet Island, and Saint Paul.

A young man with a heart condition begins a tentative love affair with a waitress. It is a tear-jerker of idealized love for teenagers.

50. *Trauma* (1993), 105m, Overseas Filmgroup/ADC (Dario

Argento); wd: Dario Argento; co-w: T.E.D. Klein, Franco Ferrini,

Giovanni Romoli; ph: Raffaele Mertes; m: Pino Donaggio; pd: Billy Jett; ed: Conrad Gonzalez; sp: Tom Savini. Featuring: Asia Argento, Christopher Rydell, Piper Laurie, Frederic Forrest, James Russo, Brad Dourif, and Minnesota actors Dominique Serrand, Isabell Monk O'Connor, Peter Moore, Stephen D'Ambrose. A gruesome movie about a serial killer, a specialty by Italian filmmaker Dario Argento. Film sites include: Hopkins, Minneapolis, and Irvine Park in St. Paul.

51. ***Little Big League*** (1994), 119m, Rank/Castle Rock/Lobell/ Bergman; d: Andrew Scheinman; co-w: Schienman, Gregory K. Pincus; ph: Donald E. Thorin; m: Stanley Clarke; pd: Jeffrey Howard; ed: Michael Jablow. Featuring Jason Robards as the Grandfather, Luke Edwards, Timothy Busfield, John Ashton, Ashley Crow, Kevin Dunn, Billy L. Sullivan, and Minnesota actors Allen Hamilton, Tim Russell, Peter Syvertsen, and Vincent Kartheiser.

Film sites include: Lakewood Cemetery at 3600 Hennepin Avenue South and the Hubert H. Humphrey Metrodome at 501 Chicago Avenue in Minneapolis; Valley Fair Amusement Park at One Valley Fair Drive, Shakopee; and Energy Park Studio at 1515 Brewster Street in St. Paul, and Edina.

A baseball team-owning grandfather leaves the ownership to his grandson who decides to take over as manager. Very watcher-friendly. The grandpa role is molded in the image, roughly, of dear Calvin Griffith whose team building skills built the Minnesota Twins into World Series Champions in 1987 and 1991.

52. ***Iron Will*** (1994), 109m, Buena Vista/Disney (Patrick Palmer, Robert Schwartz); d: Charles Haid; co-w: John Michael Hayes, Jeff Arch, Djordje Milicevic; ph: William Wages; m: Joel McNeely; pd: Stephen Storer; ed: Andrew Doerfer; featuring Mackenzie Astin, Kevin Spacey, August Schellenberg, Brian Cox, John Terry, Penelope Windlust, George Gerdes, David Ogden Stiers (of *M*A*S*H** fame*)* as James J. Hill, founder of the Great Northern Railroad and Minnesota actors James Cada, Wayne A. Evenson, and Michael Laskin.

Film sites include: Two Harbors, Brookstone, Kerrick and Cloquet; Duluth City Hall, and the Lutsen Mountain Ski Area.

A boy enters a 500-mile dog-sled race in 1917, winning against the odds. A heart warming tale.

53. ***Grumpy Old Men*** (1993), 104m, Warner/Lancaster Gate (John Davis, Richard C. Berman); d: Donald Petrie; w: Mark Steven Johnson; ph: Johnny E. Jensen; m: Alan Silvestri; pd: David Chapman;

ed: Bonnie Koehler; starring Lack Lemmon, Walter Matthau, Burgess Meredith, Ann-Margaret, Darryl Hannah, Ossie Davis, Kevin Pollak, Buck Henry, Christopher McDonald and Minnesotans Charles Brin, Isabell Monk O'Connor, Oliver Osterberg, and Buffy Sedlachek.

Film sites include: Red Wing, Stillwater, Faribault, Center City and the whole town of Wabasha; Lake Rebecca, Rockford; Paisley Park Studio at 7801 Audobon Road in Chanhassen; and Divine Redeemer Hospital at 724 19th Avenue North, South St. Paul.

Two old neighbors have been feuding for years. The feud intensifies when a beautiful widow moves across the street from them. Perfect Jack Lemmon - Walter Matthau film. This film was so popular, grossing over $150 million, that a sequel was done in 1995.

54. *The Mighty Ducks II* (1994), 106m, Buena Vista/Walt Disney; d: Sam Weisman; w: Steven Brill; ph: Mark Irwin; m: J.A.C. Redford; pd: Gary Frutkoff; ed: John Lund, Eric Sears; featuring Emilio Estevez again as Coach Gordon Bombay, Kathryn Erbe, Michael Tucker, Jan Rudes, Carsten Norgaard, Marcia Ellingsen, Joshua Jackson, Brandon Quintin Adams, Garette Ratliff Henson, Matt Doherty, Marguerite Moreau, Elden Henson, Shaun Weiss, Vincent Larusso, Columbe Jacobson Derstine; plus new players "Dean Portman (the Enforcer)," "Ken Wu (ex figure skater)," "Julie Gaffney (the great goalie)," "Luis Mendoza (a speed skater)" and "Dwayne Robertson (cowboy, great puck handler)" who says the line, "It's a great day for hockey, ain't it?" Jesse answers, "It sure is, Cowboy." This line honors Bob Johnson, former coach of the Pittsburgh Penguins after winning their 1991 Stanley Cup.

Film sites include: Blake School, 511 Kenwood Parkway; Parade Ice Arena, 600 Kenwood Pkwy; Nicollet Island, Harriet Island, Lake Harriet, Lake of the Isles; Emerson School, 1421 Spruce Place; Theodore Wirth Park, 1339 Theodore Wirth Pkwy – all in Minneapolis; Irvine Park, St. Paul; and Camp Snoopy, Mall of America in Bloomington.

55. *The Good Son* (1993), 87m, TCF (Mary Anne Page, Joseph Ruben); w: Ian McEwan; d: Ruben; ph: John Lindley; m: Elmer Bernstein; pd: Bill Groom; ed: George Bowers; featuring Macaulay Culkin, Quinn Culkin, Elijah Wood, Wendy Crewson, David Morse, Daniel Hugh Kelly, Jacqueline Brooks. Film sites include: Palisade Head on Lake Superior and Two Harbors, MN.

A peculiar thriller in which a seemingly sweet-tempered ten-year-old boy is really a sick, murderous child.

56. *Aswang: (The Unearthling)* (1993), m, Warner/Elektra/ Atlantic, Purple Onion, Young American Films, Image Entertainment; p/d: Wrye Martin, Barry Poltermann; w: Martin, Poltermann from a story by Frank L. Anderson; ph: Jim Zabilla; m: Ken Brahmstedt; ed: Barry Poltermann; ad: Margot Chulewicz; featuring Flora Cokes, Norman Moses, Victor Delorenzo, John Kishline, Tina Ona Punkstelis, Mildred Nierras, James Jacobs Anderson, Lee Worrell, Rosalie Seifert, John Gamakis, Daniel Demarco.

57. *With Honors* (1994), 100m, Warner/Spring Creek (Paula Weinstein, Amy Robinson); d: Alek Keshishian; w: William Mastrosimone; ph: Sven Nyquist; m: Patrick Leonard; pd: Barbara Long; ed: Michael R. Miller; featuring Joe Pesci, Brendan Fraser, Moira Kelly, Gore Vidal, Patrick Dempsey, John Hamilton. Film sites include the University of Minnesota campus.

58. *She Led Two Lives* (1994, NBC-TV), 88m, p: Bernard M. Kahn; d: Bill Corcoran; w: Kathleen Knutsen Rowell; m: Misha Sigel; ph: Frank Tidy; ed: David Campling; pd: Tamara Melloy, Diana Stoughton. Featuring Connie Sellecca, Perry King, A. Martinez, Patricia Clarkson, J. Smith-Cameron, David Whol, George Martin, and Minnesota actors J. C. Cutler, Sally Wingert, Signe Albertson, John Patrick Martin, Barbara Kingsley, Richard Anson, George A. Farr, Peter Thoemke, Terry O'Sullivan, and Sue Scott.

Film sites include: Galtier Plaza in downtown St. Paul, the Union Depot at 214 E. 4th St.; and the U of St. Thomas on Summit Avenue.

59. *The Cure* (1994), 98m, Polygram/Universal/Island (Mark Burg, Eric Eisner); d: Peter Horton; w: Robert Kuhn; ph: Andrew Dintenfass; m: David Grusin; pd: Armin Ganz; ed: Anthony Sherin, Saar Klein. Featuring Joseph Mazzello, Brad Renfro, Bruce Davison; Aeryk Egan, Annabella Sciorra, Diana Scarwid and Minnesota actors Stephen D'Ambrose, Shirley Venard, Peter Moore, and Bill Shoppert.

Film sites include: Stillwater, Marine-on-St. Croix, Edina, and Divine Redeemer Hospital at 724 19th Avenue North in South St. Paul. It is shot entirely in Minnesota.

Two boys search for a cure for AIDS which one of them has contracted through a blood transfusion. Well acted but unrealistic.

60. *Angus* (1994), 90m, Entertainment/ Atlas/ BBC/ Syalis/ Tele– München/ Quality/ Turner (Dawn Steel, Charles Roven); d: Patrick Read Johnson; w: Jill Gordon from a story by Chris Crutcher; Ph:

Alexander Grusynski' m: David Russo; pd: Larry Miller; ed: Janice Hampton. Featuring Kathy Bates, George C. Scott, Charlie Talbert, Rita Moreno, Ariana Richards, James Van Der Beek, Chris Owen, Lawrence Pressman. Film sites include the city of Owatonna, MN.

An overweight teenager, mocked at school, gets up the courage to fight back. A feel-good comedy about "the outsider" who earns his way into the community.

61. *World and Time Enough* (1994), 90m, Strand Releasing/1 in 10 Films (Julie Hartley, Andrew Peterson); d/w: Eric Mueller; ph: Kyle Bergesen; m: Eugene Huddleston; ed: Laura Stokes; sound: Johnny Hagen; featuring Matt Guidry, Gregory Giles, John Patrick Martin, Peter Macon, Kraig Swartz, Kathleen Fuller, Jennifer Jordan Campbell, Bernadette Sullivan, Adam Mickelson.

62. *Street Gun* (1994), 92m, Ardustry Home Entertainment LLC/ Nu Image Films/ Visionary Productions (Travis Millroy, Michael Jentsch); d: Travis Millroy; w: Millroy, Timothy Lee; m: Michael Wandmacher, ph: Joel King; ed: Steven Elbert, Omer Tel; ad: Jennifer L. Stumm; featuring Justin Pagel, Larry Roupe, Scott Cooke, Michael Egan, Ken Green, Leslie Ball, Timothy Lee, Philip Ray, Doug Fisher, Ed Jirak, Art Jentsch, C. Todd Griffin, Joey Metzger, Hilary Soltz. The alternate title is THUGS.

63. *Embrace of the Vampire* (1994), 93m, New Line Cinema/ Turner Home entertainment/Image Entertainment, Inc/General Media Entertainment/Ministry of Films Inc.(Marilyn Vance, Alan Mruvka); Alternate title: NOSFERATU DIARIES: EMBRACE OF THE VAMPIRE; d: Anne Goursand; w: Nicole Coady, Halle Eaton, Rick Bitselberger; m: Joseph Williams; ph; Suki Medencevic; ed: Terilyn A. Shropshire; pd: Peter Stolz; stunts: Peter Moore. Featured are: Martin Kemp, Rebecca Ferratti, Harold Pruett, Jordan Ladd, Alyssa Milano, Jennifer Tilly, Greg Vance, Ladd Vance, John Riedlinger, David Portlock, Charlotte Lewis, Lynn Philip Seibel, Glor Gold, Seana Ryan, Sabrina Allen, Rachel True.

64. *In the Line of Duty: Hunt for Justice* (1995), 90m, NBC-TV (Dick Lowry, Stephanie Hagan); d: Dick Lowry; w: John Miglis; m: Mark Snow; ed: William Stich; ph: Henry M. Lebo; pd: William Strom. Featuring Adam Arkin, Clyde Lund, Nicholas Turturro, Susan V. Hansen, and Minnesota actors John Paul Gamoke, Garth Schumacher, Emil Herrera. Film sites include general shots of Minneapolis.

The FBI launches a massive search to track down an underground cadre of revolutionary terrorists. There is lots of violence.

65. *Stuart Saves His Family* (1995), 95m, Paramount Pictures, Constellation, Mount Blanc, Worldwide (Lorne Michaels, Trevor Albert); d: Harold Ramis; w: Al Franken based on his book *I'm Good Enough, I'm smart Enough, and Doggone it, People Like Me*; m: Marc Shaiman; ph: Lauro Escorel; ad: Thomas Wilkens; ed: Craig Herring, Pembroke J. Herring. Film locations: Mpls, Chicago and Mundelin, IL, Hollywood Hills and Paramount Studios, CA for exterior shots.

The *Saturday Night Live* character of Stuart Smalley teaches the discipline of the Twelve Step Program as the best way to deal with life's injustices. Every one of his family has a major problem making him or her unstable.

66. *Mallrats* (1995), 108m, Gramercy/Alphaville,/View Askew (James Jacks, Sean Daniel, Scott Mosier); w/d: Kevin Smith; ph: David Klein; m: Ira Newborn; pd: Dina Lipton; ed: Paul Dixon. Featuring Ben Affleck, Shannon Doherty, Jeremy London, Jason Lee, Claire Forlani, Michael Rooker, Priscilla Barnes, Joey Lauren, Renee Humphrey, Jason Mewes, Kevin Smith and Minnesota's Josh Hartnett. Film sites include Eden Prairie's Prairie Center Mall; the Mpls-St. Paul International Airport. A group of teenagers hang out at the mall. A cult favorite for the those who were teens at that time.

67. *Grumpier Old Men* (1995), 100m, Warner/John Davis/Lancaster Gate; d: Howard Deutch; w: Mark Steven Johnson, m: Alan Silvestri; ph: Tak Jujimoto; pd: Gary Frutkoff; ed: Bill Weber, Seth Flaum, Maryann Brandon; starring Jack Lemmon, Walter Matthau, Ann-Margaret, Sophia Loren, Burgess Meredith, Kevin Pollak, Darryl Hannah, and Minnesota actors James Cada, Wayne A. Evenson and Ann Morgan Guilbert. Guilbert was very good and convincing as Loren's mother.

Film sites include: Wasbasha, Marine on St. Croix for wedding scenes; Stillwater for fishing scenes; Minneapolis for general shots and specifically for "Slippery's;" Energy Park Studio at 1515 Brewster Street in St. Paul and other general shots in St. Paul.

In this sequel of old neighbors feuding, Sophia Loren joins the cast as Walter Matthau's romantic interest. (Jack Lemmon won Ann-Margaret in the first *Grumpy* movie.) An extra comic scene has Burgess Meredith (Lemmon's dad) courting Ann Morgan Guilbert.

68. *Feeling Minnesota* (1995), 95m, Entertainment/New Line/Jersey (Danny DeVito), Michael Shamberg, Stacy Sher); w/d: Steve Baigelman; ph Walt Lloyd; pd: Naomi Shohan; ed: Martin Walsh. Featuring Keanu Reeves, Cameron Diaz, Tuesday Weld, Courtney Love, Vincent D'Onofrio, Dan Aykroyd, Levon Helm, Minnesota actors Dale Dunham, Peter Syvertsen and adopted Minnesotan Delroy Lindo. Escaped prisoner flees with his brother's wife to a small town; about double-dealing gangsters. Film sites include: general shots of Minneapolis, St. Paul and Crystal; The Thunderbird Motel, 2201 E. 78th Street, Bloomington.

69. *Fargo* (1995), 98m, Polygram/Working Title (Ethan Coen); d: Joel Coen; co-w: Joel and Ethan Coen; ph: Roger Deakins; m: Carter Burwell; pd: Rick Heinrichs; ed: Roderick Jaynes (Joel and Ethan Coen); featuring Frances McDormand, Harve Presnell, William H. Macy, Steve Buscemi, Peter Stormare, Kristin Rudrüd, Tony Denman and Minnesota actress Michelle Hutchison.

Film sites include: Embers Restaurant, 7525 Wayzata Blvd, St. Louis Park; Hallock, Stillwater, Richfield, Willernia, Brainerd; Edina City Hall, (Brainerd Police interior shots), 4801 W. 50th St. Edina; Minneapolis Club parking ramp at 8th St. and 3rd Ave. S.; and the Minneapolis-St. Paul International Airport (where Carl gets a license plate).

A car salesman in a small Minnesota town hires two criminals to kidnap his wife so that his wealthy father-in-law will pay a big ransom that get him out of debt. A pregnant rural police chief pits herself against two city-slickers. A original and witty thriller laced with the Coens' black humor.

70. *Beautiful Girls* (1995), 107m, Buena Vista/Miramax (Cary Woods); d: Ted Demme; w: Scott Rosenberg; ph: Adam Kimmel; m: David A. Stewart; pd: Dan Davis; ed: Jeffrey Wolf. Featuring Matt Dillon, Tim Hutton, Noah Emmerich, Natalie Portman, Annabeth Gish, Lauren Holly, Rosie O'Donnell, Mira Sorvino, Uma Thurman, Max Perlich, Martha Plimpton.

Film sites include: The Bryant-Lake Bowl at 810 W. Lake St. in Minneapolis; Hopkins (reunion location), Stillwater, Marine-on-St. Croix; and the Divine Redemmer Hospital at 724 19th Avenue North, South St. Paul.

Thick-headed boy-talk tolerated by the girls. A barroom pianist meets his old friends at a high school reunion to talk about dead-end jobs and women problems.

71. ***And the Earth Did Not Swallow Him*** (1995), m, American Playhouse, Kino International Corp; p: Paul Espinosa; David d: Severo Perez, w: Perez from a novel by Tomas Rivera; m: Marcos Loya; ph: Virgil L. Harper; pd: Norine Joy Francis; ed: Howard Heard, Susan Heick; featuring Joe Alcala, Art Bonilla, James Jude Courtenay, Evelyn Guerrero, Jeremy Howard, Richard Keats, Jeffrey Licon, Sid Lopez, Lupe Oliveros, Rose Portillo, Sam Vlahos, Del Zamora, Marco Rodriguez, Miguel Rodriguez, Daniel Valdez.

Marcos is a young Texan, the second son of a migrant worker. He goes up to Minnesota to help with harvesting of crops and works his way south to Texas, the final stop. He is assigned to live with an unstable couple and is dismissed from school for defending himself in a fight. A fairly accurately portrait of the socio/political conditions of the migrant workers in the mid-20th Century and the socio-religious values of the Hispanic workers.

72. ***Mystery Science Theatre 3000: The Movie*** (1996), 73m, Gramercy /Best Brains (Jim Mallon; d: Jim Mallon; co-w: Michael J. Nelson, Trace Beaulieu, Mary Jo Pehl, Kevin Murphy, Paul Chaplin, Mallon; ph: Jeff Stonehouse; m: Billy Barber; pd: Jef Maynard; ed: Bill Johnson; featuring Michael J. Nelson, Trace Beaulieu, Jim Brady, Kevin Murphy, Mallon. A mad scientist forces an astronaut and his robots to watch an edited version of the sci-fi movie, ***This Island Earth***. Some think the film infectiously funny, others find it irritating. Film sites include: Energy Park Studio, 1515 Brewster Street, Saint Paul.

73. ***The Mighty Ducks III*** (1996), 104m, Buena Vista/Walt Disney; d: Robert Lieberman; w: Steven Brill from a story by Kenneth Johnson; m: J.A.C. Redford; ph: David Hennings; ed: Colleen Halsey, Patrick Lussier; pd: Stephen Storer; featuring Estevez as Gordon Bombay, Joss Ackland, Joshua Jackson, Elden Henson, Shaun Weiss, Brandon Quintin Adams, Garette Ratliff Henson, Marguerite Moreau, Vincent Larusso–returning Ducks, plus Lane Smith, Heidi Kling, Josef Sommer, M.C. Gainey, Aaron Lohr Christopher Orr, Michael Cudlitz, Ty O'Neal, and Guthrie and Jungle Theatre actress Claudia Wilkens.

In the third and final episode, the Ducks go to Eden Hall Academy, a top-notch prep school, through scholarships. As freshman they are hazed by the snotty varsity hockey team. Charley is the focus as he behaves a lot like Gordon when he was a kid-star with the self-loathing that led Gordon to becoming a loser. Tagline: "No fear, no limits, no breaker, just Ducks!!!" The Ducks, in glory, return to Minnesota.

74. *Jingle All the Way* (1996), 88m, TCF (Chris Columbus, Mark Radcliffe, Michael Barnathan); d: Brian Levant; w: Randy Cornfield; ph: Victor J. Kemper; m: David Newman; pd: Leslie McDonald; ed: Kent Byeyda, Adam Weiss, Wilton Henderson. Starring Arnold Schwarzenegger, Sinbad, Phil Hartman, Rita Wilson, Robert Conrad, Martin Mull, Jake Lloyd, James Belushi, Harvey Korman, and Minnesota actor Peter Syvertsen. Action comedy about a salesman's frantic search for a special toy his son wants for Christmas.

Film sited include: Zumbro Café at 4302 Upton Ave. S in Linden Hills, Nicollet Island, Minneapolis; Edina; Camp Snoopy at the Mall of America; 7th Place Mall at St. Peter and Wabasha Street, the Hamm Plaza at St. Peter and 6th Street, Mickey's Diner at 36 W. 9th St., Energy Park Studio at 1515 Brewster Street, and Kellogg Park all in St. Paul; Falcon Heights Elementary School at 1393 Garden West Avenue in Falcon Hghts.

75. *The Criminals* (1996), p: Criminal Pictures (Nelle Stokes); 93 min.; ; film sites include Lake Elmo, Oakdale, and Minneapolis; ph: Vincent Morgenstern; m: Gamma Supinsky.

76. *Snow* (1996), 81m, Int'l Entertainment Enterprises/Winter Light Film LLC; d/m: Chan Poling; ph: Philip Harder; ed: Daniel Geiger; ad: Heather Keena; featuring Shane Barach, Rose Mialutha, Lars Miklesevics, Eric Remillard, John Cozier, Khalil Jamal Battle.

77. *Martha, Meet Frank, Daniel & Laurence* (1997), 90m, Film Four/ Channel 4/Banshee (Grainne Marmion); d: Nick Hamm; w: Peter Morgan; ph: David Johnson; m: Edward Shearmur; pd: Max Gottlieb; ed: Michael Bradsell; featuring Rufus Sewell, Joe Fiennes, Monica Potter, Ted Hollander, Ray Winstone. Film sites include some general shots of Minneapolis.

An American woman visiting London attracts three friends in this romantic comedy.

78. *Dill Scallion* (1997), 91m, The Asylum/Brady Oil Entertainment/Conspiracy Entertainment/Pedestrian Films (Kimberly Jacobs, Joe Blake, Jennifer Amerine); d/w: Jordan Brady; m: Sheryl Crow; ph: Jonathan Brown; ed: Sam Citron; pd: Chris Dileo; featuring Henry Winkler, Billy Burke, Lauren Graham, Kathy Griffon, Peter Berg, Willie Nelson, Travis Tritt, LeAnn Rimes, Scott Rudolph, Robert Wagner, dozens more.

79. **Major League III** (Back to the Minors)(1998), 100m, Warner/ Morgan Creek (David S. Ward, James G. Robinson); d: John Warren; w: David S. Ward (characters), Warren (story); ph: Tim Suhrstedt; m: Ken Tamplin, Robert Folk; ed: O. Nicholas Brown, Bryan H. Carroll, pd: David Crank, Barbara & Gus Cantrell. Featuring Scott Bakula, Corbin Bernsen, Dennis Haysbert, Jensen Daggett, Erick Bruskotter, Walter Goggins, Ted McGinley, Judson Mills, Lobo Sebastian, Thom Barry, Peter MacKenzie, Tim DiFillipo, Tom DiFillipo and Takaaki Ishibashi.

Gus (Bakula), an aging pitcher, is snatched from retirement to coach the Salt Lake City Buzz, the farm team for the Minnesota Twins. He accepts the challenge but finds that he is "nine players short of a dream team." Much of the film was shot at the Hubert H. Humphrey Metrodome, 501 Chicago Avenue in Minneapolis.

80. **Overnight Delivery** (1998), 87m; d: Jason Bloom; w: Mark Sedaka, Stephen Bloom; with Paul Rudd, Christine Taylor, Reese Witherspoon, and Minnesota actress Buffy Sedlachek.
Film sites include: Ayd Mill Road and Embassy Suites, 175 E. 10th St., and University of St. Thomas, in St. Paul; a Waconia gas station; the OK Corral in Jordan; Hastings, Stillwater and Maplewood; and the Minneapolis-St. Paul International Airport.

A man has just 24 hours to retrieve a letter he sent by mistake to his girlfriend who was, he thought, cheating on him. He brings a woman companion along to help and inadvertently falls in love.

81. **A Simple Plan** (1998), 120m, Paramount/ Mutual/ Savoy (James Jacks, Adam Schroeder); d: Sam Raimi; w: Scott B. Smith from his novel; ph: Alar Kivilo; m: Danny Elfman; pd: Patrizia von Brandenstein; ed: Arthur Coburn, Eric L. Beason. Featuring Bill Paxton, Billy Bob Thornton, Bridget Fonda, Brent Briscoe, Gary Cole, Becky Ann Baker, Chelcie Ross, and Minnesota actors Wayne A. Evenson, Jack Walsh, and Peter Syvertsen.

Three frends find a bundle of cash in a crashed plane, and decide to keep the money. "Halliwell calls it "a deft, chilling thriller of corruption and greed, charting an inexorable slide from integrity to betrayal and worse." Thornton and screenwriter Smith were nominated for Oscars. Film sites include Delano, Golden Valley, Energy Park Studio, 1515 Brewster Street in St. Paul.

82. *A Chance of Snow* (1998), 87 m, Lifetime Television (Nicholas Batchelor); d: Tony Bill; w: Michele Cook; m: Van Dyke Parks; ph: Bing Sokolsky; ed: Axel Hubert; pd: Cliff Cunningham; featuring JoBeth Williams, Michael Ontkean, Barbara Barrie, Charles Durning, Dey Young, Dina Merrill, Angelica Chitworth, Travi Christofore, Evan Gabriel, Tony Jackson, Kelly Bertenshaw, Rebecca Kolls, Patrick Coyle, Edgar Davis, Mary Rehbein, and Minnesota actors James Cada, Peter Syvertsen, John Paul Gamoke, Joe Minjares, Marquetta Senters, Jim Westcott, and Buffy Sedlachek. The chief film site was the Twin Cities Int'l Airport.

After signing divorce papers, a woman is stranded at the airport during a blizzard. She runs into her ex-husband there and the estranged couple takes a fresh look at their broken marriage.

83. *Drop Dead Gorgeous* (1998), 98m, New Line/Capella/KC Medien (Gavin Pallone, Judy Hofflund); d: Michael Patrick Jann; w: Lona Williams; ph: Michael Spiller; m: Mark Mothersbaugh; pd: Ruth  Ammon; ed: David Codron, Janice Hampton. Features Kirsten Dunst, Ellen Barkin, Allison Janney, Denise Richards, Kirstie Alley, Amy Adams, Sam McMurray, Tara Redepenning, Shannon Nelson, Sarah Stewart, Michael McShane, and Minnesota actress Michelle Hutchison.

Film sites include: Eden Prairie, Chaska, Farmington, Waconia, Hopkins, New Germany; the Ardmore Village (trailer park), Lakeville; Energy Park Studio at 1515 Brewster St., the Scott View Estates (Leeman home), the Sheraton-Midway Hotel at Dale St. and Interstate 94, Airport Hojos in St. Paul; Wayzata Junior High auditorium at 149 Barry Avenue in Wayzata, Minnesota.

A film crew documents events leading up to a beauty contest. The town's wealthiest woman is obsessed with her daughter winning. A satire on small town life and the beauty business.

84. **Homo Heights** (1998, aka Happy Heights), 92m, Lehman-Moore Productions (Kate Lehman, Christine K. Walker); d/w: Sara Moore; m: Evan Lurie; ph: David Doyle; ed: Vaughn G. Smith; pd: Elizabeth Fine: ad: Kevin Egeland; featuring Quentin Crisp, Stephen Sorrentino, Lynn Sain, Grant Richey, Michelle Hutchison, Emil Herrera, Barbara Kingsley, David Fenley, Lee DeLaria, Tim Tuelin, Daniel Alexander Jones. Christine K. Walker, the executive producer, was nominated for a Producer's Award by the Independent Spirits Award (2000, also for Walker's **Backroads**).

85. **With or Without You** (1998), 104m, Double-U Productions/ Mount Curve/ Wardenclyffe Entertainment (Robert Schwartz, Julie Hartley); d/w: Wendell Jon Andersson; m: Michael Wandmacher; pd: Gregory M. Cummins; ed: Laura Stokes; pd: Jack Ballance; ad: Donovan M. Hake; featuring Kristoffer Ryan Winters, Marisa Ryan, Rachel True, Sally Wingert, Margi Simmons, Amy Parks, Dylan Roy, Trace Beaulieu, Mark Mallman, G-Sharp, Theresa Hegler, Jim Lichtscheidl, Isabell Monk O'Connor, Elizabeth Montgomery.

86. **The Naked Man** (1998), 98m, Albatros Film (Japan)/Mars Distribution (France)/Naked Man Productions/October Films (Ben Barenholz); d: J. Todd Anderson; w: Ethan Coen, J. Todd Anderson; ph: Jeff Barklage; ed: Mark Crecher; m: Edward Bilous; ad: Marie L. Baker, featuring: Michael Rapaport, Nancy Plank, Michael Jeter, Doug Fisher, Donald Murphy and Minnesota actors Rachael Leigh Cook, Peter Thoemke, Terry O'Sullivan, Dale Dunham, Wayne A. Evenson, Charles Brin, Steve Shaffer, Traci Christofore, Isabell Monk O'Connor and cast of dozens. Chiropractor by day and a wrestler by night. A man takes matters into his own hands when a pharmaceutical kingpin moves into his town to muscle out competition.

87. **Mulligan** (1999), Vandy Productions (Tim VandeSteeg, Jason Wallace); d: Tim VandeSteeg; w: Bill Borea, Joshua Will, Kevin Ross, VandeSteeg; m: Michael Whalen; ph: Afshin Shahidi; ed: Rodney G. Johnson, Jason Wallace; featuring Steve Lattery, Joshua Will, Cedric Yarbrough, Teri Michaels, Bill Borea, Alex Cole, Hidric "Rick" Booker, Mikki Daniels, Eve Overland, Jame Hammill, Roger R. Johnson, Charles Hubbell, Jim Jorganson, Kari Yun Stiff.

88. **Here on Earth** (1999), m, 20th Century Fox (David T. Friendly); d: Mark Piznarski; w: Michael Seitzman; ph: Michael D. O'Shea; m: Kelly Jones, John Stephens, Andrea Morricone; ed: Robert

Frazen; pd: Dina Lipton; ad: James F. Truesdale; featuring Minnesota's Josh Hartnett, Leelee Sobieski, Annette O'Toole, Bruce Greenwood, Chris Klein, Michael Rooker, Annie Corley, Elaine Hendrix, Stuart Wilson, Ronni Saxon, Maureen O'Malley, Tac Fitzgerald, Jessica Stier, Eric Eidem, Zach Fehst, and other Minnesota actors Peter Syvertsen, Isabell Monk O'Connor, and Garth Schumacher.

Film sites include: Welch, Red Wing, Miesville and Goodhue County; Summit Hill in St. Paul; and Shattuck-St. Mary's School at 1000 Shumway Avenue in Faribault. A rich college kid learns a lesson after his joy ride destroys a country café.

89. **Sugar & Spice (& Semiautomatics)** (2001), 84m, New Line Cinema (Wendy Finerman); d: Francine McDougall; w: Mandy Nelson; Michael Nelson; featuring Marla Sokoloff, Marley Shelton, Melissa George, Mena Suvari, Rachel Blanchard, Alexandra Holden, James Marsden, Claudia Wilkens, Kevin Kling.

Film sites include: Anoka High School; Arlington High at 1495 Rice St. and Grand Avenue in St. Paul; Eastview High at 6200 140th St. W. in Apple Valley; and locations in Eagan, Welch, Roseville, Falcon Heights, New Brighton, West St. Paul, and Minneapolis.

The prettiest girl in her high school class becomes pregnant by the star quarterback of the football team. She transforms herself from a pert, sweet, cheerleader to a careless individual with violent ways and an increasingly dangerous lifestyle.

90. **Herman, USA** (2001) alternative title: *Taking a Chance on Love*, 89m, Porchlight Entertainment/St. Anthony Films/Herman Productions (Patrick Wells, John & Sage Cowles); w/d: Bill Semans; ph: Ross Berryman; m: Stephen D. Graziano; ed: David S. Geiger, Michael N. Knue; pd: Bernard Hides; featuring Michael O'Keefe, Kevin Chamberlin, Enid Graham. Ann Hamilton, Garth Schumacher, Terry O'Sullivan, Jim Cada, Barbara Kingsley, Shirley Venard, Mark Benninghoffen, Peter Syvertsen, Michelle Hutchison, Kristin Rudrüd, Jay Hornbacher, Mary Rehbein, Lavinia Erickson, Stephen D'Ambrose, Richard Anson, Tony Mockus, Jr, Anthony Mockus Sr. Clyde Lund, Marvette Knight and a cast of 1000s. Most of the above actors are Minnesotan.

Note: the film was not shot in Herman because of shortage of hotel/motel rooms for cast and crew, but New Germany.

Seventy-eight bachelors from Herman, Minnesota, place an ad in the papers, and busloads of women from thirty-seven states and four countries descend upon the town. The men are slightly stereotyped as country bumpkins with a few warts here and there. Besides all the dancing and revelry we see a variety of relationships develop, some comic and some romantic, and one tragic. Thanks, Pat Wells.

91. *The Wooly Boys* (2000), 99m, Promersberger/Berzinski (Robert Schwartz, Julie Hartley); d; Lesdek Burzinski; co-w: Max Enscoe, Annie de Young, Ed Hansen, Glen Stephens, George "Buck" Flower; m: Humie Mann; ed: Andrew S. Eisen, Stephen E. Rivkin; ad: Lindin Snyder; ph: Stephen Storer; featuring Peter Fonda, Keith Carradine, Kris Kristopherson, Joseph Mazzello, Robin Dearsden and Minnesota actors James Cada, Lana Schwab, Wayne A. Evenson, Jim Westcott, Mark Benninghoffen, Stephen Pelinski, and Marquetta Senters.

"Sheep ranchers' visit to the big city triggers a mischievous adventure with his grandson, a computer whiz. It's about fight'n, steal'n, shoot'n and other lessons from grandpa." Film sites include: McGinty Road east of Wayzata; Woodwinds Health Campus (hospital), 1925 Woodwinds Drive, Woodbury; Minneapolis Convention Center, 1301 2nd Ave. S. (the bus station) in Minneapolis.

92. *Joe Somebody* (2001), 98m, 20th Cent.-Fox (Brian Reilly, Arnold Kopelson, Anne Kopelson, Matthew Gross, Ken Achity; Arnon Milchan, exec. p); d: John Pasquin; w: John Scott Shepherd; ph: Daren Okada; m: George S. Clinton; pd: Jackson de Govia; ad: Scott Ritenour; starring Tim Allen, Minnesota's Kelly Lynch, James Belushi, Julie Bowen, Tina Lifford, Robert Joy, Wolfgang Bodison, Ken Marino, Hayden Panettiere, Greg Gerrmann, Cristi Conaway, and Patrick Warburton. Among the many Minnesotan actors: Jim Westcott, James Cada, Marquetta Senter, Peter Syvertsen, Claudia Wilkens, Emil Herrera, and former Minnesota Governor Jesse Ventura.

Joe (Tim Allen), is beaten up by a bully co-worker. Finally, he fights back. Film sites include: Conner's Deli, 5411 Penn Ave. S., Nicollet Mall, Gaviidae Commons at 555 Nicollet Ave., Grumpy's Bar and Grill at 2200 4th St. N.E., the Grand Hotel for thirteen scenes at 615 2nd Avenue South, and the Target Center, 600 First Avenue North in Minneapolis; St. Agnes School at 530 Lafond Avenue in St. Paul; and the Fine Arts Interdisciplinary Resource School, 3915 Adair Avenue North, Crystal.

93. *No Direction Home: Bob Dylan* (2001), 208m; BBC, PBS, Box TV, Spit Fire Pictures; p/d: Martin Scorcese; co-p: Susan Lacy, Jeff Rosen, Nigel Sinclair, Anthony Wall; ed: David Tedeschi; ph: Mustapha Barat; ad: Mike Pollard. Shot in Hibbing, MN. and New York City, NY.

A chronicle of Bob Dylan's evolution from folk singer/protest singer (1961-1966) to the "voice of a generation" and rock star. Archival footage is intercut with interviews about his style changes, influences on his music; his tours with other singers. This film won an Emmy, five wins in all among seven nominations.

94. Sweet Land (2005), 110, p: James Bingham, Alan Cumming; d: Ali Selim; w: Ali Selim based on a short story by Will Weaver entitled "Gravestone Made of Wheat"; ph: David Tumblety; ed: James Stranger; m: Thomas Lieberman; pd: James Bakkom; ad: Emily Davis; featuring Elizabeth Reaser, Tim Guinee, Lois Smith, Alex Kingston, John Heard, Ned Beatty, Alan Cumming, Patrick Coyle, Tim Gilroy, Jodie Markell, James Bakkom, Paul Sand, Sage Kermes, Patrick Heusinger. Among the Minnesota actors: Jim Westcott, James Cada, Stephen Pelinski and Will Weaver.

Film sites include Chippewa County's Pioneer Village in Montevideo, Minnesota, Heritage Hill and its antique farm machinery, the Swensson Farm Museum, and the Milwaukee Road Depot all in Montevideo but also sites in Dawson and Madison, MN.

A German mail-order bride comes to the "land of opportunity" to find love with a Norwegian immigrant farmer. (For details see the entry on Ali Selim.) The world première was at the Hamptons International Film Festival on Oct. 25, 2005 while the première for the general public was at Minneapolis' Riverview Theater.

95. A Prairie Home Companion (2005). 105"; P: Bill Pohlad, River Road Entertainments; D: Robert Altman; Story/co-w: Garrison Keillor, Ken LaZebnik; featuring Kevin Kline, Meryl Streep, Tommy Lee Jones, Woody Harrelson, Lily Tomlin, and the shows' founder and host, Garrison Keillor and super talented sound effects man, Tom Keith. Others featured: Robin Williams, Jeralyn Steele, Rich Dworsky on piano, Peter Oustroushka - guitar, Butch Tompson-clarinet, Andy Stein-violin, Arnie Kinsella–drums, "Spider" John Koerner–guitar, Gary Raynor-bass; Sue Scott, Tim Russell and Jim Westcott.

Film sites are: Fitzgerald Theater, 10 Exchange St. E. and Mickey's Diner, 36 W 9th St. in St. Paul and general St. Paul ambiance shots.

The film—Robert Altman's last—explores the interplay between various performers before and during a live radio broadcast of *A Prairie Home Companion.*

96. *North Country* (2005), 126min; p: Warner Bros Pictures; d: Niki Caro; co-w: Michael Seitzman from Clara Bingham's book; m: Gustavo Santaolalla; ed: David Coulson; ph: Chris Menges; pd: Richard Hoover; ad: Gregory S. Hooper; c: Cindy Evans; featuring Charlize Theron (as Josey Aimes), Frances McDormand, Sean Bean, Woody Harrelson, Sissy Spacek, Tom Bower, J.C. Cutler, Elle Peterson, Thomas Curtis, Richard Jenkins, Rusty Schwimmer, Linda Emond; among Minnesota actors: Chris Mulkey, Sally Wingert, James Cada, Katherine Ferrand, and Bruce Bohne. Film sites include the environs of Chisholm, Eveleth, Virginia, Minnesota, and the Iron Range.

A fictionalized account of the first major successful sexual harassment case in the United States, Jenson v. Eveleth Mines, where a female miner who had endured abuse won a landmark 1984 lawsuit. Tagline: "All she wanted was to make a living. Instead she made history."

97. *Aurora Borealis* (2005), 110m; d: James C.E. Burke; w: Brent Boyd; m: Mychael Danna; ed: Richard Nord; pd: Taavo Soodor; ph Alar Kivilo; ad: Barry Isenor; c: Anne Dixon; featuring Don Sutherland and Louise Fletcher (Mr. & Mrs. Shorter), Joshua Jackson (Duncan Shorter), Juliette Lewis (as Kate, the home companion). Film sites include: the Mall of America in Bloomington, MN; the Walker Sculpture Garden at 725 Vineland Place, Minneapolis.

A young man is emotionally crippled by the premature death of his father and has difficulty staying employed. He gets a job as a handyman to be near his grandparents (Sutherland and Fletcher). His grandpa (Sutherland) suffers from Alzheimer's.

[This list was compiled with the aid of Ben Nelson, formerly of the Minnesota Film Board.]

About the Author

Rolf Canton was born and raised in Minneapolis. He attended Washburn High School and graduated from the University of Minnesota in 1969 in Theatre Arts and Humanities. He has been a film buff since kindergarten and has met eighty-some film stars at various film events. He has worked as a lumber salesman, a law clerk, a massage therapist, and a writer. He holds degrees in Herbal Studies and Pastoral Wellness Counseling, and has taught English as a second language in Salonika, Greece.

His book, *The Moriarty Principle*, was published by Galde Press in 1997. He wrote and co-produced the video, "Conversations with Ancient History," and wrote, produced and directed the video "The Pipe Dream Continues (An Irregular Look at Sherlock Holmes in Minnesota)."

After living most of his first fifty-five years in Minneapolis, Rolf moved in 2002 to Bonn, Germany, with his wife, Nahid, and sons, Wahid and Yusuf. Rolf is an English teacher in Bonn.

In 2006 Nodin Press published the companion to this volume, *Minnestans in the Movies*, which deals with the lives, careers, and Minnesota-connection of a wide array of actors and actresses.

Rolf is currently working on *Minnesotans in the Media: TV – Radio – News*. Public input is welcome. If you know of someone who should be in his books, please contact the publisher with as much biographical information as possible.